The Battle of
Heligoland Bight 1939

The Battle of Heligoland Bight 1939

The Royal Air Force and the Luftwaffe's Baptism of Fire

ROBIN HOLMES

GRUB STREET · LONDON

For Sheelagh with much love

Published by
Grub Street Publishing
4 Rainham Close
London
SW11 6SS

Copyright © Grub Street 2009
Copyright text © Robin Holmes 2009

British Library Cataloguing in Publication Data
Holmes, Robin
 The Battle of Heligoland Bight: the Royal Air Force and
 the Luftwaffe's baptism of fire
 1. Great Britain. Royal Air Force. Squadron, No. 149 –
 History. 2. World War, 1939-1945 – Aerial operations,
 British. 3. Harris, Paul. 4. Wellington (Bomber) 5. World
 War, 1939-1945 – Regimental histories – Great Britain
 I. Title
 940.5'44'941-dc22

ISBN-13: 9781906502560

All rights reserved. No part of this publication may be reproduced, stored in a retrieval system, or transmitted in any form or by any means electronic, mechanical, photocopying, recording, or otherwise, without the prior permission of the copyright owner.

Typeset by Pearl Graphics, Hemel Hempstead

Printed and bound by MPG, Bodmin, Cornwall

Grub Street Publishing uses only FSC
(Forest Stewardship Council) paper for its books.

Contents

Preface by Group Captain P.I. Harris DFC	6
Introduction to Vickers Wellington Mk 1A 'R for Robert'	8
1. A very good cottage on the foundations of a castle	9
2. La Drôle de Guerre	19
3. 149 (East India) Squadron – Mildenhall	46
4. The Battle of Heligoland Bight	56
5. Blood, toil, tears and sweat	107
6. Hidden away for all time	126
Appendix A Personal recollections of the Battle of Heligoland Bight	129
Appendix B Memories of Peace by C.G. Grey	153
Appendix C The Marienkäfer (Lady-Bug) Squadron by Wolfgang Falck	156
Appendix D Claims and Losses	160
Vickers Wellington Mk III cutaway drawing with key	164
Glossary	166
Acknowledgements	168
Picture Acknowledgements	171
References	173
Index	176

Preface

This book records the very earliest air battles between the Royal Air Force and the Luftwaffe. These raids took place in daylight and one proved fateful. On that particular raid I flew a new Wellington, N2980 or 'R for Robert'. Like all Wellingtons she was a joy to fly and an object of affection to her crew. Much is owed to the genius of the late Sir Barnes Wallis, who gave us this superb aeroplane to help us through the dark and difficult times of the early war years. I flew her on that fateful raid to Wilhelmshaven on 18th December 1939, an intensely exciting experience that shattered the long held belief that 'the bomber will always get through'.

I was fortunate that day to survive the battle because Wing Commander (as he was then) Richard Kellett's leading was immaculate. Our ten Wellingtons stuck closely together in tight formation, our guns worked and our very young crews exhibited the true 'bulldog spirit'. In those early days we lumbered along at about 200mph and defended ourselves with guns that were little better than pea-shooters. Today, the young men who guard our island fly at twice the speed of sound and tackle the enemy with sophisticated guided missiles. How different things were in 1939. The 'Phoney War' overshadowed all our operations in those days, when very strict orders forbade us from attacking anything that might result in German civilians being hurt, the last vestige of a decade of appeasement thinking.

A couple of weeks after the disaster of the Battle of Heligoland Bight a squadron of Messerschmitts attacked three Wellingtons on a daylight armed reconnaissance sweep over the North Sea. This was the last nail in the coffin of Bomber Command's cherished philosophy of daylight precision raids by self-defending bomber formations. A whole new technology had to be learned.

Today, the public image of Bomber Command in World War II is one of huge dark shapes taking off at dusk with the survivors limping home at the break of dawn. *The Battle of Heligoland Bight 1939* tells us why it had to be done that way – by night.

Group Captain P.I. Harris DFC

Introduction to
Vickers Wellington Mk 1A, 'R for Robert'

The contribution of the bomber to the defeat of Nazi Germany was significant, but in securing the unconditional surrender of Imperial Japan it was decisive. The curtain fell on World War II to the drone of a Superfortress over Nagasaki, a curtain that had been raised almost exactly six years earlier to the roar of Wellingtons over Brunsbüttel and Blenheims over Wilhelmshaven. Whereas the story of Colonel Tibbets' Enola Gay over Hiroshima on 6th August and Major Sweeny's Bock's Car over Nagasaki on 9th August 1945 is legend, the story of Squadron Leader Harris and Squadron Leader Lamb over Brunsbüttel and Flight Lieutenant Doran over Wilhelmshaven on 4th September 1939 is virtually unknown.

On 2nd September 1945 462 B-29s staged a fly-past over the USS *Missouri* during the Japanese surrender ceremonies. With a bomb-load of 20,000lbs and a defensive armament of 12 0.5 inch machine guns and a 20mm cannon, the Boeing Super-Fortress was the most modern and efficient Allied bomber when World War II finished.

On 2nd September 1939 the Royal Air Force was placed on War Establishment. With a bomb-load of 4,500lbs and a defensive armament of six .303 inch Browning machine guns, the Vickers Wellington Mk 1A was the most modern and efficient British bomber when World War II started.

The story of the first British bombing raid of the war, of why Bomber Command flew by night and of the Wellington Mk 1A are all closely linked together. It is a story of the Stone Age of strategic bombing. Out of the total 11,461 Wellington bombers produced, Paul Harris' old Wimpy from the Battle of Heligoland Bight is now the only one left that fought back against Nazi tyranny and survived.[1] All the others were shot down, ditched in the sea, crashed on training flights or were melted down into saucepans.

---

[1] Wellington bomber MF628, beautifully preserved in the Royal Air Force museum at Hendon, is a late T Mk 10 that saw no active service in the war.

1
A very good cottage on the foundations of a castle

'G for George' skims the surface of the water, lower and lower until the two spotlights meet and the bomb aimer peers through his sights at the twin towers of the Möhne dam. Streams of tracers arc up towards his Lancaster as Wing Commander Guy Gibson steadies his aircraft on its run up to the target. As Barnes Wallis's bouncing bomb skips across the surface, the Lancaster claws itself upwards through a hail of flak. A mighty explosion is followed by a huge fountain of water. The dam holds. The rest of 617 Squadron take their turn, and there are more explosions, more fountains of water, till finally the dam face cracks and the deluge pours through. Every time they re-run *The Dam Busters* you get a lump in your throat, but by May 1943 the writing was on the wall for Nazi Germany. By then Bomber Command was a truly formidable organisation equipped with the most efficient aerial sledgehammers – the Lancaster and the Halifax. From then on, in partnership with the US Eighth Airforce's Liberators and Flying Fortresses, the cities of Germany were subjected to an ever-increasing pounding that eventually resulted in vast areas being reduced to piles of rubble, the bomber's contribution to the final defeat of Nazi Germany. Nostalgia, however, tends to distort our view of history by recalling the better times at the expense of the bad ones. Perhaps that is why the Lancaster and Mosquito are remembered with such affection. Big, tough and menacing – fast, daring and deadly – these two epitomise today's image of Bomber Command during World War II. They belong to the better times when our backs were no longer against the wall and when, with the help of our American and

Russian allies, victory was on the horizon. Model shops abound with plastic kits of Lancasters, Mosquitoes, Halifaxes, Flying Fortresses and Liberators. You have to search hard to find a Whitley or a Wellington. They belong to the dark days when Britain stood alone, invasion and defeat staring us in the face. The 'Flying Barn Door' and the 'Wimpy' however were the two aircraft that laid down the firm foundation upon which both Bomber Command *and* the US Eighth Airforce built their huge self-defending bomber formations, a concept that relied upon a major British advance in armament technology – the power-operated gun turret. More than any other bomber, the Wellington proved this to be a formidable defensive weapon. Until the advent of long-range escort fighters in 1944, big bomber formations had to rely for their survival upon mutual supportive cross-fire from their power-operated gun turrets.

The *raison d'être* for the big bomber formations that were later to become such familiar sights as they headed out over the sea towards Germany, night after night, can be traced back to the very beginnings of the RAF in 1918. Its founder, Sir Hugh Trenchard, was a fervent advocate of the philosophy that 'offence is the best form of defence'. Through the lean years of the 1920s and the early 1930s this was the guiding light that motivated senior officers in the RAF, officers who were finally given the go-ahead to rebuild their run-down service in July 1934 when it eventually dawned on a reluctant British Government that Herr Hitler meant business. Just prior to leaving to present a new British disarmament plan to the Reduction and Limitation of Armaments Conference at the League of Nations in Geneva, Stanley Baldwin expressed his growing concern to the House of Commons on 10th November 1932.

> I think it well also for the man in the street to realise there is no power on earth that can protect him from bombing, whatever people may tell him. The bomber will always get through.

Baldwin, oft accused of having an 'Air Armada' complex, was not alone in fearing the growing power of the bomber. 'In those days everyone believed that aerial bombardment would reduce the cities of Europe to ruin within a few weeks. European civilisation would come to an end.' So wrote the famous historian A.J.P. Taylor in his book, *History of World War II*. Memories of the raids by German Gothas on London in 1917 and the predictions of doom from H.G. Wells in his book *The War in the Air* combined to stir up strong anti-bomber feelings. Throughout Europe (with the exception of Germany, where freedom of speech was in the process of being extinguished) and in the United States of America, groups of vocal women organised petitions and presented them to the League of Nations with the clear message 'Ban the Bomber'. In response to Hitler's growing strength in the air the cry went up for Britain to give a moral lead and set an example by adopting a policy of unilateral disarmament.

Hitler's answer to this universal cry for peace and stability was to withdraw from the League of Nations, repudiate the Treaty of Versailles, reintroduce conscription and reveal to the world, on the 1st March 1935, his new Luftwaffe which he claimed had already reached parity with the RAF. For those with eyes to see, the reality was now terrifyingly apparent. War in Europe was inevitable – Britain and France *had* to set about defending themselves from Hitler's bombers – but how?

The answer was given at the time by C.G. Grey in an article in *The Aeroplane*. 'The real defence of this country must rest on counter-offensives by which the enemy is prevented from leaving his aerodromes, and his supplies of aircraft and armaments are destroyed.' The Royal Air Force was in complete agreement with this sentiment but was unsure as to how it could be implemented.

> In theory, there were three principal methods by which the day bombers might hope to pass safely through the opposing air defences. Firstly they might travel at such great speed that the opposing fighters and flak would seldom be able to get on terms with them. In this way they would also be able to exploit the elements of surprise to the full. A 'speed bomber' did not, however, exist in 1939.
>
> Secondly, the bombers might be covered by long-range fighter escort but, as in the case of the speed bomber, no

long-range fighter existed at that time, and the years which followed were to show the difficulties of producing one. It was possible that Spitfires might afford support in an attack on the Ruhr, if flight over the Low Countries was possible, but it was unlikely that any would be available for this purpose.

Thirdly, and this was the only immediately practical proposition, the bombers might concentrate in tight tactical formations and rely for their protection upon collective fire power. The defensive strength of these formations might be increased by equipping some aircraft with more guns or guns of larger calibre and, possibly, by providing them with special armour plating. 'Self-defending' bomber formations might also, of course, gain a certain advantage by surprise, or at times they might be protected by cloud cover.

The success of self-defending formation tactics would depend upon whether the necessary concentration of fire power could be generated and sustained. This, in turn, would depend upon whether the bombers could keep station in the face of enemy attack from the air and the ground and after manoeuvring over the target. Any advantage to be gained from cloud cover might be a disadvantage to station keeping, and whether surprise could be achieved or not would largely depend upon the extent to which the Germans had developed a system of radar early warning. These problems and many others, such as the performance and armament of the German fighters, the accuracy and strength of their anti-aircraft fire and the comparative advantages and dangers of high-and low-level attack, were either unknown or untested when, on 4th September 1939, 15 Blenheims and 14 Wellingtons took off between three and four o'clock in the afternoon to attack German warships reported to be off Brunsbüttel and in Wilhelmshaven.[i]

Having settled on the 'means', the next decision that had to be faced was the 'end' to which it should all be directed, i.e. the target. Before the war, the RAF considered themselves capable of hitting a specified target from 10,000 feet with an average bombing error of no more than 225 yards. It goes without saying of course that this was in good weather, with no cloud, no opposition and above all in *daylight*. The possibility of having to hit a precision target at night was not considered because it was thought that 'appreciable results' would not be forthcoming.[2]

The Air Ministry duly formulated a whole series of proposals which culminated in the Ruhr Plan. This envisioned a strike at the heart of German industry in the Ruhr valley to destroy precision targets like power stations, synthetic oil plants and aircraft factories. When first informed of this plan, the Air Minister, Sir Kingsley Wood, declared with affronted decency that factories were private property. Later, the German blitzkrieg on Warsaw demonstrated that Hitler did not concern himself with such niceties.

The four corner-stones on which pre-war Bomber Command was built were the idea that offence was the best form of defence, that the bomber would always get through, that bomber formations would be self-defending and that attacks on precision targets would be made in daylight.

To implement these four policies the organisation and equipment of the RAF were completely overhauled. Safe behind their Maginot Line, the French reaction to Hitler's sabre-rattling was different. From 1933 to 1935 the French Government placed panic orders with their aircraft industry (nationalised in 1936) which resulted, by 1938, in the French Air Force being stocked with obsolete machines unfit to fly against the Germans. The 'family firms' of the British aircraft industry on the other hand resisted the pressures from government to produce unimaginative bomber designs to the undemanding specifications issued by the Air Ministry. One firm in particular was working on a revolutionary new form of construction against considerable opposition from the traditionalists. Vickers Armstrongs at Weybridge had come up with an idea for 'knitting holes together' called geodetics, and its inventor, Barnes Wallis, was so convinced of its merits that the company went ahead and built a prototype at their own expense and called it the Wellesley. So good was the geodetic

---

[2] Minutes of Air Ministry Conference (ACAS in chair), 30th Nov. 1938.

design concept that, in 1938, two Wellesley aircraft won the world long distance record for Britain.[ii] That same year its big brother, the Wellington, entered squadron service with the RAF when a Mk 1, number L4215, was taken on charge by 99 Squadron at Mildenhall. Barnes Wallis's faith in his geodetics was later to be fully justified when hundreds of aircrew were bought back safely from over Germany by Wimpys with battle damage that would have destroyed lesser machines.

1938 was a momentous year in European politics. In March, Hitler annexed Austria and called it *Anschluss*. Later the Führer announced his intention of doing the same thing to the Sudetenland in Czechoslovakia. In an unprecedented diplomatic initiative, the British Prime Minister, Neville Chamberlain, flew to Berchtesgaden in September to dissuade the Führer from further territorial acquisitions. Although not a phrase in use at the time, Chamberlain started 'shuttle diplomacy' between Britain and Germany. His third and last meeting with Hitler took place in Munich, and he succeeded in getting joint signatures on a document symbolising the desire of Britain, France, Germany and Italy never to go to war with one another again. Upon his return to Britain, Chamberlain alighted from his aircraft at Heston aerodrome and, in the midst of a tumultuous welcome, waved aloft the piece of paper that was to bring 'peace for our time'.

Historians have argued at length over Chamberlain's motives for his policy of appeasement that culminated in the Munich Agreement. The rapturous welcome he received from the British public, however, testified to the mood of the nation that September, and a few members of parliament were observed to weep openly with relief upon hearing the news. Hopelessly outmatched and later accused of being hoodwinked by the devious Adolf, Chamberlain was to see everything he had worked for crash in ruins, but as to whether or not he was fooled by Hitler can be judged from his speech to the House of Commons on 3rd October, four days after he returned from Germany.[iii]

> Let no one think that because we have signed this agreement between these four powers at Munich we can afford to relax our efforts in regard to that programme

(i.e. rearmament) at this moment. Disarmament on the part of this country can never be unilateral again. We have tried that once and we very nearly brought ourselves to disaster. If disarmament is to come it must come by steps, and it must come by agreement and have the active co-operation of other countries. Until we know we have obtained that co-operation and until we have agreed upon the actual steps to be taken, we here must remain on guard.

There is no argument however about the outcome of Neville Chamberlain's initiative at Munich – it bought the Royal Air Force the year it so desperately needed to 'gird up its loins' and face what was becoming increasingly apparent, even to the most ardent supporters of appeasement as 1939 wore on, that Britain and Germany were set on a collision course.

Ten years after he relinquished his post as Chief of Air Staff, Lord Trenchard watched the fruits of his labour at an RAF display in the spring of 1939. As the squadrons of fighters and bombers flew in formation overhead, the father of the Royal Air Force looked up secure in the knowledge that he had provided, as he said in his own words, 'a very good cottage on the foundations of a castle'.

When the siren first sounded over London its shield had been greatly strengthened. Fighter Command stood ready to enter the lists with 500 Hurricanes and Spitfires and pick up the gauntlet thrown down by the challenger with the swastika-emblazoned fuselage.

While the shield was to prove only just adequate, the lance was as yet no more than a toothpick. Bomber Command could not contemplate a thrust at the heart of German industry. More time had to be bought. Sir Edgar Ludlow-Hewitt, its Commander-in-Chief, had at his disposal only a fraction of the enemy's strength.

Recalling the devastation visited on London, Coventry and Clydebank, it is hard to comprehend that Hitler had made no preparations for a bombing war. The Luftwaffe was never intended as a strategic weapon. Its original function was to act as handmaiden to the German army. There was plenty of time to build up the Luftwaffe into a strategic force, should it prove necessary, for Hitler had promised Göring in 1938 that his beloved air force would not be required for such a role before 1942; any earlier war with Britain, the Führer had positively assured him, could be ruled out. Born in secret and nurtured at a clandestine base called Lipetsk in Russia, the Luftwaffe was above all a propaganda weapon intended to intimidate those who opposed Germany's expansionist policies. In 1936 the Spanish Civil War provided an ideal opportunity to test the aircraft, equipment and organisation of the new Luftwaffe under the most rigorous operational conditions. Many deficiencies were bought to light and rectified. For instance in 1937, a year after the war started, it was found that the Luftwaffe (like the RAF) did not possess a single modern bomb. Steps were taken to rectify this omission, and new aircraft such as the Heinkel 111, Dornier 17, Junkers 87 dive bomber and the incomparable Messerschmitt 109 received their baptism of fire in the Condor Legion. In the skies over Spain they reigned supreme.

The Heinkel 111 was similar to the Wellington and proved ideal in continental operations, but it had to struggle to reach targets in the north of England, where its lack of fighter escort or power-operated turrets proved fatal. The Dornier 17, nicknamed the 'Flying Pencil', was similar in appearance and performance to the Hampden and it suffered the same fate; neither could defend themselves against fast, well-armed fighters. The Junkers 87, frequently referred to as 'the scourge of Europe' or 'the aircraft that conquered nations', proved as big a disaster as the Fairey Battle, for the gull-winged 'Stuka' fell easy prey to RAF fighters and was quickly withdrawn to less well-defended theatres.

All in all, as August 1939 drew to a close, the scales were just about equally balanced as regarded quality, performance, range and bomb-load on the opposing sides.

The big disparity lay in numbers. Sir Edgar Ludlow-Hewitt could muster a maximum of 17 operational squadrons of strategic bombers (Whitleys, Hampdens and Wellingtons), a total of 272 aircraft (Battles and Blenheims were considered tactical bombers). Availability of crews reduced this even further to an average of 140 bombers. Ranged against this, Jeschonnek, Göring's chief-of-staff, had at his disposal between 1,200 and 1,600 bombers and this did not include hundreds of dive bombers. The Royal Air Force desperately needed a *deus ex machina* (a divine intervention) and it came on the day Germany invaded Poland. The President of the United States, Franklin D. Roosevelt, appealed to the belligerents to refrain from unrestricted aerial bombardment of civilian populations. The British accepted this restriction that same day. The Germans, for their own good reasons, welcomed the appeal 18 days later, once their victory in Poland had been assured.

To Chamberlain's government the logic was sound. The RAF desperately needed to conserve its precious aircrews and bombers while new machines issued from the factories and men were trained to fly them. The Ruhr plan was placed temporarily on the shelf. New targets had to be found that would not provoke instant retaliation on British civilians. A glance at the map of Europe reveals Bomber Command's dilemma. Holland and Belgium wanted nothing to do with the looming hostilities and opted for neutrality, thereby denying Bomber Command direct access to Germany's industrial heartland via their airspace. The Royal Air Force had strict instructions not to overfly neutral territory. The French requested the British to refrain from attacking land targets in Germany because *L'armée de l'Air* had precious few modern bombers to deter an attack or fighters to defend their people. While they were confident that the Maginot Line would stop the Wehrmacht, French politicians, like all other European leaders, were haunted by the spectre of skies darkened by hordes of enemy bombers intent on destroying their cities.

At the Air Ministry they had prepared numerous thick files of possible targets in the event of war with Germany. One of these plans, Western Air Plan 7B, called for the bombing of the German fleet in and around its base at Wilhelmshaven. In the German battleships, the British saw the biggest threat to their vital ocean supply arteries. Besides this, battleships were obviously legitimate targets and, if they could be found clear of land, they could be attacked without the risk of stray bombs killing civilians. Denied direct access to the Ruhr over France and the Low Countries, and fearful of the repercussions from being the first to harm civilians, the British Government seized enthusiastically upon WAP 7B.

The only way into Germany then was via the Heligoland

Bight and the only unmistakeable military targets were battleships. At the Air Ministry it became fashionable to view this new situation as 'keeping the gloves on'. Let the Germans incur the odium of being the first to break Roosevelt's humanitarian appeal; the Royal Air Force would go for the *Scharnhorst*, *Gneisenau*, *Emden*, *Admiral von Scheer*, *Nürnberg*, *Leipzig* and the rest of the German fleet at Wilhelmshaven.

A quarter of a century before, as August 1914 drew to its close, HMS *Arethusa* engaged the German light cruisers *Stettin* and *Frauenlob* in what developed into the first full scale fleet engagement of World War I. In history books this is referred to as the first Battle of Heligoland Bight.

2

La Drôle de Guerre

Early on the morning of 1st September 1939, Hitler unleashed his Stukas on Poland. The Germans called their new form of warfare *blitzkrieg*. In support of their Panzer divisions the Luftwaffe rained down death and destruction, first on the airfields, later on the cities. The Poles resisted gallantly for 27 days but, with half their obsolete airforce destroyed on the ground, cavalry pitted against tanks and Warsaw ablaze from end to end, resistance soon crumbled.

In accordance with treaty obligations, the British Ambassador delivered an ultimatum in Berlin at 9.00 a.m. on 3rd September. It is reported that Hitler, Göring and Goebbels received it with stunned surprise. An answer was demanded within two hours. None was received.

> Everything that I have worked for, everything that I have hoped for, everything that I have believed in during my public life, has crashed in ruins.

So said the British Prime Minister to a silent House of Commons at noon. That evening Chamberlain re-formed his Cabinet with Churchill as First Lord of the Admiralty.

Forty-eight minutes after Chamberlain broke the news to the world, a MkIV Blenheim bomber, N6215, took off from Wyton to reconnoitre the great German naval base at Wilhelmshaven. Several enemy warships were spotted, but when the pilot tried to transmit this information back to base he found that the intense cold at 24,000 feet had frozen up his wireless transmitter. By the time he returned to Wyton it was too late in the day to do anything about it. Early next morning Flying Officer McPherson took off once again and headed his

Blenheim towards the great naval base. As he approached his target low cloud forced him to fly at only 300 feet above the waves. He photographed warships lying in the Schillig Roads near Wilhelmshaven and at Brunsbüttel at the mouth of the River Elbe. Immediately he transmitted this information by wireless but only a garbled account was received back at base. When the Blenheim eventually touched down, just before noon, the aerial photographs were processed to reveal two battle cruisers, the *Gneisenau* and *Scharnhorst* at Brunsbüttel and the 'pocket battleship' *Admiral von Scheer*, with cruisers and destroyers, anchored in the Schillig Roads.

The time had come to test Stanley Baldwin's oft repeated maxim: 'The bomber will always get through'.

The Royal Air Force launched their first bombing raid of the Second World War shortly before 3.00 p.m. on 4th September 1939. In response to Flying Officer McPherson's photographic reconnaissance, eight Wellington bombers of 149 Squadron, under the command of Squadron Leader P.I. Harris, took off from Mildenhall to be joined by a further six Wellingtons of 9 Squadron from Honington under the command of Squadron Leader L.S. Lamb. Their targets were the battleships *Scharnhorst* and *Gneisenau* at Brunsbüttel.

Ten Blenheim bombers of 110 and 107 Squadrons under the command of Flight Lieutenant K.C. Doran also took off from Wattisham, to be joined by a further five Blenheims of 139 Squadron from Wyton. Their target was the *Admiral von Scheer* at Wilhelmshaven. In Doran's words, 'The weather in the Heligoland Bight was bloody, a solid wall of cloud seemed to extend from sea-level and we flew in and out of clouds between 50 and 100 feet'.

So bad was the weather that five of the Wellingtons from 149 Squadron turned back but Squadron Leader Harris pressed on regardless with his other two remaining Wellingtons piloted by Flying Officer Macrae and Flight Lieutenant Stewart. The five Blenheims of 319 Squadron also turned back because of poor visibility.

Before take-off all the pilots had been instructed to bomb only naval ships found clear of land. If any of the warships were tied up alongside in harbour, they were not to be attacked. Under no circumstances were bombs to be dropped on land where civilian casualties could result. These orders were very explicit and stemmed from the War Cabinet's insistence that Bomber Command should do nothing to provoke retaliation on British or French civilians.

President Roosevelt's appeal would be respected, the gloves would stay on. But to young men, ready, willing and able to demonstrate their prowess in battle, the orders seemed crazy. They had no way of understanding just how weak Bomber Command really was. The stage was being set for what would later become known as La Drôle de Guerre – the Phoney War.

Detailed to lead 149 Squadron's eight aircraft that day was Squadron Leader Paul Harris. His second pilot was Pilot Officer Billy Brown, standing in for Pilot Officer Sandy Innes who was convalescing from an appendix operation. They had been with 149 for only a week having both just been posted from the crack 214 Squadron at Feltwell. What they found on arriving at Mildenhall gave rise to considerable misgiving; 149 Squadron was quite unprepared for war. This fact manifested itself only too soon as they ran towards their aircraft – they had no idea where Brunsbüttel was. No prior warning had been given of the target. No time had been allowed to study maps or prepare a plan of attack. No instructions had been issued to the captains other than the fact that there were two cruisers at the entrance to the Kiel Canal – 'go and take a crack at them'. After climbing aboard their aircraft they carried out the pre-flight checks only to find that their machine was unserviceable and so they had to hunt around for another. Flying Officer Bill Macrae, a Canadian, very nearly took off without any bombs onboard; he just looked in the off chance and found none. On the way, Squadron Leader Harris ordered that the guns be tested, only to make the horrifying discovery that not one of them worked. He was flying to Germany in an aircraft that was completely defenceless. Not wanting to turn back on the first raid of the war he made the decision to press on regardless.

Typical of the lack of understanding which existed in the early days of the war is the personal recollection of the Brunsbüttel raid by Sergeant 'Bunny' Austin, the navigator in Paul Harris's Wellington.

> I recall vividly standing by for up to 24 hours or more in the crew room with the crew waiting to go somewhere, we knew not where but assumed it would be Germany. When the call did in fact come we all dashed out to the aeroplane. There was no briefing for crew members other than, I think, the captains, and when we got in the aeroplane and took off I asked the captain, Paul Harris, where we were going, as navigator of the lead machine I would find it useful to know. After handing over to the second pilot, Pilot Officer Brown, he came back to the navigation table and said we were going to the Kiel Canal and I fortunately had all the available charts that one could have at that time in my navigation bag. Taking it out we found the Kiel Canal or rather, we didn't find the Kiel Canal, it was an old admiralty chart and it was labelled Kaiser Wilhelm Canal. I recall saying to Paul, 'Well, that's it', and he said, 'No, no, it's the Kiel Canal', and by some freak of fate a short distance off the Kaiser Wilhelm Canal there was a little tiny tributary marked Kiel Canal. Paul said, 'that's where we're going, that's where we're going'. So I then said, 'do we go straight there?' and he said, 'no, no, we must fox the enemy, we go up north-east then across and then cut down', in other words make a deviation, and we duly set course!

There was no sign of 9 Squadron, and after a couple of hours two of Harris's Wellingtons lost formation and returned to base, dropping their bombs in the sea. 149 Squadron's other three Wellingtons, led by Flight Lieutenant Duguid, got as far as Wangerooge then turned back because of the adverse weather. Bunny Austin goes on to say.

> I also remember on that trip that it was cloudy and on the second leg, which would have led us straight on into Denmark, we lost one of the aeroplanes, by lost, I mean we lost sight of him, he didn't crash or anything, and in fact he didn't quite know what he was doing and he went on and was undoubtedly the crew which was later reported in the papers as having bombed Esbjerg in Denmark. Meanwhile we proceeded, looking for warships

at the entrance to the Kiel Canal.

Paul Harris and his crew didn't find the battleships *Scharnhorst* and *Gneisenau*. Suddenly their Wimpy shuddered; they had taken a direct hit by flak and the rear gun turret was damaged. Fortunately the gunner, Jimmy Mullineaux, had vacated it earlier because the guns were not working. The third aircraft was no longer in view having disappeared into the low cloud. Alone, with a damaged and defenceless aircraft, the Germans alerted and the weather poor, Paul Harris aimed his bombs at a bridge over the River Eider above Tönning and turned for home. He nursed L4302 the 300 miles back and landed at Mildenhall six and a quarter hours after taking off.

But 9 Squadron from Honington found Brunsbüttel, and the three aircraft led by Flight Lieutenant Grant flew into a hail of flak from the battleships' iron ring of anti-aircraft defences. On the approach of the bombers, Luftwaffe fighters from II/JG77 under the command of Oberstleutnant Schumacher took off from Nordholz near Cuxhaven. Feldwebel Hans Troitsch spotted Squadron Leader Lamb's three Wellingtons flying low over the water. As he dived to the attack, two of the bombers turned and disappeared into low cloud. Troitsch pursued the remaining Wellington and shot it down in flames.[3] A second Luftwaffe pilot, Feldwebel Alfred Held, observed burning wreckage on the water and took it to be two twin-engined English bombers, (probably 107 Squadron Blenheims). While circling above this wreckage Held saw, far in the distance, a single Wimpy which he pursued, and after a short battle it crashed into the sea in flames. Meanwhile the Blenheims under Flight Lieutenant Doran at Wilhelmshaven were faring even worse. Flak bought down four and Leutnant Metz, another of Schumacher's pilots, shot down a fifth.[4] *Scharnhorst* and *Gneisenau* escaped unscathed, and *Admiral von Scheer* was hit by three bombs, none of which exploded. The only serious damage caused by the RAF that day occurred when a stricken

---

[3] In April 1963, Generalmajor a. D. (Retired) Carl Schumacher said that he had always believed that Feldwebel Troitsch was the first to shoot down an RAF aircraft.

[4] The Air Ministry denied that any of these losses were due to fighter action, and attributed them all to flak.

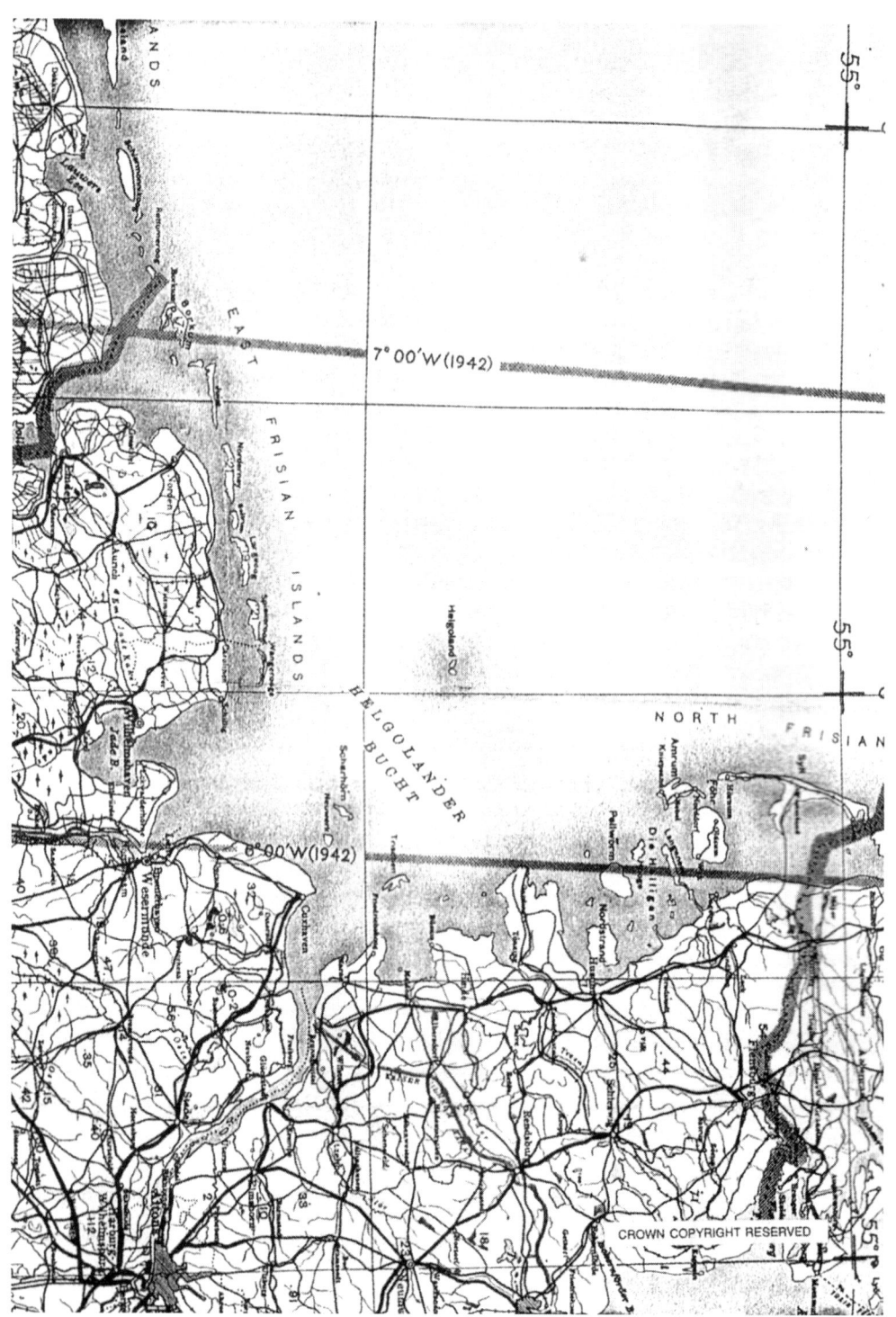

LA DRÔLE DE GUERRE

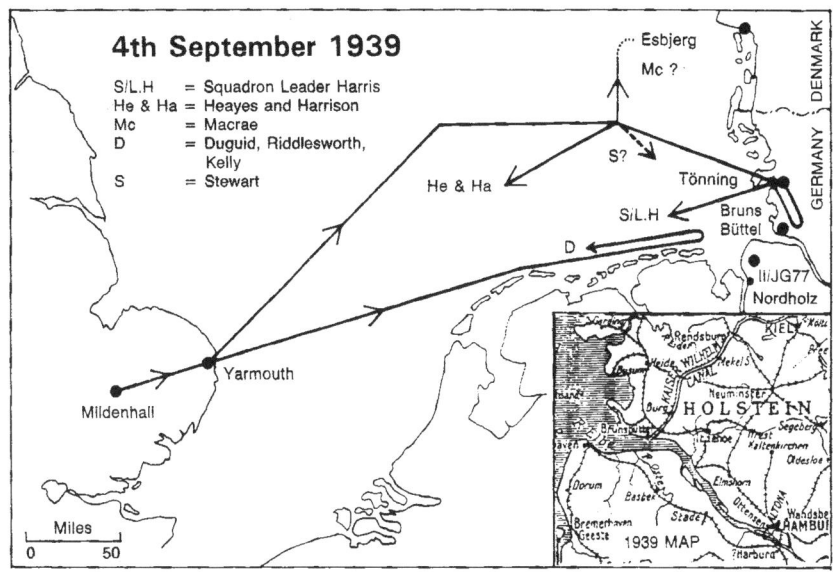

No. 149 Squadron, Mildenhall
L4302 S/Ldr Harris	Dropped bombs on bridge over river Eider.
L4265 F/O Macrae	Dropped bombs on Brunsbüttel (?)
L4271 Sgt Heayes	Turned back, dropped bombs in sea.
L4229 F/Lt Stewart	Dropped bombs off Cuxhaven (?)
L4263 Sgt Harrison	Turned back, dropped bombs in sea.
L4272 F/Lt Duguid	Turned back, dropped bombs in sea.
L4374 F/O Riddlesworth	Turned back, dropped bombs in sea.
L4270 F/Sgt Kelly	Turned back, dropped bombs in sea.

No. 9 Squadron, Honington
Section No.1	Attacked by 9 Messerschmitt Bf 109E-1s.
L4320 S/Ldr Lamb*	Dropped bombs on merchantman (claimed a fighter).
L4268 F/Sgt Borley	Shot down.
L4275 F/Sgt Turner	Shot down.
Section No.4	Encountered heavy A.A. fire from ship's defences.
L4278 F/Lt Grant	Claimed hits on a Battleship in harbour but German
L4287 Sgt Purdy	records mention no damage to either
L4262 Sgt Bowen	*Scharnhorst* or *Gneisenau*.

Luftwaffe
II/JG77 under Oberstleutnant Carl Schumacher at Nordholz (near Cuxhaven).

Feldwebel Alfred Held received the Iron Cross, Second Class, and his victory was widely proclaimed in the German and world press at the time and subsequently related in all historical accounts, as the first victory of a German fighter over a British bomber. Squadron Leader Lamb's Section was the only one that reported being attacked by fighters that day and Feldwebel Troitsch relates that he attacked a formation of THREE Wellingtons, one of which he shot down. Held attacked and shot down a SINGLE Wellington, which could only have been a survivor from Lamb's Section. It appears from this that Generalmajor Schumacher's assertion was correct and it was Troitsch and not Held who merited the laurels. [iv]

---

*S/Ldr Lamb and his crew perished in a flying accident less than a month later (30.10.39).

Blenheim crashed, either accidentally or as a last gallant attempt by its pilot, into the cruiser *Emden*, tearing a huge hole in the bows and inflicting the first casualties of the war on the German navy, 11 sailors were killed and 30 injured.[v]

A week later the first decorations of the war were gazetted; to Flying Officer McPherson and Flight Lieutenant Doran, the DFC for their part in the Brunsbüttel and Wilhelmshaven raids.

The War Cabinet, however, was not unduly impressed with Bomber Command's performance on its first raid against the enemy, and decreed that in future bombers operating from home bases would confine their attacks to German naval ships at sea and not attempt to penetrate heavily defended naval bases. So the 'honour' of sinking the first capital ship of the war fell to Leutnant Schuhart commanding U-29 when his submarine torpedoed and sank the aircraft carrier HMS *Courageous* on 17th September. By the 19th, Bomber and Coastal Command had carried out seven reconnaissance missions into the Heligoland Bight with single aircraft. Little could be achieved by these individual planes because wireless contact with base was proving a chancy business, and, even if they had succeeded in calling up a squadron of bombers, it would have taken several hours for them to arrive. In the meantime, any warships that had been spotted would be safely back in harbour. So a new policy was adopted whereby the Bight would be patrolled by nine or more fully armed bombers under orders to attack any units of the German fleet found in the area. This policy of reconnaissance in force started on 26th September. Whereas Bomber Command had an uneventful trip that day, the Luftwaffe was presented with the opportunity of a lifetime, an opportunity to put the Bomber vs. Battleship controversy to the test.

A Dornier 18 flying boat of the coastal squadron 2/106 based at Nordeney was flying a long-range reconnaissance mission over the North Sea. The pilot could see little because of the heavy cloud cover. Suddenly his observer started; he had just seen a warship through a gap in the clouds. No, he was wrong; it was not one warship, it was a whole battle fleet. The pilot circled the gap in the clouds and counted four huge battleships and an aircraft carrier accompanied by cruisers and destroyers. At once the Do. 18 transmitted back this information. The time was 10.45 a.m. and the Luftwaffe had just found the British Home Fleet at sea and far from the safety of its base. Presented with this golden opportunity, nine He 111s of the 'Lion' Geschwader under the command of Captain Vetter and four of the new Ju 88s of the 'Eagle' Geschwader under the command of Leutnant Storp took off to do battle. Here was a chance in a million to cripple the Royal Navy, and only 13 aircraft were sent to attack HMS *Nelson*, *Rodney*, *Hood*, *Renown* and the aircraft carrier *Ark Royal*, with its screen of cruisers and destroyers. Captain Vetter and Leutnant Storp did no better than Squadron Leader Harris, Squadron Leader Lamb and Flight Lieutenant Doran. One bomb from a Ju 88 hit HMS *Hood* but did not explode and bounced overboard. One bomb from another Ju 88 was seen to throw up a great fountain of water alongside the *Ark Royal*, but the pride of the Royal Navy sailed on and the chance of a lifetime was gone. Göring later claimed that the *Ark Royal* had been sunk, and dismissed as propaganda the British press photographs of her steaming into harbour.

Several days later, on 29th September, 11 Hampdens from 144 Squadron left Hemswell in two sections. One, consisting of five aircraft led by the CO, Wing Commander J.C. Cunningham, took off at 4.05 p.m. and was never seen again. The other, comprising six aircraft led by Squadron Leader W.J.H. Lindley, found two German destroyers steaming at 20 knots in line astern and attacked from 300 feet, but the defensive screen was too effective and no damage was inflicted on the ships. Lindley's section got back safely but Cunningham's fell victim to Me 109s from II/JG 77. After that the theory of reconnaissance in force became less popular.

In both Britain and Germany disillusionment set in. The realities of modern warfare bore no relationship to the textbooks written by veterans of the 1914-18 war. Foul weather, poor navigation, inadequate training, wireless transmitters that froze up, guns that jammed, bombs that didn't explode – *that* was the reality. In modern jargon both adversaries were right at the bottom of the learning curve.

The next move was up to the German navy. In an incredible act of bravery, Leutnant Gunter Prien in U-47 sneaked past the defences into Scapa Flow, torpedoed and sank HMS *Royal*

Oak, and then made good his escape. This attack led to increased surveillance of the east coast of Scotland by German reconnaissance aircraft. Next day HMS *Hood* was spotted heading for the naval base at Rosyth in the Firth of Forth. Göring's chief-of-staff, Jeschonnek, gave orders for an attack to be made on the *Hood* and telephoned Captain Pohle at Westerland with a personal order from the Führer.

> Should the *Hood* already be in dock when KG 30 reaches the Firth of Forth, no attack is to be made. I make you personally responsible for acquainting every crew with this order. The Führer won't have a single civilian killed.

There we have it! La Drôle de Guerre. Exactly the same orders that had been given to Harris, Lamb and Doran prior to the first British raid on Germany were now being issued to Pohle before the first German raid on Britain.

In Germany it was believed that Britain would soon 'see sense' and be prepared to sue for peace, or at least remain a supine observer cowed by the might of the invincible Luftwaffe, an air force that had been instrumental in subjugating Poland two weeks previously. The Führer considered it important not to antagonise the British populace at this stage of the game by bombing their cities, apart from which, the vast majority of his bombers were still tied up in Poland.

On the morning of 16th October, the Luftwaffe set off for its first raid on the mainland of the United Kingdom. At 2.00 p.m. Captain Pohle's squadron of nine Ju 88s flew over Edinburgh and 12,000 feet below lay the Firth of Forth spanned by its famous railway bridge. As German intelligence had told him that there were no Spitfires based in Scotland, his aircraft flew in loose formation. HMS *Hood* had just arrived at Rosyth and was in the sea-lock, being readied for entry into the inner harbour. 'She was a sitting target but orders robbed us of our prize', reported Pohle. Out in the roadstead lay the cruiser HMS *Southampton*. Through a hail of anti-aircraft fire Pohle dived his Ju 88 and released his 1,000lb bomb. It went straight through three decks without exploding, came out of the side of the cruiser and sank an admiralty launch tied up alongside.

'Achtung! Achtung! Spitfire' was a cry later to become famous in the skies over Kent. German intelligence had got its facts wrong[5]; Spitfires thundered into Göring's new 'Wonder Bombers'. With smoke pouring from his port engine, Pohle turned seaward. Bullets slammed into his machine. He was a sitting duck. His radio-operator and rear-gunner were hit. The Spitfires came at him again. This time his observer was hit and his starboard engine packed up. Just before passing out, Captain Pohle succeeded in ditching in the sea close to Crail. Five days later he regained consciousness in Port Edgar hospital, the sole survivor from his aircraft. In accord with the sentiment prevailing at that time, Flight Lieutenant George Pinkerton, a flight leader in 602 Squadron who had shot down the Ju 88, visited Helmut Pohle in hospital. Pinkerton's ground crew, Sergeant Harry Henderson and his comrades, carried the coffins of two dead members of Pohle's crew who were buried with full military honours in Portobello Cemetery, Edinburgh. The chivalry of World War I was still maintained by both sides during the early days of the war. The results of the attack had been minimal. The cruisers HMS *Southampton* and HMS *Edinburgh* together with the destroyer HMS *Mohawk* suffered only superficial damage. I/KG30 lost two aircraft, 4D+AK and 4D+DH. First Brunsbüttel and Wilhelmshaven now Rosyth, both were daylight raids on heavily defended naval bases. Bomber Command didn't get the message but the Royal Navy did. That very next day I/KG30 took off again under its new commander, Captain Doench. Their target was the British Home Fleet at Scapa Flow, but the birds had flown and were safely out of range in Loch Ewe on the west coast of Scotland. All that remained at Scapa Flow was the old depot ship HMS *Iron Duke*, whose sides were damaged by near misses. On the island of Hoy the first German bombs of the war fell on British soil.

October wore on into November with little activity from either the Luftwaffe or Bomber Command. By mid-November German aircraft had started sowing magnetic mines round the British coast. At sea, enemy U-boats were exacting a mounting

---

[5] 603 City of Edinburgh Squadron was based at Turnhouse and 602 City of Glasgow Squadron had just arrived on 13th October at Drem near Haddington.

toll on shipping, and the First Lord of the Admiralty was becoming increasingly restive. On the 17th, a reconnaissance plane patrolling the Wilhelmshaven area reported that it had spotted several warships exercising in the area. Because bombers could not reach the area before dusk, no action was taken. The First Lord of the Admiralty raged at such 'tepid indecision'. Things were truly grim. Shipping losses were mounting and the Germans were using magnetic mines to which we had no counter. Why, demanded Winston Churchill, did the RAF not venture to Wilhelmshaven? Bomber Command accordingly received instructions to mount 'a major operation with the object of destroying an enemy battle-cruiser or pocket-battleship'. This order removed the restriction on attacking enemy warships in the immediate vicinity of German naval bases. However, the 'greatest care' was still to be exercised to ensure that there would be no casualties to German civilians; 'no bombs are to be aimed at warships in dock or berthed alongside the quays'. This was an echo of the Führer's order to Captain Pohle. Both sides were still intent on keeping the war within bounds.

At the same time as Winston Churchill demanded a more aggressive policy from Bomber Command, a brand new Mk 1A Wellington bomber was winging its way from the factory towards RAF Mildenhall. A few days previously it had been rolled on to the tarmac at Weybridge. At 4.30 p.m. on 16th November, Vickers chief test pilot Mutt Summers took it up and put it through its paces. After ten minutes it landed, had a few minor adjustments made, and took off again. This time everything worked perfectly. The new Wimpy was taken on charge of 149 Squadron at Mildenhall on 20th November and given the squadron letter 'R for Robert'. As the large white letters OJ R were painted on the sides of its fuselage, Wellington N2980 was ready to go to war. It didn't have long to wait.

3RD DECEMBER 1939

Bomber Command's response to Churchill was to mount a major raid on the German island fortress of Heligoland, two tiny rock outcrops in the German Bight, 75km north of Wilhelmshaven. Twenty-four of the RAF's latest Mk 1A

Wellingtons from 38, 115 and 149 Squadrons were detailed to attack any enemy naval vessels found in the area. The raid was led by the CO of 149 Squadron, Wing Commander R. Kellett, AFC. 149 Squadron provided 12 aircraft, grouped into four sections of three. Leading the attack, Kellett positioned his section well out in front. Following some distance behind and leading the remainder was Paul Harris with his section. Off to his right and behind flew the third section led by a young Canadian, Flight Lieutenant J.B. Stewart in a brand new Wimpy, OJ R. Directly behind Stewart flew the fourth section led by Flight Lieutenant A.G. Duguid.

Sitting next to Paul Harris was the second pilot, Pilot Officer Herome Alexander Innes, a handsome young Scot from Perth. The events of that day were later recorded in his little hardbacked notebook.

> 3.12.39 The amazing has actually happened. We have been on a real live raid and what is more dropped our bombs with success and come away with no casualties except damage from AA fire and we went out 24 aircraft, 12 of ours and 12 of 38 Squadron. Up to a point off Denmark and then south to Heligoland and then to Schillig Roads. Object to find and bomb any enemy warship – Wing Commander Kellett leading and separated from us to reconnoitre Heligoland. Leaving Paul Harris and I to lead remainder. We were joined by rest of formation over Thetford where they were waiting – most impressive sight and awe inspiring seeing so many Wellingtons spoiling for a fight and without doubt the most efficient bombing plane in existence. The formation on these trips is amazing. No point in close up so we were spread back for several miles. I often wonder what the population think when we pass overhead heading for the North Sea. Anyhow when we got to the separation point after a very good trip north, grand weather 5/10 cloud. Threw out sea markers in case they were hit by bullets and flew on. Suddenly we saw Kellett's formation swing round and at same time got code signal saying that Cruisers were at Heligoland. We swung round after having passed within two-three miles of it. Amazing thing we were quite clear,

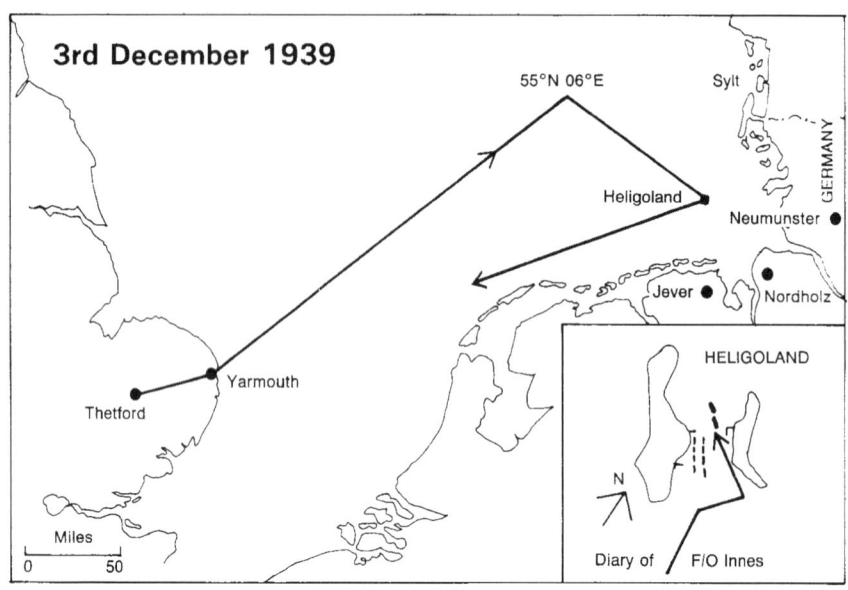

No. 149 Squadron

N2960 W/Cdr Kellett, AFC	Bombed the two cruisers, all bombs missed.
N2892 F/O Turner	Bombed the two cruisers, all bombs missed.
N2946 F/Sgt Way	Bombed the two cruisers, all bombs missed.
N2893 S/Ldr Harris	Bombed the two cruisers, three hits claimed on one.
N2868 F/O Briden	
N2943 F/O Bulloch	Attacked by four ME 109s, hits claimed on one.
N2980 F/Lt Stewart	Made a second attack on a ship outside the harbour.
N2945 Sgt Heayes	
N2867 F/O Smith	
N2984 F/Lt Duguid	Attack baulked by cloud. Returned with bombs on.
N2944 F/O Riddlesworth	Returned independently due to petrol running low.
N2894 F/Sgt Kelly	

Luftwaffe
4 Me 109Ds of I/JG26 Jever led by Hauptmann Dickore intercepted.
1 Me 109 shot down by Cpl Copley (38 Sq.), Pilot Lt Günter Specht survived.*

4 Me 109Ds of 10(N) /JG26 Jever	Took off too late
4 Me 109Es of Jagd. Gruppe 101, Neumünster	to intercept the
8 Me 109Es of II(J) /Tr.Gr.186, Nordholz	Wellingtons.
8 Me 110Cs of I/ZG26 Jever	Luftwaffe Report
	for 4th Dec. '39.

---

*Günter Specht lost his left eye in this action but survived and went on to become one of the Luftwaffe's top aces with at least 32 confirmed victories, 15 of which were American four-engined bombers. He was reported missing in action on the 1st January 1945 during 'Operation Bodenplatte'.

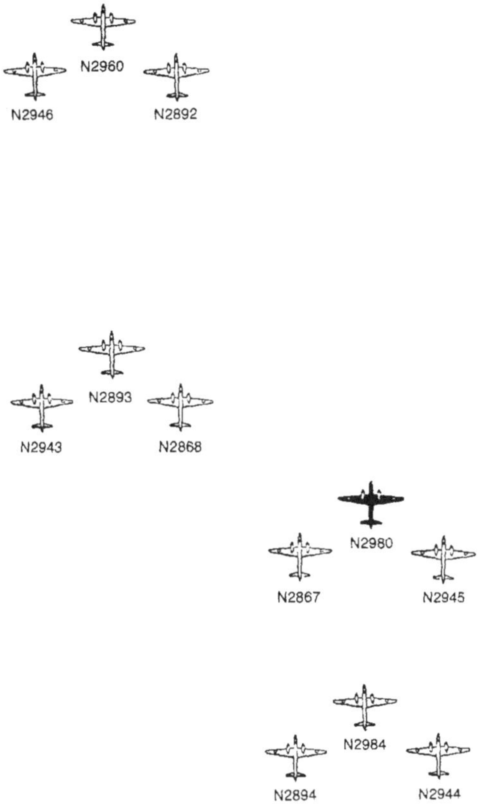

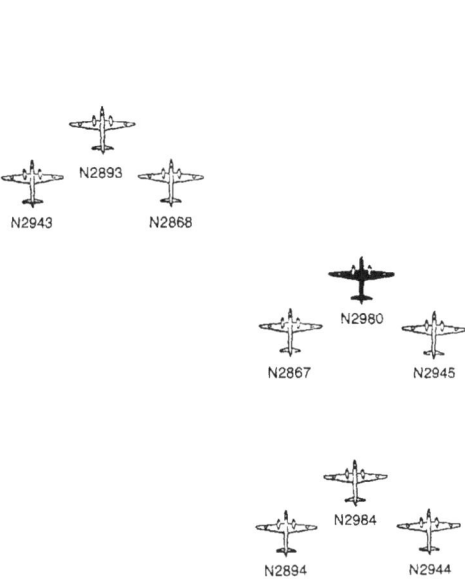

149 Squadron, 3rd December 1939

no cloud yet no AA fire. Passing round west side we swung round and ran up to the north. Sure enough there in between the two islands were several ships. So I gave the usual orders for bombing. Amazing thing but it seemed exactly the same as bombing with practise bombs at Berners Heath. Apparently no ack-ack fire which seemed odd – into cloud so had to go almost over target before release – I gave usual orders – left left, steady when Squadron Leader suggested altering course to avoid AA fire. So we turned right and then left and ran up and bombed. Not a good release for a bit to left of target but when they hit I saw first one bomb over ship by 20-30 yards then in quick succession the remaining three 500 SAP[6] fell amidship on the ship, all three appeared to land at same time – so sleepy.

---

[6] Semi Armour Piercing.

4.12.39 Dog tired yesterday and fell asleep writing it up. The bombs went off three in a bunch and one just after – not a good release – but as it turned out very fortunate for all three appeared to hit direct. Funny thing but I saw the last bomb strike and explode just before the first three – probably due to the three having to pierce the ship before exploding. I don't see how the ship could survive long after that. Unfortunately the clouds came up and though I took photos none of them showed the right place for immediately after release we turned off and took evasive action. Anyhow all this time while I was at the bomb window blissfully bombing we were apparently under the most intense AA fire. They were exploding short of leader and just ahead of us. In fact we apparently went straight through one burst in the run up. Also they had got our height to within 100-200 feet, some of the squadron had small damage from AA but no harm. Stewart had cloud at the critical moment so made it a dummy run and came up a second time. He deserves a medal if anyone does. Someone says they blew up an AA battery with an inaccurate bomb. Some gunners even peppered the island from 10,500 feet (2 miles) – optimistic. Anyhow we skidaddled as soon as possible and when some five-ten miles away from island fighters appeared. Great excitement. Every tail gunner in the formation had a go. We were about a mile away and at least four-five formations between us but no one was going to miss such a chance and the first we have had, tracer bullets everywhere. I saw three Me 109s climbing to attack, then one attacking and one going away with black smoke pouring out so it may have been got. Remainder saw formation of 24 aircraft with four guns apiece to the rear and thinking better of it broke off attack at least 600 yards away. We were very sick for we wanted to really test these aircraft and turrets. After that there was no more excitement and we arrived home at 1410 after 5h 10m trip. Late for lunch. Heard today that Marham Squadron saw a direct hit on cruiser – but still no photographs. When we got back, went immediately to intelligence officer where questioned, filled in forms, handed in logs etc. I was hauled off to ops room, questioned by group captain then put onto the phone and had to tell it all again to senior air staff officer. I couldn't tell much except that it was the largest ship there and I got it. Very tired that night and bed early.

5.12.39 I was thinking this evening on the dangers of aerial bombing. How one does not give a jot to the nature of a target (anyhow for high bombing). All you worry about is that it *is* the target. It might just as well be a mark on the ground. So there is a great danger of bombing targets involving immense loss of life and just because you can't see detail it doesn't worry you one bit. For instance there may have been 200-300 on that ship on Sunday and yet am I thinking about them? – No not a bit. War perhaps, but a most impersonal war.

An official source[vi] states that the result of this raid was one minesweeper[7] sunk by a bomb which passed through the bottom of the vessel without exploding, some accidental damage on land to an anti-aircraft emplacement and one enemy fighter shot down. Not a single German, service or civilian, was killed in the attack, which a German report describes as 'cleverly delivered from the sun and executed with great certainty in avoiding the residential area of the island'.

Group Captain Harris and Wing Commander Austin both personally confirm that they hit a German warship that day. Bunny Austin relates:

> Again looking at my logbook I find that we did do another operation before the December 18th raid. This was against Heligoland over Heligoland on December 3rd and again on this occasion Paul Harris was the skipper and Sandy Innes, Pilot Officer Innes, was our second pilot. It was really a successful raid in the sense that the German ship, the *Brummer* I think it was, was hit by a salvo of bombs and Sandy Innes did the bombing. I remember that I was a little upset on this particular occasion because Paul ruled

---
[7]German Situation Report West No. 104, 4th December 1939, states: 'A lugger was sunk by an unexploded bomb'.

that Sandy Innes should do the bombing if the ships were moving and I would do it if the ships were stationary. Before the arrival of observers and NCO observers on the squadrons it had been the practise that the second pilot did the bombing and in all fairness Sandy Innes was a skilful bomb aimer. I think he would be the first to admit that he was extremely lucky, a salvo of bombs actually fell on the rear-end of the *Brummer*. In fact the bomb stick setting was not adjusted correctly and he'd actually salvoed the whole darned lot and he was lucky they hit. This raid led High Command up the garden path a little; although there was a fair amount of anti-aircraft fire we saw fighters but were certainly not seriously attacked and I don't think there were any losses at all, certainly not by our squadron. Some people I think gained the impression that the Germans held-off because we were too formidable a target, wishful thinking I fear.

The war diary[8] of the commander of the North Sea Defence (BSN) on 3.12.39, states that a minesweeper M1407[9] was sunk by a bomb which holed the forward section without exploding. No mention is made of any hits on a cruiser or on a Artillerieschulschiffe called *Brummer*.

During the action, Squadron Leader Harris's number three aircraft (to the left and behind) became detached from his section and was set upon by four Me 109s. Three did not come any closer than 600 yards but the fourth ventured into range and was fired at by the ventral and rear gun turrets. The Me 109 was observed to fall away to one side emitting black smoke but later righted itself before it reached the water and flew off. In the first section, flak damaged Kellett's number two and number three aircraft but did not prevent them from reaching home. Leading Aircraftman J. Copley, in the rear turret of a 38 Squadron Wimpy, first learned of a hostile presence when an armour piercing bullet lodged in the quick release box of his parachute harness. He was credited with shooting down a Messerschmitt that ventured too close and

---

[8]Bundesarchiv – Militärarchiv: Ref. No. RM61 II/v./M/149/35064.
[9]A converted trawler, formerly called the *Johann Schulte*.

was later awarded the DFM. By accident, a Wellington from 115 Squadron released over land a bomb that had been 'hung-up' in its bomb-bay. By good fortune it hit a military target, an aircraft gun emplacement, the first British bomb of the war to land on German soil. All 24 Wellingtons headed for home – four stragglers bringing up the rear.

Back at Mildenhall, Wing Commander Kellett turned to Paul Harris as they strolled away from their aircraft and asked, 'Did I lead all right?' to which Paul replied, 'Go a little slower next time'.

14TH DECEMBER 1939

In the North Sea, His Majesty's submarine *Salmon* had torpedoed the German cruisers *Nürnberg* and *Leipzig* the previous day and they were now limping back under their own steam to the safety of Wilhelmshaven.

At this period of the war, Coastal Command had the right to order sweeps as required and now called up Bomber Command to go and finish them off. A large force of Hampdens and Wellingtons were brought to 'stand by'. The Hampdens took off at dawn on the morning of the 14th but found nothing and returned. Just before 11.45 a.m., 12 Wellingtons from 99 Squadron under the command of Wing Commander J.F. Griffiths, flying in the leading aircraft piloted by Squadron Leader McKee, took off from Newmarket. The weather was bad. As they passed over Yarmouth at 1,000 feet the aircraft were flying just below 10/10 cloud. Proceeding out over the sea the weather deteriorated. Approaching the Dutch coast just before 1.00 p.m. the squadron had to descend to 600 feet because of low cloud and they flew on through drizzle and fine rain. Experience on 4th September and 3rd December indicated that the fighter defences of north-west Germany were weak and apparently half-hearted. The 12 aircraft were formed up into four sections of three, as 149 Squadron had been on the previous Heligoland raid. Terschilling was sighted at 1.05 p.m., and the formation turned slightly northwards as though heading for Heligoland to put the flak ships off the scent. They were thought to have been the early warning source on Kellett's raid. Actually the Germans had been using a form of early-warning radar called 'Freya' which had given the defences eight minutes warning of the attack.

When they reached the map references 54°N 07°30′E the squadron swung round in the direction of the Schillig Roads. By now the weather had deteriorated to such an extent that they were flying only 200 feet above the waves and just below the cloud base. The Wimpys were armed with three 500lb SAP bombs that had to be dropped from at least 2,000 feet to enable them to penetrate armoured decks, and Griffiths had been ordered not to drop his bombs unless he could see his target from that height. At 2.15 p.m., the island of Wangerooge was sighted about two miles dead ahead. The bombers then turned due east and flew parallel to the coast until they spotted a submarine on the surface. The submarine fired a red-ball signal cartridge. In response, Griffiths fired two red signal cartridges on the off-chance that it might be the required recognition signal. The submarine promptly crash-dived. The course was then altered to a north-easterly heading and at 2.25 p.m. two cruisers were observed steaming due south about a mile away. The heading was changed to north to enable Griffiths to fly parallel with the ships so that he could examine them for torpedo damage inflicted by HM submarine *Salmon* the previous day. One of the cruisers was the *Nürnberg* doing about ten knots, but they passed one another too quickly for any damage assessment to be made. To give himself enough time to prepare for an attack, Griffiths continued to head north then turned in a wide arc to port until his squadron pointed southwards on the same heading as the cruisers. At 2.29 p.m., three escorting destroyers appeared dead ahead. They opened fire immediately on the Wellingtons as they flew overhead at a height of only 200 feet. Five minutes later the two cruisers came into view putting up a fierce barrage of flak from main and secondary armament along with pom-pom fire. Prudently the Wellingtons skirted the cruisers and, knowing that they could not attack with their 500lb SAP bombs from such a low level, decided to call it a day. The aircraft turned westward towards home and, as the island of Wangerooge loomed up out of the mist half a mile ahead, three tiny specks were observed climbing towards the formation.

Harry von Bülow's Messerschmitts were now stationed on Wangerooge and his new Bf109E-1s were more potent than the

LA DRÔLE DE GUERRE   39

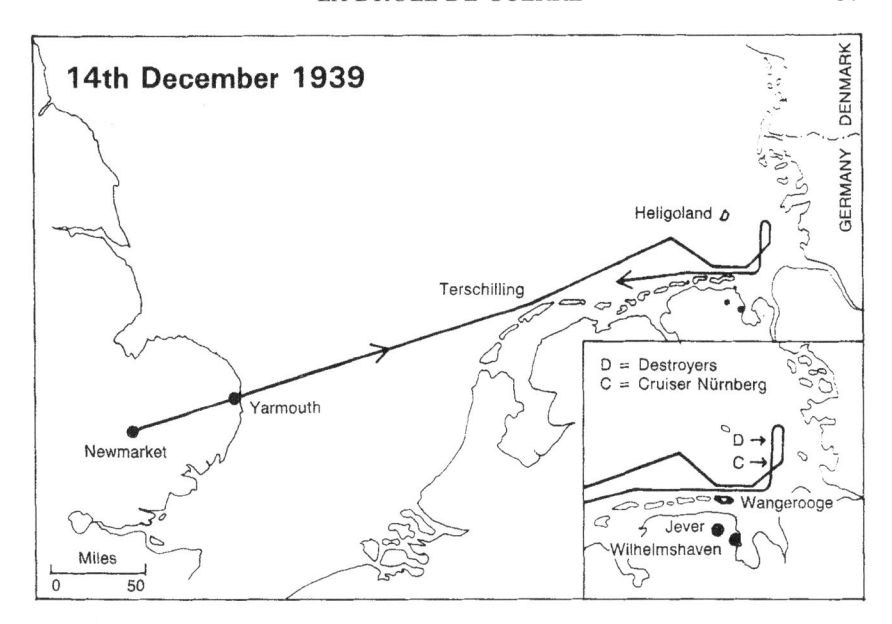

14th December 1939

[Map showing flight path from Newmarket/Yarmouth across to Terschilling, Heligoland, and the German coast area including Wangerooge, Jever, Wilhelmshaven. Inset shows D = Destroyers, C = Cruiser Nürnberg.]

No. 99 Squadron

N2958 S/Ldr McKee	Claimed a fighter shot down by Cpl Bickerstaff.
N2887 F/O Dyer	
N2870 P/O Lewis	Collided with N2911 and crashed into the sea.
N2913 F/Lt Brough	
N2886 F/Sgt Healey	Shot down in flames.
N2911 F/Sgt Downey	Collided with N2870 and crashed into the sea.
N2912 S/Ldr Catt	
N2914 F/O Smith	
N2999 F/Sgt Williams	
N2957 F/Lt Hetherington	Crash landed at Newmarket, three killed including captain.
N2986 Sgt Brace	Shot down in flames. Possibly shot down a Me109.
N2956 F/O Cooper	Last seen heading for German coast with undercarriage down.

Luftwaffe[vii]

II/JG77: 3 Squadrons of Me109E-1s based at Jever.

Staffel 4.
Oberleutnant Henz	Claimed one Wellington.
Feldwebel Sawallisch	Claimed two Wellingtons.
Leutnant Demer	Claimed one Wellington
Leutnant Brankmeier	Shot down and killed (possibly by N2986).

1/ZG26: 1 'Schwarm' (4 aircraft) of Me110Cs at Jever.

Staffel 2.
Captain Restemeier (CO)	Claimed one Wellington. His fighter was badly damaged and the pilot was wounded in the head.
Hauptgefreiter Schulze	Claimed one Wellington.

Note: Most history books assert that the RAF first encountered Göring's new Me110 'Destroyers' during the Battle of Heligoland Bight on the 18th of December 1939. In fact, Restemeier's 'Schwarm' of Me110s attacked 99 Squadron on the 14th of December 1939. Two days later, 2/ZG26 was transferred from Jever to Crailsheim (Würzburg area) and was replaced by twenty-three Bf 110s of 1/ZG76.

Bf109Ds that had intercepted Kellett 11 days earlier. The Messerschmitts formed up in line astern from below and attacked the right-hand aircraft in the last section. Sergeant Brace's aircraft was hit and fell away in flames towards the sea. On his left, Flying Officer Cooper was seen to be in trouble. His undercarriage came down and he broke away from the formation and disappeared into the clouds, heading south towards the German coast. The rear and under turrets of the two rearmost sections blazed away at the attackers. One of the Messerschmitt 109s spiralled down trailing black smoke and was seen by several observers to crash into the sea. From above and behind the leading aircraft of Squadron Leader McKee, a Me 110 dived into the attack and opened fire at a range of 250 yards. In the rear turret, Corporal Bickerstaff aimed his two Brownings and fired directly into the cockpit. Tracers were seen to drill into the fuselage at the pilot's position and emerge out of the other side. The German aircraft burst into flames and was last seen diving towards the sea where it was claimed to have been seen hitting the water. Directly behind the first section, Flight Lieutenant Brough fought off another Me 110 which was also claimed to have crashed into the sea.

Meanwhile in the leading section, Pilot Officer Lewis's Wellington was observed to falter and turn towards the rear where he collided with the Wellington flown by Flight Sergeant Downey. Both aircraft crashed into the sea. Another Wellington, flown by Flight Sergeant Healey, was seen to be on fire and it heeled over to show the geodetic members on the underside of the aircraft well exposed. Crews in the third section could see four blazing wrecks on the water and at first assumed they were twin-engined Messerschmitt 110s until it was realised that six of the Wellingtons had vanished from the formation. The blazing twin-engined wrecks were Wellingtons, not 110s. Later a Wellington reappeared out of the clouds once they were well on the way home. It was Flight Lieutenant Hetherington, the leader of the ill-fated rear section. The last attack occurred as the now much-depleted formation crossed the Dutch frontier just after 3.00 p.m. Arriving back at Newmarket, six of the Wellingtons landed safely but Hetherington's aircraft had been badly damaged and crashed in a field just off the racecourse killing the pilot and two of his crew.

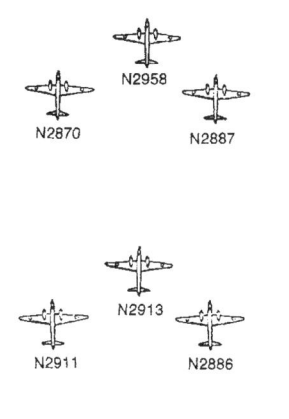

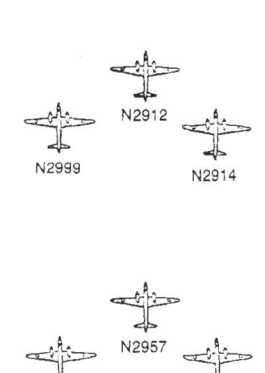

99 Squadron, 14th December 1939

Yet again the German navy had escaped unscathed. For the price of one fighter shot down, Bomber Command lost six precious Wellingtons and five-and-a-half irreplaceable crews. How on earth could the concept of daylight raids by self-defending bomber formations survive in the face of a loss rate of 50 per cent? The official report[viii] came out with this surprising comment:

> After careful analysis of individual reports by all members of crews, it seems almost possible to assume that none of our aircraft were brought down by fire from the Messerschmitts.

Jackie Baldwin who was the cheerful and popular AOC of 3

Group got it just about correct when he referred to the events of the 14th thus: 'I place it somewhat on a par with the Charge of the Light Brigade'. Air Commodore Norman Bottomley, Bomber Command's senior air staff officer and the future deputy chief of air staff from 1941, wrote in his covering letter[viii]:

> **Formation Flying**
> It is now by no means certain that enemy fighters did in fact succeed in shooting down any of the Wellingtons. Considering that enemy aircraft made most determined and continuous attacks for 26 minutes on the formation, the failure of the enemy must be ascribed to good formation flying. The maintenance of tight, unshaken formation in the face of the most powerful enemy action is the test of bomber force fighting efficiency and morale. In our service it is the equivalent of the old 'Thin Red Line' or the 'Shoulder to Shoulder' of Cromwell's Ironsides.

Down at the sharp end, Sandy Innes jotted down some comments in his notebook.

> 14.12.39 The other side of war with a vengeance tonight – aircraft lost left, right and centre. First of all Jimmy Carter and Forbes Irving came over from Methwold and told us they had lost a plane last night – straight in while night flying. No apparent reason. Three dead. And then tonight came news of 99 and the result of their sweep in the Heligoland Bight. Clouds 900 feet so too low to bomb though they saw some cruisers. However they came round again in hope but no good and the fighters came in, Me 110 and 109. Seven attacks delivered, so Germans must have got over the shocks at the dustbins.[10] We got three of them, maybe four and they got one of ours down. Another one hit which collided, both being lost. Two missing on way back and one went in near Newmarket – total six aircraft and about five and a half crews. What a shambles, in practically every case it was the unarmoured port wing which caught alight. Why in heavens name they didn't bung on armour there as well beats me.

---

[10]Dustbins: the name given to the Mk 1A Wellington's ventral (underneath) gun turret.

LA DRÔLE DE GUERRE

With six aircraft lost out of a force of 12, the part played by the German fighter defences should have been the subject of the closest scrutiny. Comments in Bottomley's letter such as '...it is remarkable that our casualties were so light' and 'Had it not been for good leadership, losses from enemy aircraft might have been heavy' do not seem to tally with the facts.

> 1. The surviving Wellingtons (including Hetherington's) were found to be full of *bullet* holes.
> 2. The report clearly states: 'Enemy fighters were difficult to see when below near the sea, owing to the overcast sky, poor visibility and the effective camouflaging of the upper surfaces of the aircraft'.
> 3. At least three Wellingtons were *seen* to have been brought down by the action of enemy fighters (Sandy Innes's diary).

So the myth of the Wellington's invulnerability to fighter attack when flying in 'tight, unshaken formations' was to be upheld – for another four days anyhow:

> It may be argued that Wellington formations are quite capable of defending themselves successfully against fighter attack. That is certainly true...[viii]

The culprit on the 14th was decreed as flak. Henceforth, daylight raids on heavily defended targets would take place from heights out of range of anti-aircraft guns.

Across the North Sea, the Luftwaffe report was more precise. Lagebericht[11] West No. 115, Luftwaffe HQ, 15th December 1939 states:

> German pilots registered five kills, plus one probable but unconfirmed kill. One German fighter shot down.

The German naval flak gunners did not submit one single claim for an aircraft shot down.

---

[11] Situation Report.

At 3 p.m. on the afternoon of 17th December, Baldwin telephoned on the scrambler to Air Commodore Bottomley at Bomber Command HQ at High Wycombe, to urge a further operation against the German fleet.

The group commander pointed out the importance of seizing the very first suitable day in view of the few such occasions which were likely to present themselves under winter conditions. He stated that from the point of view of preparation, the details of the plan had been thoroughly considered by all concerned, and he was satisfied that if Monday 18th December were given as zero day, there would be no undue haste in planning and preparation right down to the crews engaged.

Air Chief Marshal Sir Edgar Ludlow-Hewitt, commander-in-chief of Bomber Command, concurred. He approved Baldwin's proposal to mount a new attack on the German fleet at Wilhelmshaven on the 18th, subject only to a proviso that the Wellingtons bomb from at least 10,000 feet, which should take them above effective flak. Group Captain Goodwin, senior air staff officer at Group HQ, drafted orders for the operation to be carried out by 24 Wellingtons. Nine aircraft would come from 149 Squadron at Mildenhall, including that of the formation leader, Wing Commander Richard Kellett, who had also led the 3rd December sweep; nine would come from 9 Squadron at Honington; the remaining six from 37 Squadron at Feltwell. 'Task: to attack enemy warships in the Schillig Roads or Wilhelmshaven', began the operation order. 'Great care is to be taken that no bombs fall on shore, and no merchant ships are to be attacked. Formations shall not loiter in the target area, and all aircraft are to complete bombing as soon as possible after the sighting signal has been made.'

'Not only did I have all the leaders into the operations room the night before the mission went out,' wrote Baldwin to Ludlow-Hewitt a few days later, 'but I personally explained to each of them my ideas on formation flying and what I meant by mutual assistance, and they all professed that they agreed and understood.'

Late in the afternoon of Sunday 17th, the order went out to the squadrons taking part in the operation to stand-by at two hours notice for take-off from 0730 hours on the morning of the 18th. Pilots and observers were briefed by squadron and station commanders. Before dawn on the 18th, a Whitley of 4 Group, from 78 Squadron at Dishforth in Yorkshire, flew out across the North Sea, approaching the island of Heligoland at 0800 in patchy cloud, ideal cover for a daylight bomber operation. The crew signalled their weather report, and turned homewards towards England. 3 Group HQ passed the final readiness order to the Wellington squadrons: take-off would be at 0930; squadrons would take up formation over King's Lynn before crossing the North Sea. The attack on Wilhelmshaven was on.[ix]

The first full-scale fleet engagement of World War II was less than six hours away. Over that self-same little bit of North Sea where the *Arethusa* had chased the *Stettin* and *Frauenlob* a quarter of a century before, a fleet of Messerschmitts would shortly tear into a fleet of Wellington bombers. In this forthcoming battle, the Royal Air Force would be the first to learn that daylight raids over heavily defended targets were untenable and this would lead them to seek safety in the hours of darkness.

> It was not until December (1939) that the Wellingtons were again involved in a serious encounter with the German air defences and, from the point of view of the effect which they had upon subsequent operations, the three actions which were fought on 3rd, 14th and 18th December were among the most important of the war.[x]

3
149 (East India) Squadron – Mildenhall

'F for Freddie' was a very famous film star in 1941. Those of us who were around at the time will have no difficulty remembering the name of the picture that featured this celebrity. If, as is more likely, that era is familiar only through the pages of history books or post-war films, then 'F for Freddie' was a Wellington bomber of 149 Squadron based at Mildenhall. The name of the film was *Target for Tonight* and it was made at a time when the morale of the nation was at a very low ebb. Britain stood alone. Poland, Norway, Denmark, Holland, Belgium and France had fallen under the heel of the Nazi jackboot. Only the Battle of Britain had saved us from a similar fate. Huge areas of London, Coventry, Clydebank and many other cities lay in ruins. Over four million tons of shipping had been sent to the bottom between June 1940 and March 1941. We dearly wanted to know that we could 'give it' as well as 'take it'.

Along to the local cinema came *Target for Tonight*. There, the public was treated to the spectacle of a 'typical' RAF raid on an enemy rail junction and secret fuel dump. Spirits soared as 'F for Freddie' dived through a hail of tracer shells and flak to drop its bombs – bang on target. We thrilled as the young bomb aimer pressed the 'tit' and reported 'bombs gone'. But it was all pure hokum. There is no record of 'F for Freddie' ever having been used operationally. In a secret report to the Air Ministry on 18th August 1941 it was revealed that Bomber Command was lucky to get one bomb in ten within *five* miles of its target. Fortunately for national morale, the Butt Report and its scandalous findings were kept secret. Every night as people gathered round the wireless to listen to Alvar Liddell, Bruce Belfrage, or John Snagge read the nine o'clock news, names like Mannheim, Gelsenkirchen, Frankfurt, Hamburg, Cologne, Essen and Dortmund became synonymous with the growing determination to repay Hitler for the havoc he had wrought. Satisfaction at hearing the marshalling yards at Hamm had been bombed (yet again) was always tinged with apprehension as everyone waited to hear the price that had been paid. The news that 'One of our aircraft is missing' always brought forth a sigh and a shake of the head; secretly all hoped it was not 'F for Freddie'. Hokum perhaps, but in 1941 *Target for Tonight* was immensely popular and just what the doctor ordered. So what if the aircraft never fired a shot in anger? It was worth its weight in gold. 149 Squadron probably did more for the war effort with that one film than all the bombs it had dropped on Germany up till then. Though only acting in the film, the pilot of 'F for Freddie', Group Captain P.C. Pickard, DSO DFC, later played the role of real life hero when he led his Mosquito squadron in the legendary attack on Amiens prison in 1944. Sadly he did not survive the attack.

It is not surprising that 149 Squadron should have been chosen to lift the nation's spirits in 1941. The squadron had played a prominent role in a much earlier propaganda film made during the early days of the Phoney War. This film was called *The Lion has Wings*, and starred Ralph Richardson and Merle Oberon. Films made during the war portraying the exploits of Bomber Command are very few and far between. After the war, cinema audiences were deluged with celluloid reruns of the stiff-upper-lip exploits of the RAF and the rather less formal missions of the USAAF. Without doubt the most famous of all these post-war films was *The Dam Busters*. Made with the benefit of hindsight it provides a realistic insight into the workings of Bomber Command in 1943. By then the threads were beginning to be pulled together. Experienced aircrews, radio-navigation, four-engined heavyweight bombers, all combined to fulfil Lord Trenchard's vision of the RAF as a powerful strategic weapon of war. Over four years the RAF matured into a dedicated, highly professional and, above all, lethal organisation. How different things were in 1939. *The Lion has Wings* grants us a rare glimpse into the past. It allows us to see the RAF as it was in the beginning. Present-day audiences, conditioned by slick camera work and spectacular special effects, would find it more than a little hammy if not downright hilarious in places. The important thing is not to look at the actors but at the faces of the airmen, young, eager and – dare one say it – naïve. These were faces that belonged on the school rugby pitch or bending over the oars as Oxford and Cambridge pulled for the finishing line. Paul Harris is there, laughing and joking with his comrades as they stand by their Wimpys in mock readiness to take off and teach the jolly old Hun a lesson. Less than a month after the film was released in November, those same young innocent faces climbed aboard their aircraft in earnest and headed out over the North Sea towards Wilhelmshaven where the jolly old Hun shot them out of the sky.

149 Squadron, along with 9, 37, 38, 99 and 115, made up the operational squadrons of No. 3 Bomber Group together with 214 and 215 Squadrons in reserve. Formed initially as a night bomber group equipped with Handley Page Heyfords, Handley Page Harrows and Fairey Hendons, there had been no requirement and hence no training for formation flying. By the summer of 1939 the group had been re-equipped with the Vickers Wellington Mk 1, and its role suddenly switched to that of day bombing in preparation for carrying out the Ruhr Plan.

That summer saw Europe having a fit of the jitters. To counter the massive propaganda the Germans were giving their Luftwaffe, the Air Ministry instructed No. 3 Group to lay on a series of formation flights over Europe for the purpose of 'Showing the Flag' and helping to bolster French morale. Selected squadrons did three flights to Marseilles and one to Bordeaux, flew over Paris on Bastille Day and put in an appearance at the XXVth International Aviation Exhibition in Brussels where the RAF pilots warily exchanged chivalrous compliments with their Luftwaffe counterparts. The results of this flag-waving exercise were most revealing. Out of all the squadrons that took part, only two could fly in perfect formation, 9 and 214. All the others gave the impression of competing in a race, with some squadrons scattered all over the sky and showing little semblance of any formation at all. The problem stemmed from the fact that every squadron had its own ideas and whimsies about formation flying. Every squadron acted independently and subscribed to one of two schools of thought. The first held that a formation of bombers should fly as tightly together as possible thereby forfeiting individual manoeuvrability but gaining the advantage of mutual supportive crossfire from the power-operated turrets of the nearby aircraft. 214 Squadron belonged to this school of thought. The alternative school felt that bomber formations should only be held together loosely thereby retaining the manoeuvrability of individual aircraft albeit at the expense of mutual support. (Apart from this, it took a great deal of skill and concentration to hold a group of bombers in tight formation.) One of the few joint exercises with Fighter Command did nothing to convince the 'loose formation' school of the immense superiority in speed and manoeuvrability of modern fighters.

Another problem confronting the group was that many of their squadron COs were of 1914-18 vintage and did no flying whatever. As a consequence they had no experience or knowledge of modern, fast, well-armed bombers or how to deploy them. The lessons of the formation flights over France were ignored.

On 28th August one of the flight commanders who had led 214 Squadron to Marseilles and Bordeaux in July was posted from 214 reserve squadron at Feltwell to be flight commander of 'B' Flight in 149 operational squadron at Mildenhall. His name was Squadron Leader Paul Harris. He had had five years experience of flying in Egypt, Palestine and the Sudan and was a firm believer in the tight formation theory. As was customary in those days he requested that his crew be transferred with him, and his navigator, Bunny Austin, has this to say.

> Paul himself was a highly respected flight commander. He was rather more serious perhaps than most officers at that time perhaps because, at 32, he was a little older than the average. He commanded considerable respect from all because of his ability and his modest manner. He was a stickler for discipline and insisted that the crew practised at all times their safety procedures. An interesting side light is that, rather typical of Paul, he was larger than the average and with his Irvin flying jacket on he had the

greatest difficulty in getting through the escape hatch which was underneath the Wellington. We had a special drill for this, I recall it vividly. The drill was that the rest of the crew went first then Paul would leave the controls, get down into the escape hatch and I would put both feet firmly on his shoulders and I would push him through the hatch and I would then follow.

Peacetime drills and exercises were put into practise for real at 11 a.m. on 3rd September 1939 when Britain declared war on Germany.

At 5 p.m. 149 Squadron received orders to send 12 aircraft to attack part of the German fleet reported in the North Sea. An hour-and-a-half later three Wellingtons of 'A' Flight led by Squadron Leader H.I. Dabinett took off to commence the operation. Ten minutes later the remaining nine Wellingtons from 'A' Flight had their take-off cancelled on orders from Group Headquarters. For three-and-a-half hours Squadron Leader Dabinett and his three aircraft searched for the elusive German fleet but could not find it because of adverse weather conditions and approaching darkness. Dabinett, Turner and Way dropped their bombs in the sea and headed home for Mildenhall. Next day, 4th September, the two battle cruisers were reported at Brunsbüttel and it was the turn of 'B' Flight under the command of Squadron Leader Harris (see also p.21).

Of 149 Squadron's eight aircraft that headed out over the North Sea towards Brunsbüttel on that first raid, five turned back early having lost formation in low cloud, leaving their flight commander and two others to press on to the target. In the event, the Vickers gun turrets proved useless because the sights did not follow the guns and the ammunition belts were forever getting stuck in the ducts. Flight Lieutenant Stewart's Wimpy developed a leak in a fuel tank and had to make a forced landing at Honington. Valuable lessons had been learned. Better gun turrets, stricter discipline and self-sealing fuel tanks were top of the priority list. In the three month lull between 4th September and 3rd December two of the problems were put right. The Mk 1s were replaced by Mk 1As and the squadron got a new commanding officer. Nothing was done about the vulnerable fuel tanks. During these months, 149

Squadron practised formation flying. Squadron Leader Harris was a fully qualified flying instructor with eight year's flying experience behind him, five having been spent operationally in the Middle East. Promoted to squadron leader in Flying Training Command in February 1939, he had to leave because there was no appointment for him. Had he not left the command before the outbreak of war he would probably never have got out, as flying instructors were 'frozen' because they were needed so desperately. A firm believer in the 'tight formation' philosophy, he set about ensuring that all *his* aircraft could defend themselves. Another problem that occupied his mind was bombing accuracy. At the time, the Luftwaffe Ju87B-1 'Stukas' were enjoying tremendous success as high-accuracy dive bombers, and this, thought Paul Harris, was the way to sink a battleship. The story is taken up by his navigator, Bunny Austin.

> Paul was particularly keen that we should improve our bombing and our gunnery and on every conceivable occasion he could, we went to Berners Heath, the local range, and practised. Paul had a lot of courage and obviously a lot of conviction that the Wellington was a magnificent aeroplane which indeed it was. He certainly believed that it could operate as a dive bomber and on one particular occasion over Berners Heath in that September, in fact I see from my logbook that it was 21st September, we were practising high altitude dive bombing which he, on each dive, made steeper and steeper. My job was to stand in the astrodome and watch the aeroplane to see that we were not losing any fabric from the wings as we got steeper and steeper. On the final dive, a tremendous sheet of fabric on our top main-plane burst out and we had to limp back to Mildenhall with both wings severely damaged. I think Paul lost some of his enthusiasm thereafter for high altitude bombing.

As the Mk 1s were put out to grass, they were replaced by the very latest Mk 1As having new turrets produced by Frazer-Nash, and in this respect 149 Squadron was particularly fortunate. Archie Frazer-Nash frequently drove up in his

Bentley and climbed aboard Paul Harris's new Mk1A to be taken up to test the three turrets and their Browning machine-guns. Occasionally Frazer-Nash's partner, Captain E.G. Thompson, would go up as well and do a bit of experimenting. Many of the bugs were ironed out on these flights and Aircraftman First Class Doxsey in the front turret, Aircraftman First Class Mullineaux in the rear turret and Sergeant Austin in the ventral turret picked up a lot of valuable experience on how to operate and look after their defensive armament. The retractable ventral turret was intended as defence for the underside of the aircraft. Capable of rotating a full 360 degrees when lowered, it could also fire two degrees above the horizontal when trained aft, very useful in backing up the rear gunner against attacks from astern. Unfortunately it knocked 15 knots off the aircraft's speed just when it was needed most and demanded additional power from the engines when it could be least afforded.

After three months of comparative inactivity pressure started to build up for some kind of response from Bomber Command to Churchill's call for action. As November drew to its close, the first indication that something was afoot became apparent when 149 Squadron got a new commanding officer, Wing Commander Kellett, AFC. Richard Kellett was very well known in aviation circles, having won the World Long Distance record with the RAF Long-Range Development Flight in 1938. This feat had been a great boost for British aviation in what were otherwise pretty depressing times. On 5th November, Squadron Leader Kellett led a flight of three Vickers Wellesley monoplanes from Ismailia in Egypt to Darwin in Australia, non-stop. Adverse winds caused one Wellesley, piloted by Flight Lieutenant H.A.V. Hogan, to land at Kupang in Timor to refuel. The two remaining Wellesleys, piloted by Squadron Leader Kellett and Flight Lieutenant A.N. Combe, reached Darwin on 7th November having flown 7,162 miles in just over 48 hours. In 1938 this was an incredible feat.

Wing Commander Kellett had scarcely settled into his new command when he received orders on 2nd December to prepare his squadron (together with 38 and 115 Squadrons) for a major raid on the German island fortress of Heligoland. Winston Churchill's call for more vigorous action was to be answered and next day the weather promised well. The outcome of that raid gave much encouragement to Bomber Command and appeared to vindicate their policy of self-defending formations tackling heavily defended targets in daylight. The few German fighters that had turned up seemed unable to shoot down any of the bombers. Were enemy fighters impotent against power-operated turrets in tightly packed formation? Was this proof of one of the cornerstones of Bomber Command policy: 'The bomber will always get through'? That day everything certainly seemed to point to those conclusions.

Exactly a week after getting back from Heligoland Paul Harris took charge of 'R for Robert'. This was the same aircraft in which Flight Lieutenant Stewart had so bravely turned back for a second try at the German cruisers on the 3rd. Training was resumed in their new aircraft, and that day they took off with Pilot Officer Swift as second pilot to practise formation flying, air firing and high level bombing. They did the same again three days later, this time with Pilot Officer Innes as second pilot and practising low level bombing. The mood changed abruptly however when the news of 99's heavy losses filtered through on the night of the 14th. They now perceived that the events on the 3rd at Heligoland had been a fluke. Next time they might not be so lucky. Sandy Innes jotted down his thoughts in his notebook.

> 15.12.39 Naval officers arriving to stay here. There is a really big push coming off shortly. An auspicious moment to think of it after Thursday's effort. However, given reasonable conditions it shouldn't be too bad. Apparently only five people know what it is. I would like to know but could guess pretty well I think.

On the morning of the 17th, Paul Harris opened his Sunday newspaper over breakfast to reveal the headlines:

THE KING HONOURS GRAF SPEE VICTORS
Commodore Harwood, leader of the attack on the German pocket battleship *Admiral Graf Spee*, knighted and promoted Rear-Admiral. Captains of the cruisers

Achilles, *Ajax*, *Exeter* – Companions of the Order of the Bath.

After breakfast Harris and his crew climbed aboard 'R for Robert' and took off to do some more training in formation flying and high level bombing. After landing, Sandy Innes opened his notebook and wrote one line:

17.12.39 Tomorrow's the day – Standby from 7 a.m. Soon know now.

That evening, Wing Commander Kellett and Squadron Leader Harris were summoned to group headquarters along with the squadron commanders and section leaders of 9 and 37 Squadrons for a briefing. In the words of a later 3 Group report the group commander 'stated that from the point of view of preparation, the details of the plan had been thoroughly considered by all concerned...'[12]

Richard Kellett, the officer detailed to lead the raid, was a newcomer to 149 Squadron. He had never flown with 9 or 37 Squadrons before as a group. He had never had a chance to practise formation flying or bombing with the other two squadrons he was to lead. He had never been given the opportunity to discuss or formulate any kind of plan for bombing or fighting, whether as a group or by squadrons or by flights. Neither had he been given time to discuss the tactics to be followed in the event of fighter attacks. In short, he was not given the chance to impose his will on what was otherwise an incoherent assortment of squadrons. In particular, one of the squadrons he was to lead had never faced the enemy before, and had a non-flying commanding officer who believed in the 'loose formation' theory and intended experimenting with a new kind of formation – flying stepped down in pairs – on their first ever encounter with the enemy. As Paul Harris later said, 'group headquarters laid on no group formation training – a fatal error'.

As it transpired, two chance remarks were to prevent the forthcoming raid from degenerating into a total massacre. After the 3rd December raid Kellett had asked if he had led all right,

---

[12] Comment by Group Captain Paul Harris – 'What utter rubbish'.

to which Paul Harris had replied, 'Go a little slower next time'.

At the briefing on the evening of 17th December, Paul Harris was told that Flight Lieutenant Peter Grant would be flying with him with three of 9 Squadron's aircraft. This was the first time they had ever flown together and Paul Harris's parting words to Peter Grant were, 'Stay close to me whatever happens'.

No. 149 (East India) Squadron
Badge: A horseshoe and a flash of lightning interlaced.
Motto: *Fortis nocte* ('Strong by night')
Authority: King George VI, February 1938.
The horseshoe is indicative of good fortune in the First World War when the squadron flew extensive operations with the loss of only one pilot and observer. A further reason for the horseshoe is that much of the squadron's work was in connection with the cavalry. The flash of lightning is symbolic of the speed with which work was done during a comparatively brief history.

No. 9 Squadron
Badge: A bat.
Motto: *Per noctem volamus* ('Throughout the night we fly')
Authority: King Edward VIII, November 1936.
Unofficial World War II name:
'Ipswich's "own" squadron'.

No. 37 Squadron
Badge: A hawk hooded, belled and jessed, wings elevated and adorned.
Motto: 'Wise without eyes'
Authority: King George VI, April 1943. This badge is indicative of the duties of blind flying.

4

The Battle of Heligoland Bight

It was the season of 'peace on earth, good will towards men'. Christmas Eve was less than a week away. It was also the coldest winter on record for half a century. At Boulogne the Channel froze. In places the ground temperature dropped to 40 below and tins of anti-freeze solidified. That morning of 18th December, *The Times* headlined: GRAF SPEE SCUTTLED WITHOUT A FIGHT.

At Mildenhall the weather was overcast, mainly cloudy with visibility between two and four miles. In accordance with Group Operations Order B. 60 dated 17th December, Wellington bomber N2960 took off at 9.27 a.m., with Wing Commander Richard Kellett AFC at the controls. Next was N2892 piloted by Flying Officer F.W.S. Turner, followed by N2962 flown by Flying Officer J.H.C. Speirs.

Waiting his turn at the head of the runway sat Paul Harris at the controls of N2980. The windsock indicated a 10-20 mph wind from the east-north-east. As he sat there with his hand on the throttles his mind flashed back to the time almost 25 years before when, as a small boy of eight, he had been walking down a country lane near Oxford one day in 1915. Suddenly, over the hedge flew an aeroplane – narrowly missing the little lad as he gazed up in open-mouthed wonder. At that instant he knew what he wanted to be more than anything else in the world – a pilot. As soon as he was the right age he applied to Cranwell but his mathematics let him down. Reluctantly he chose the law as his profession and qualified as a solicitor in 1930 but his heart just wasn't in it. In the summer of 1931 he tried the RAF again. This time fortune smiled on him and he was accepted for a short service commission. Starting at No. 2 Flying Training School at Digby in December of that year he was already a fortnight over the top age limit, but Europe was unsettled and the RAF desperately needed good pilots. At the commissioning board his keenness carried the day and a blind eye was turned to the fact that he was over age.

In a Wellington the second pilot sat on a folding seat to the right of the pilot. Pilot Officer Herome Alexander Innes came from a service family. His father had been the commanding officer of the 2nd Battalion of the Black Watch. The army though was not for Sandy because he had always longed to be a pilot. Upon leaving school (Rugby) he joined the General Accident, Fire and Life Assurance Company Limited but slowly came to the conclusion that office life did not suit his temperament. He was the outdoor type and loved a day on the hill with his shotgun and his dog Astra or driving his little MG round the Perthshire countryside or better still, skiing in the Alps. Towering above all, however, was his passion to fly. In 1938 he joined the Royal Air Force. From Peterborough he was posted to Stradishall and thence to 214 Squadron at Feltwell. There he joined Paul Harris's crew flying Handley Page Harrow bombers. As it became more obvious that war was on the way, crews were transferred from the highly trained and disciplined 214 Squadron to less well prepared operational squadrons. Along with the rest of Paul Harris's crew he was posted to 149 Squadron at Mildenhall – 'to hot up the squadron's formation flying and prepare it for battle'.

The wireless operator sat in a tiny compartment directly behind the pilot. Aircraftman First Class 'Jock' Watson was a very quiet pleasant young chap, never known to flap and too self-effacing to catch the eye, but his skill as a wireless operator was quite exceptional. One of Paul Harris's original crew from 214, he rarely engaged in social mixing but had an affinity for a good pint of beer.

The navigator sat in his own little cubicle behind the wireless operator. He also doubled as the gunner in the ventral turret and occasionally as bomb aimer. Sergeant Austin was never referred to as anything other than 'Bunny' (after the pre-war tennis champion 'Bunny' Austin). His father was a warrant officer in the RAF and his son decided to carry on the tradition, joining as a wireless operator/mechanic apprentice in 1932. On passing out in 1935 he was posted to 16 Squadron where, to his delight, he became an air-gunner almost immediately. His one aim was to fly and his sights were set on becoming an air-observer. After a tour of duty with 36 Squadron in Singapore he returned to Britain where he eventually joined Paul Harris's crew in 214 Squadron, transferring to 149 Squadron three days before the Germans invaded Poland.

The tail gunner sat in isolation at the rear of the aircraft. Politely referred to as 'tail-end-charlie', his was the loneliest job of all, without even a parachute for company. Jimmy Mullineaux had falsified his age to join the RAF. On leaving school he started work in a Birmingham factory only to find that he wasn't happy there. He then found a job in another factory but once again left after a short stay. A third try at factory life convinced him that he was not cut out for that kind of life so, unbeknown to his parents, he joined the RAF in 1937. There he was truly happy.

The front gun turret was manned by Aircraftman First Class Doxsey. He was very young and was the only one who had not transferred from 214 Squadron as part of the original crew. All gunners were volunteer ground crew and no special emphasis was placed on their training. There were no gunnery leaders then and the only training they got amounted to what they picked up on training flights or actual missions. Very occasionally they were allowed to fire 200 rounds on training flights, but otherwise they spent their time attending to their ground duties.

'R for Robert' was clear for take-off. Paul dragged his thoughts back to the matter in hand and eased the throttle levers gently forward. The two Pegasus XVIII engines responded and N2980 turned into the wind and gathered speed down the runway. By the time the wheels had cleared the ground and been retracted into their housing in the engine nacelles, N2943 with Flying Officer H.L. Bulloch at the controls was lined up at the head of the runway. Behind him waited Flying Officer M.F. Briden in N2961. The remaining three Wellingtons, N2984 piloted by Flight Lieutenant A.G. Duguid, N2866 piloted by Flying Officer A.F. Riddlesworth and N2894 piloted by Flight Sergeant Kelly, followed three minutes later. 149 Squadron was airborne and circled over Mildenhall aerodrome as it waited for the rest of the formation.

At Honington, 12 miles away, the scene was repeated exactly as 9 Squadron's nine aircraft took off. The two squadrons joined up over Mildenhall and set course for King's Lynn. Feltwell's six Wellingtons were late. They missed the rendezvous and caught up with the main formation about an hour later, 100 miles out over the North Sea. The course set from the Wash was 040° True, as far as Latitude 55° North. The plan was to avoid the concentration of flak ships around the Frisian Islands, thought to have been the source of early warning on previous raids. As they climbed steadily to 14,000 feet, Paul observed with some concern that the broken cloud over England was gradually thinning out. By the time 37 Squadron caught up, the cloud had disappeared completely and left them in a bright, crystal clear sky. Looking out of his cockpit Paul estimated that he could see as far as 50 miles – not a good omen, for German fighters would have no trouble in spotting them. Sergeant Hough, in the lead aircraft, completed his calculations and informed his pilot, Wing Commander Kellett, that they had reached their first turning point. The compass was set to a new heading of 091° True. As they droned steadily eastwards at a speed of 140mph, Jimmy tried traversing his turret and noticed how sluggish it had become. The hydraulic oil was thickening up in the freezing temperature. It was one of the coldest winters on record and everyone onboard 'R for Robert' was becoming acutely aware of the numbing December chill. Bunny hugged his Irvin jacket tight about him as the icy draughts spilled in through the turret gaps and blew relentlessly down the unheated fuselage.

It was just coming up for noon when Paul glanced out of his cockpit and saw two Wellingtons peel away from Kellett's formation and head for home. Flight Lieutenant Duguid, leading the second vic in the first formation, was having trouble maintaining the revs on his starboard engine. With his speed dropping he could no longer hold position so he ordered Sergeant Murdoch to send a signal by Aldis lamp to his number two and number three. Off on his starboard side, Flying Officer Riddlesworth dutifully obeyed and closed up on Kellett. Flight Sergeant Kelly could not have noticed Duguid's signal because he too broke away from the formation and followed the ailing Wimpy down and on to the heading for the

18th December 1939

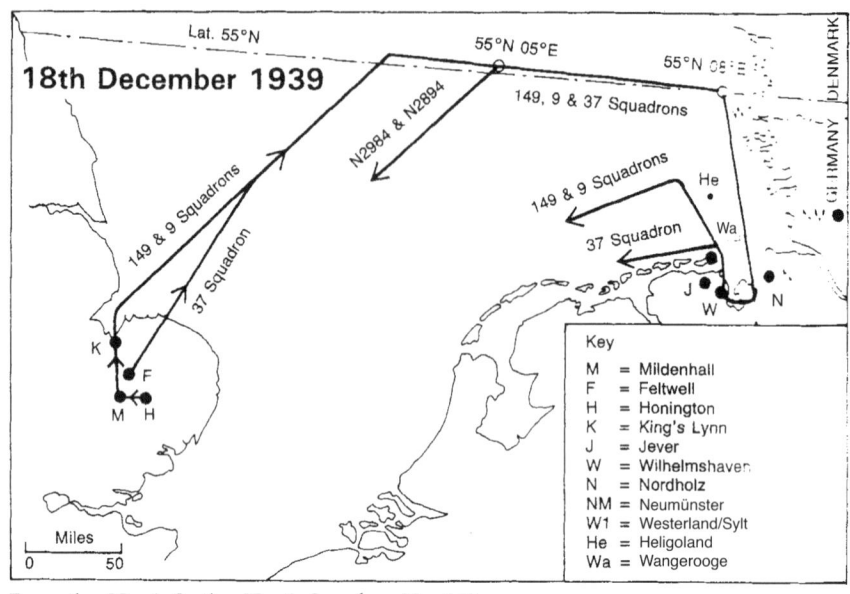

Formation No. 1, Section No. 1. Squadron No. 149
N2960 W/C Kellett   Landed Mildenhall 1600 hrs.
N2892 F/O Turner   Landed Mildenhall 1610 hrs.
N2962 F/O Speirs   Shot down, no survivors.

Formation No. 1, Section No. 2. Squadron No. 149
N2984 F/Lt Duguid   Returned Mildenhall early. Reported engine trouble.
N2866 F/O Riddlesworth Landed Mildenhall 1600 hrs.
N2894 F/Sgt Kelly   Returned Mildenhall early. Accompanied N2984 back.

Formation No. 2, Section No. 1. Squadron No. 149 (+500 ft on Formation No. 1)
N2980 S/Ldr Harris   Landed Coltishall 1600 hrs.
N2943 F/O Bulloch   Landed Mildenhall 1600 hrs.
N2961 F/O Briden   Ditched near Cromer Knoll, no survivors.

Formation No. 2, Section No. 2. Squadron No. 9 (+500 ft on Formation No. 1)
N2964 F/Lt Grant   Landed Honington 1600 hrs.
N2981 Sgt Purdy   Landed Honington 1600 hrs.
N2983 Sgt Ramshaw   Ditched 100 miles from the Wash, 4 survivors.

Formation No. 3, Section No. 1. Squadron No. 9 (+500 ft on Formation No. 1)
N2872 S/Ldr Guthrie   Shot down, no survivors.
N2871 F/O Macrae   Landed North Coates Fitties, 1600 hrs.
N2873 Sgt Petts   Landed Sutton Bridge, 1600 hrs.

Formation No. 3, Section No. 2. Squadron No. 9 (+500 ft on Formation No. 1)
N2941 F/O Allison   Shot down, no survivors.
N2940 P/O Lines   Shot down, no survivors.
N2939 F/O Challes   Shot down, no survivors.

Formation No. 4, In pairs, stepped down, Squadron No. 37 (+1,000 ft on Formation No. 1)
N2904 S/Ldr Hue-Williams Shot down, no survivors.
N2903 F/O Lemon   Landed Feltwell, 1540 hrs.
N2888 F/O Wimberley   Shot down, 1 survivor.
N2889 F/O Lewis   Shot down, no survivors.
N2935 F/O Thompson   Shot down, no survivors.
N2936 Sgt Ruse   Shot down on the island of Borkum, 3 survivors.

THE BATTLE OF HELIGOLAND BIGHT 61

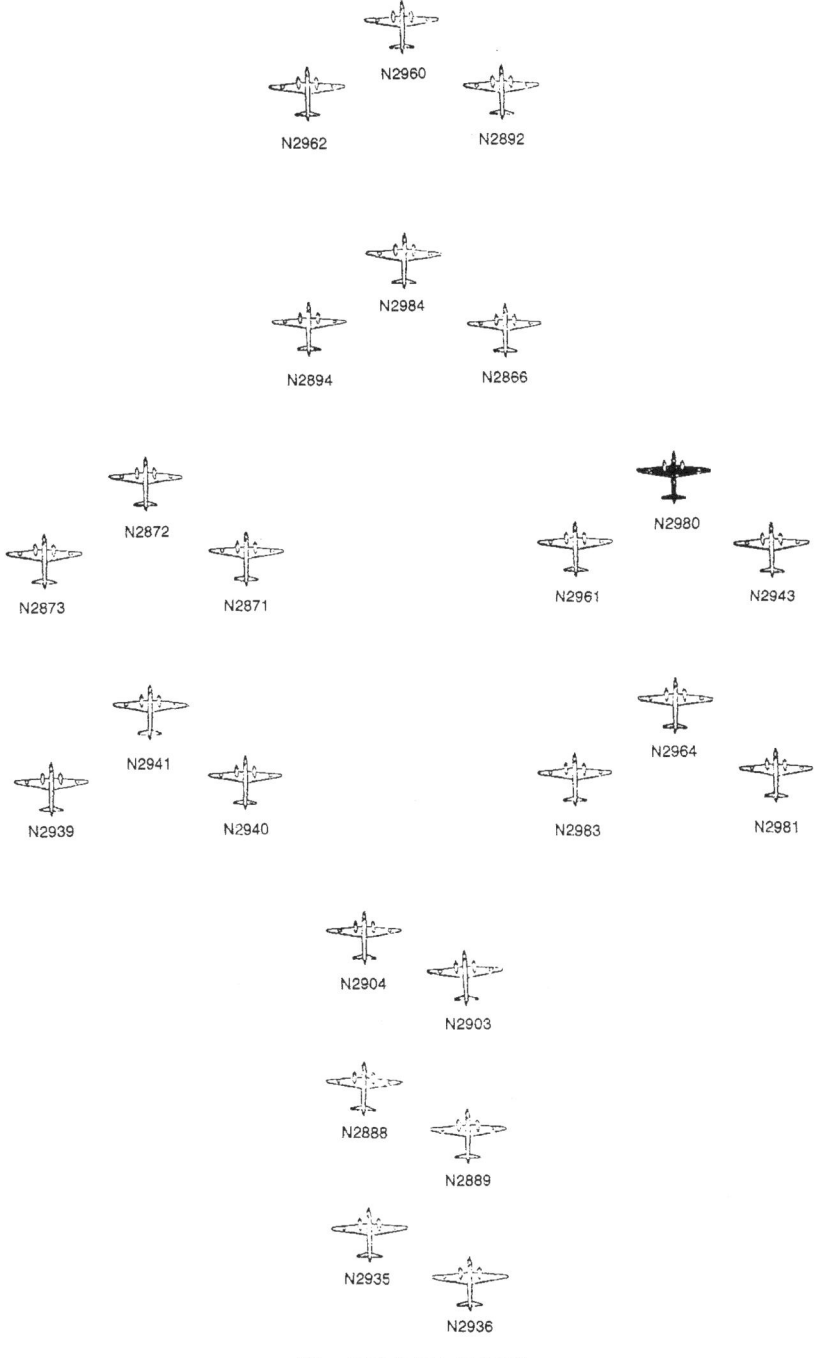

'The BIG DIAMOND'
149 Squadron, 9 Squadron and 37 Squadron, 18th December 1939.
Time 11.30 hrs; Position 55°N; 4°30'E; Height 14,000 feet.

homeward journey. N2984 and N2894 arrived back at Mildenhall a little before 1.30 p.m. Duguid reported that his starboard engine had been surging. With the loss of these 12 guns, Kellett's formation was now considerably weakened.

Three hours after taking off from Mildenhall, Richard Kellett spotted a hazy smudge on the horizon. Fifty miles ahead, across a gin-clear sky, lay the Danish-German border and the enemy island of Sylt. Paul gave the order to lower the 'dustbin' and Bunny climbed down and tested his guns.

In the leading aircraft, Sergeant Hough plotted the position of the second turning point and, when he estimated that they were within 12 miles of Sylt, Kellett gave the order for the formation to wheel to starboard for the long run down the coast to Schleswig-Holstein. The plan had been to nip in the back door of the German defences. In the event, this dog's leg was to afford the enemy almost an hour's warning of their coming. Now cruising due south, with the mainland about 30 miles off on their port beam and Heligoland clearly visible ahead on their starboard bow, the British airmen did not realise that they had just tripped an invisible alarm. A blip on German radar had given them away. In those days the RAF pilots had only the faintest glimmer that there was a frightfully 'hush-hush' British invention that could detect aircraft by radio waves. They never dreamed that the Hun might also have perfected a similar capability.[13]

The tiny island of Heligoland slipped past beneath the starboard wing as Sandy scanned the sky for enemy fighters. No flak from Heligoland, that was a good sign. At his position in the astrodome, Sandy could see for miles. The land was white with snow and there was ice in the estuaries. Beneath them, Bunny noticed a convoy of half a dozen merchant ships, a tempting target but strictly out of bounds. Suddenly Sandy spotted a couple of tiny black dots about a mile away on the port beam. More of them followed, they were Me 109s, and one swung in to attack 'R for Robert'. Jimmy opened up to be joined by Bunny in the 'dustbin'. The fighter broke away in the face of such concentrated fire. More attacks followed but again they were successfully beaten off. One Messerschmitt was seen

---

[13] The Oslo Report, which confirmed the existence of 50 cm radar at Wilhelmshaven, was not received in London until early November 1939.

to spiral seaward trailing black smoke after it attacked Flying Officer Turner's aircraft. The tail gunner, Aircraftman First Class Coalter, claimed first blood. In Flying Officer Lemon's Wellington all the gunners reported hitting another and confirmed that it flew off with smoke billowing from the engine. Fifteen thousand feet below, Bunny could clearly make out several large merchantmen lying at anchor in the Schillig Roads but that was all; there were no battleships to be seen. A convoy was heading for either Brunsbüttel or Cuxhaven.

Looking dead ahead Paul could see Kellett's formation flying into a wall of black splotches. A few minutes later, 'R for Robert' was itself enveloped in the flak barrage. By now, the fighters had peeled away to hang-off on the flanks till their turn came round again. Kellett had made a feint towards Bremerhaven and, as the bombers crossed the coast just to the west of Cuxhaven, another convoy of merchant ships could be seen heading up the river Weser towards Bremerhaven. The leading aircraft was carrying a Royal Navy observer, Lieutenant Commander Rotherham, to help identify German battleships. He spotted a very large passenger liner with two funnels, tied up in the harbour, which he took to be the *Bremen*. Off to starboard could be seen the great naval base of Wilhelmshaven, but they were too far away to make out anything clearly. As the bombers passed to the south of Bremerhaven, it became obvious that there were no major naval targets at Brunsbüttel, in the Schillig Roads or in the Jade Busen. Kellett ordered a signal to be sent, a series of dashes followed by the letter W. Their target would be Wilhelmshaven but they needed to fly over it to get a closer look. The whole formation turned to starboard and headed west across the Jade.

Just to the south of Wilhelmshaven, Kellett wheeled again in another arc to the north on a course set to bring them directly over Bau Haven. As a result of this manoeuvre, the formation out on the port side of the big diamond had to open up to full throttle in an effort to keep up. The two Wellingtons on the outside of this formation were struggling and Sergeant Petts made repeated calls to his leader, Squadron Leader Guthrie, to slow down – but got no reply. By now, the flak had really thickened up as the battleships in the harbour joined in. The flak was accurate for height but trailed behind the bombers. Over the intercom Jimmy kept up a running commentary. On several occasions he exclaimed excitedly, 'Hurry up Sir, hurry up, it's catching up on us'. Sandy watched fascinated as the jet-black splodges suddenly appeared and immediately expanded and there was a bump if it was too close. As he looked back, he could see all the bursts hanging about in the sky and it reminded him of coming out of a large wood and seeing all the tree tops on the sky line. For ten minutes they flew straight and level over Wilhelmshaven. In the harbours and docks below him, Sandy could make out three large warships and four destroyers.[14] The order was given to open bomb doors. In the leading aircraft, Wing Commander Kellett had an agonising decision to make. There beneath him lay the pride of the German Navy, the battleships *Scharnhorst* and *Gneisenau*.

> A pocket battleship, then thought to be a cruiser, and a battleship, were then noticed in the inner harbour. The position of the target was not clear until the visual signal for attack commencing (diving 1,000 feet) had been made. As it was then realised that there was risk of dropping bombs on land, particularly from that direction, no bombs were dropped.[xi]

Wing Commander Kellett's orders were quite specific: 'Great care is to be taken that no bombs fall on shore, and no merchant ships to be attacked.'

From their vantage point, 15,000 feet up in the cloudless sky, it was painfully obvious that there were no enemy battleships 'clear of land' at the expected anchorages at the mouth of the Elbe or in the Schillig Roads. Their prey was safely tied up alongside the quays and jetties in Bau Haven. Since it would have been impossible to aim bombs at the battleships without killing civilians on shore, Kellett had no alternative but to abandon his mission.

Looking down from the cockpit of 'R for Robert' Paul Harris spotted four big ships anchored in the middle of the outer harbour. They looked like merchantmen but intense anti-

---
[14] Aerial photographs later revealed a fourth large warship in the harbour.

aircraft fire arched skyward from their decks. Paul reasoned that they had to be fleet auxiliaries, and therefore legitimate targets. He gave the order to Pilot Officer Innes to attack them. In great haste, Sandy took aim and pressed the bomb release. Following his leader's example another aircraft in Harris's section dropped its bombs on the four ships. A total of six 500lb SAP bombs, dropped in haste in the middle of the harbour, was all there was to show for the RAF's first major attack on the German mainland. The results were not observed.

Paul was not the only one to drop aimed bombs that day. Sergeant Herbie Ruse was concentrating on keeping formation with Flying Officer Thompson. 37 Squadron was trying out a new kind of flying formation, stepped down in pairs rather than the conventional vics of the other squadrons. Herbie Ruse was flying behind and below Thompson and as they cleared Wilhelmshaven Herbie saw his leader open his bomb doors, apparently on his own initiative, as they approached a German vessel lying in the Schillig Roads. The navigator, Sergeant May, shouted up, 'He's going for that ship! He's going to overshoot!' Recalling the punishment meted out to Squadron Leader Glencross of 214 Squadron, Ruse shouted back, 'Are you sure its naval?' Weeks before, Glencross had been taken off flying duties and given a desk job because he had had the temerity to drop bombs on a German minesweeper that had fired on him, without first making absolutely certain it was a *naval* vessel. The Wellington in front of him released its bombs. Sergeant May pressed his own bomb release. N2936 lifted as the weight of the bombs vanished. He watched three fountains shoot up into the air followed seconds later by his own three as the sticks splashed harmlessly into the sea.

The lead Wellington was just clearing the flak barrage as Kellett looked back at the disarray behind him. His own four and Paul Harris's six were still flying in tight formation, but off to port 9 Squadron's six had opened out and Squadron Leader Guthrie was some distance ahead of his formation. Bringing up the rear, 37 Squadron was straggling and Squadron Leader Hue-Williams was racing ahead to try and catch up with the leaders. Approaching Wilhelmshaven his number two, Flying Officer Lemon, had made a spectacular departure from the formation. The story is taken up by 'Cheese' Lemon:

> At about this time Pilot Officer Paul Templeman who was sitting in the second pilot's seat, made ready to return to the bomb aimer's position for the run-up on the target. On getting down from his seat he inadvertently caught his parachute harness on the flap lever, and the lever was placed in the full-flap position. Before the hydraulics could work, the main power unit had to be turned on, therefore no power had gone to the flaps, and they remained up, and I was not aware the lever was in the down position. However, as we approached the target the main hydraulic power was turned on to put the bomb doors down. This activated the flaps at the same time, causing the aircraft to climb rapidly and lose forward speed. As we were experiencing heavy flak at the time I assumed that we had received a direct hit. By the time I had located the problem, 37 Squadron was a considerable distance ahead of me. I followed in their wake and at the target area jettisoned my bombs in the bay, as no target was available. It was obvious by now that all hope of catching up the squadron had gone. I pulled the revs and the throttle levers back, stuck the nose in an almost vertical position and headed for the deck. We cleared the heavy flak but ran into intense light flak as our height decreased. The loop[15] and the aerials were torn off. The vibration and noise were nerve-racking. Our only chance was to hug the sea and get there before the fighters came in. We streamed out towards the Frisian Isles but ran into flak from the island defences and shipping. This, in actual fact, was I believe our salvation as the fighters stayed clear of the area. Just after clearing the islands the rear gunner spotted two Me 109s coming in for a rear attack. I shoved the nose down another 50 feet and we were really on the deck. The rear gunner's voice came through and said one of the Me 109s had hit the sea with his wing and cartwheeled straight in. After a while the other aircraft abandoned the attack.

Meanwhile, back at 10,000 feet, Kellett's bombers proceeded

---
[15] Radio Direction Finding loop, located in front of the astrodome.

on their northerly heading towards the open sea. Miraculously, not one of the Wellingtons was hit as they flew on, enveloped in flak. They sailed through to emerge out the other side, unscathed. The time was coming up for 1.30 p.m., an hour after they first tripped the alarm. The fighters were patiently waiting for the flak to subside. When it did, they fell on the pride of RAF Bomber Command like a ton of bricks.

Earlier that same day, around the time that Wing Commander Kellett was setting off for Wilhelmshaven, Oberstleutnant Carl Schumacher was chatting to his adjutant, Leutnant Miller-Trimbusch. 'Splendid weather for fighters', he remarked as he studied the sky over the German Bight. The day had dawned cold but sunny. The early morning mists over the East Frisian Islands had evaporated to reveal a sky of purest blue satin, clear to the horizon in all directions. 'The Tommies are not such fools – they won't come today', dutifully replied Miller-Trimbusch as he surveyed a cloudless sky that was indeed ideal for their fighters. Schumacher nodded his agreement. A month before, Geschwaderkommodore Schumacher had been appointed to command the new Luftwaffe Group JG1 set up to defend the North Sea area. At the outbreak of war he had been in command of the fighter Wing II/JG77. Now, he was responsible for the whole Air Force Group controlled from Jever, just a few kilometres to the west of Wilhelmshaven. He was feeling good, for not only was it a perfect day for his fighters but he had at last received the reinforcements he had been asking for since Heligoland had been attacked by British bombers a couple of weeks earlier. The previous day the long-range fighter Gruppe I/ZG76 had arrived from Bonninghardt after a distinguished record in Poland. Equipped with the latest twin-engined Messerschmitt Bf110-C fighters. I/ZG76 was a potent addition to his armoury. Under his command he now had between 80 and 100 single and twin-engined fighters, all ready to go at a moment's notice. Miller-Trimbusch's words hung in the cold frosty air as, a couple of hundred miles to the west, Kellett's captains set their compasses on the heading that would fly them into history.

The German fighter defences under Oberstleutnant Schumacher consisted of the following units:

II/JG77 under Major von Bülow-Bothkamp on the island of Wangerooge;
III/JG77 under Captain Seliger at Nordholz near Cuxhaven;[16]
Jagdgruppe 101 under Major Reichardt, one squadron at Westerland on Sylt;
Jagdgruppe 101 under Major Reichardt, two squadrons at Neumünster;
10(N)/JG26 (nightfighters) under Staffelkapitän Steinhoff at Jever;
I/ZG76 under Captain Reinecke at Jever.

II/JG77, III/JG77, Jagdgruppe 101 and 10(N)JG26 were equipped with the Messerschmitt 109. I/ZG76 was equipped with the Messerschmitt 110.

The second squadron of Zerstörergeschwader 76 (i.e. 2/ZG76) was commanded by Staffelkapitän Wolfgang Falck. This officer had been one of those trained at Lipetsk, the Luftwaffe's secret base near Moscow in the early thirties. He had become well known and liked in pre-war aviation circles. Indeed, such was his reputation that the prestigious magazine *The Aeroplane* published an article about him in early 1940 entitled 'Memories of Peace'.[17]

To acquaint themselves with their surroundings and get used to flying out over the sea, Wolfgang Falck and his 'Lady-Bug' squadron were exercising in the clear blue skies close by the island of Borkum. Hidden among the sand dunes on the island of Wangerooge, 80 kilometres to the east, Leutnant Hermann Diehl of LN-Vers, Regiment 3, was spending his lunch hour demonstrating the usefulness of his new 'Freya' radar to a naval officer who was visiting his experimental installation. Diehl was using Falck's flight of Messerschmitt Bf110s as a demonstration of how he could detect intruding aircraft that came within range of his equipment. After a while he swung the Freya radar beam northwards towards Heligoland. Suddenly he spotted a large echo coming from the direction of Sylt. Diehl knew that there were no German aircraft reported

---

[16]Formerly II(J)/Tr. Gr. 186 for the aircraft carrier 'GRAF ZEPPELIN' which was never completed.
[17]See Appendix B.

in that area, and so he immediately picked up his phone which had a direct line to the Geschwader HQ in Jever. It was lunchtime and Hermann Diehl received short shrift from the other end of the line. 'Tommies approaching in weather like this? You're plotting seagulls or there's interference on your set,'[xii] came the sceptical reply. Shades of Pearl Harbor! There had been no alarms from the naval radar on Heligoland or any of the patrol boats up there. In desperation, Diehl rang up the local commanding officer of II/JG77 fighter group based close by on Wangerooge. Harry von Bülow was however at that moment at the Geschwader HQ in Jever. Nobody wanted to know. Twenty minutes later, the naval radar on Heligoland (also a Freya set) reported intruding aircraft as well. But still the fighters were not scrambled. The report had first to go through the naval exchange at Wilhelmshaven and all the 'official channels' before it reached Geschwader HQ at Jever.

While the German radar was every bit as efficient as its British counterpart, the problem lay in communications. Arguments still persisted between the Luftwaffe and the Kriegsmarine about precisely who was responsible for each sector, and considerable overlap existed between the fighters and the flak ships. The British had succeeded in marrying their radar chain to an efficient fighter control organisation. No such union existed between the Luftwaffe and its long-range electronic eyes. The report from the Heligoland radar was only hesitatingly passed through the naval HQ exchange to the Luftwaffe at Jever, thus confirming Hermann Diehl's original alert. Twenty-two Wellington bombers cruised majestically down the coast of Schleswig-Holstein as the Luftwaffe struggled to overcome their simple disbelief that the Royal Air Force could flaunt itself before them 'on a brilliant day that promised only a massacre'. Fifty-seven doomed men among the 120 in the British formation were granted an hour's extra life because the Germans couldn't believe Bomber Command would be so foolish. Only when observers on Heligoland spotted the bombers through binoculars did the Luftwaffe finally grasp the fact that they were under attack. The naval observers sent a signal saying that 44 bombers were heading for Wilhelmshaven – precisely double Kellett's numbers. This is more than likely to have been an error of duplication in transmission rather than a mistake in addition. Belatedly the order went out from Jever for the fighters to scramble.

First off the ground were six Messerschmitt Bf109D-1s of 10(N)/JG26, a nightfighter squadron based at Jever. Their commanding officer was Staffelkapitän 'Mäcki' Steinhoff. One of his fighters took up position on a course parallel to the bombers about a mile away on their port beam, and radioed their course, height and airspeed back to base. One or two of the other Me 109s launched probing attacks against the intruders but were beaten off by the concentrated fire from the turrets. But Steinhoff's pilots did not have long to press home their attacks. At 1.10 p.m. the bombers crossed the mudflats of Wurst, to the west of Cuxhaven. The flak units 214 (Cuxhaven), 244 and 264 (Wesermunde) opened up. The fighters broke away and circled out of range of the flak as Kellett made his turns westward over the Jade Busen and again northward for Wilhelmshaven. By now the flak had intensified, being joined by the flak units 212, 222, 252, 262 and 272, ringing the city. From the dockyards, the battleships *Scharnhorst* and *Gneisenau* opened up, together with all the other naval ships in the harbour.

Far away to the west, Feldwebel Walz was humming quietly to himself as he relaxed in the radio operator's position of the Me 110. It was a glorious day. The sun shone through the cockpit canopy and, as he gazed back, he could make out the island of Borkum between the 110's twin tails. They were on a familiarisation flight 'to get acquainted with the sea, the coast and the islands'. Suddenly his radio crackled into life. British bombers were over Wilhelmshaven and they had been ordered to intercept them. Walz immediately informed his pilot, Staffelkapitän Falck, and the starboard wing dipped as the fighter banked steeply on to a heading of 110 degrees. Far on the horizon, Falck could make out the tiny black dots of a flak barrage as he and his rottenflieger (wing man), Unteroffizier Fresia, raced for the fray. At last, Diehl's 'seagulls' had been recognised for what they really were and the Luftwaffe was belatedly getting its act together.

'The sepia shades of Camels and Archie' still coloured the perceptions of the airmen from Mildenhall, Honington and Feltwell. Many had joined up at a time when Harrow, Heyford and Hendon bombers were looked upon in the RAF as the very latest thing and the biplane fighter was their only adversary. Lumbering northwards at less than 200mph, the crews could clearly see fighters taking off from a well-camouflaged aerodrome at Schillig Point. These were not the sedate biplanes they were accustomed to, but modern 350mph, cannon-armed, monoplane fighters. The Luftwaffe pilots that were racing to get airborne down the runways at Jever, Wangerooge and Neumünster had learned many valuable lessons from the previous encounters with the Wellingtons. They knew that the twin guns at the rear made stern attacks dangerous, but they now also knew that the turrets could not traverse to a full right-angle with the fuselage. This meant that their targets had a blind spot on the beam. JG1's squadron commanders urged their fighter pilots to knock out the rear turrets at long range with their 20 mm cannon, where the Wellington's .303s were useless, and then close in for the kill. The biggest bonus, however, was the fact that, if they managed to get hits on the bomber's wings, there was a good chance of the aircraft exploding in a great ball of fire.

Through a criminal omission on the part of the Air Ministry, the aircraft lacked self-sealing tanks. If hit in a fuel tank, especially that in the port wing, a Wellington could be transformed within seconds into a flying bonfire. Even if the tanks did not ignite, rapid loss of fuel would almost certainly bring down a crippled aircraft on a long run home.

Perhaps it was just as well that it was not generally appreciated by those who flew in Wellington bombers during those early days that this was the case. Had they known that the port wing tanks did not even have the benefit of armour plating they might have been more apprehensive as the flak barrage lifted and the fighters pounced.

First blood was credited to Unteroffizier Heilmayr in an Me 109E-1 from II/JG77 at 1.30 p.m. Immediately afterwards, 'Mäcki' Steinhoff reported attacking a Wellington and watching it spiral downwards in flames into the sea.

Racing towards the Schillig Roads from his exercise grounds close by Borkum, Wolfgang Falck spotted a close formation of Wellingtons 12 miles south-west of Heligoland at 11,000 feet. 9 Squadron, out on the left flank of the big diamond, had been left behind as the bombers wheeled northwards for Wilhelmshaven over the Jade Busen. Squadron Leader Guthrie's six aircraft were separated from the main formation and flying flat out to try and catch up. Falck and his rottenflieger, Fresia, swung in behind the bombers and Falck went for the Wellington on the right and Fresia for the one on the left. After two attempts, Falck saw the bomber disintegrate in mid-air. Fresia's victim dropped away with its port engine in flames. From Guthrie's original formation of six aircraft, only two made it back home. The captains of these two survivors reported that they had observed one aircraft in Flying Officer Allison's section catch fire and explode in mid-air while another went down with its port engine on fire. Pilot Officer Lines was flying number two position in Allison's section and Flying Officer Challes was flying the number three position. After his initial success, Falck turned his attention to the lead Wellington in the first section, but this time he did not get things all his own way. The rear-gunner got in a long burst on the attacking Messerschmitt 110 and Falck's starboard engine jerked to a standstill. With petrol streaming from his holed wing-tanks and clouds of smoke billowing from the cockpit, Falck broke off his attack to try and nurse his stricken fighter back to Jever. Unhappily, his victim had also succumbed to cannon and machine-gun fire and the blazing Wimpy flew headlong into the sea. In their reports, both Petts and Macrae described how their leader, Squadron Leader Guthrie, was last seen about 20 miles from the Schillig Roads being attacked by an Me 110 which he shot down in flames. Unteroffizier Fresia's second victim was Flying Officer Allison. Meanwhile, Wolfgang Falck was struggling to see where he was going. The ammunition in the fuselage was in flames and his cockpit was full of dense smoke. He opened the cabin window to clear the smoke and peered out searching for Jever. Shortly, his port engine packed up as well and he knew he could never reach his home base without power. He fired off all his ammunition and dumped his remaining fuel to lighten the aircraft and see if it would glide as far as Wangerooge. Fortunately, the wind was in his favour. With a great rush, the ground rose up to meet him and he quickly activated the compressed-air pump to lower his undercarriage. Falck made a skilful dead-stick landing and his machine rolled to a stop just short of the control tower. Feldwebel Walz climbed out of the rear compartment to join his pilot on the ground. The lady-bug on the fuselage had done its job well and brought them both safely back.

Bill Macrae, 'a wild, brave, passionately alcoholic Canadian short-service officer', was flying number two to Squadron Leader Guthrie. The fierce little Canadian cursed his gunner as he kicked and banked the Wellington under attack and heard no sound of answering fire from his own rear turret. 'I'm trying, skip, but my fingers are too stiff to get the guns to bear!' shouted the frozen, desperate gunner who was wounded moments later. Fabric was flapping from great gashes torn in the wing and fuselage, and fuel leaked from the tanks. Around him, 9 Squadron was disintegrating. Off on his port beam, Sergeant Petts was desperately making repeated calls to his leader to slow down. Despite opening up to full-boost, Petts was getting left further and further behind. As the fighters closed in for the kill, he decided that he would never catch up with Guthrie, and so he pushed the nose of his Wimpy down and dived as fast as he could towards sea level in an effort to shake off his pursuers. Levelling off just above the water he suddenly remembered a drill he had practised during co-operation exercises with Fighter Command. When the Messerschmitts came into the attack he slammed his throttles shut and, as the Wimpy lost speed, the fighters overshot and Robertson in the rear turret held his fingers on the triggers. On one occasion when an Me 110 closed on the Wellington due to this unexpected drop in speed, Robertson was treated to the spectacle of the German rear-gunner putting his fingers to his nose in a rude gesture before opening fire on the bomber. The gunner in the dustbin was badly wounded in the thigh, and Ginger Heathcote, the second pilot, scrambled down the fuselage and dragged Bob Kemp up out of his turret and helped him on to the rest bunk. Heathcote then scrambled forward to help Balch, who had been hit in the foot, out of the front turret. In the rear turret, Robertson emptied his guns into an Me 110 and heard the hammers click dead. He was out of ammunition, and just at that moment there were no more Messerschmitts to be seen. With two wounded gunners and with his rudder controls partly jammed, Sergeant Petts nursed N2873 the 200 miles to the English coast to land at Sutton Bridge in Lincolnshire. Macrae later made an emergency landing at the coastal aerodrome of North Coates Fitties. Petts and Macrae were the only two from 9 Squadron's port formation in the big diamond to make it back.

'R for Robert' was leading the starboard formation in the big diamond. At the briefing the previous evening, Paul Harris had been told that three aircraft from 9 Squadron, under the command of Flight Lieutenant Grant, would be flying in his formation. Fair-haired and elegant, Peter Grant was almost a Hollywood caricature of the sporting young English public school boy. After the briefing, Paul strolled across to Peter and said, 'Stay close to me whatever happens,' and fortunately this is precisely what he did. Harris's six Wimpys stuck together like a rolled up hedgehog, guns bristling all around. The Messerschmitts could not penetrate the wall of lead. Their cannons however outranged the Wimpy's Brownings, and from a safe distance they hammered fire into the tightly knit bunch of bombers. Looking out of his cockpit, Peter Grant was dismayed to see petrol pouring from one of his wing tanks. Quickly he switched on the pumps to transfer fuel from the holed tank to the ones that seemed intact. He later remarked: 'There was absolutely nothing we could do except sit there being picked off one by one.' On his port side he noticed that Sergeant Ramshaw was losing fuel from several punctures in his tanks. Later he learned that Ramshaw's turrets had jammed and the rear-gunner had been mortally wounded. Defenceless, N2983 dropped beneath the formation and limped homeward under the shelter of their guns.

Paul had little time to heed all the commotion going on around him. His eyes were firmly glued on Kellett as he struggled to hold N2980 in tight formation on his leader's vic. Bunny was manning the dustbin. He vividly recalls sitting there watching holes suddenly appear in the fabric, as if by magic, and bits of geodetic disintegrate in front of his eyes while at the same time feeling quite helpless to do anything about it. At the astrodome, Sandy was calling out the attacks as they developed. The elevator was hit and badly damaged, the wings and fuselage were holed repeatedly, and the torn and tattered

THE BATTLE OF HELIGOLAND BIGHT 75

fabric flapped in the slipstream as the fighters pressed home their attacks. Off on his port bow, Paul watched fascinated as an Me 109 swung in to attack Kellett's weakened formation. His leader had only four aircraft since the departure of Duguid and Kelly. The fighter broke away and came round again. Three times it tried to mount a beam attack and three times it missed. Oberleutnant Fuhrmann eventually got fed up with the difficult deflection shooting and, throwing caution to the winds, tried an attack from dead astern. This was precisely what the tail-gunners had been trained for – mutual supporting fire. All the tail-gunners in Kellett's vic ripped into him. Spuming smoke, Fuhrmann's fighter curled away seaward. The pilot managed to pull his machine out of its steep dive to make a perfect ditching, amid a cloud of spray, a couple of hundred metres from the island of Spiekeroog. Observers on the shore watched as the pilot clambered out of his cockpit onto the wing and jumped into the sea just as his fighter sank. He struggled desperately to swim to the shore but his heavy flying gear soaked up the icy water. Those standing on the beach watched helplessly as Johann Fuhrmann drowned a couple of hundred metres from safety.

Suddenly a twin-engined fighter streaked across N2980's path, intent on attacking Kellett's four Wimpys. Paul recalled the event 'just as if it were yesterday. The fellow shot straight across my bows blotting out the sun, jolly nearly rammed him. Young Doxsey let fly with a long burst but the so-n-so got Speirs, went up in a great huge ball of flame.' Flying Officer Speirs was flying number three in the lead formation when the Messerschmitt's fire lanced into his fuselage. There was an explosion to the rear of the cockpit, close to the wing root. Almost certainly the fighter had hit a high-pressure oxygen bottle. The bomber was immediately engulfed in flames. N2962 fell away from the formation to plunge into the sea 10,000 feet below. There were no parachutes.

Still the fighters came on. At one point Paul was alerted by a voice on the intercom from the front turret shouting, 'I'm hit, I'm hit,' but at the height of the battle there was nothing he could do about it. He watched out of the cockpit as Riddlesworth, the remaining pilot from Duguid's vic, closed up to take Speirs's place behind Kellett. Over the intercom came a report from Sandy that Flying Officer Briden had been hit and was spuming fuel out of his wing tanks. The surviving nine Wellingtons from Kellett, Harris and Grant's three vics drew closer together as they battled their way through 'The Hornet's Nest'. Aided by disciplined and determined formation flying, they pressed resolutely onward till they were out of range of the fighters.

Some distance behind the leader's formation straggled 37 Squadron. They had opened out in the barrage over Wilhelmshaven and were dangerously spread out as they emerged from the flak. Their leader, Squadron Leader Hue-Williams, was observed by Peter Grant racing far ahead of his formation in an attempt to catch up with the leaders. He had just succeeded in doing so when an Me 110, piloted by Oberleutnant Gordon Gollob, made a dive across his stern and raked the bomber with cannon and machine-gun fire. Peter Grant watched as Hue-Williams dived towards the sea with his starboard wing well on fire. Captain Reinecke, the CO of I/ZG76, later noted in his report: 'The Wellington is very inflammable and burns readily'.[xiii]

37 Squadron's experiment with the 'stepped down in pairs' formation can be considered a failure by results. 'Cheese' Lemon, flying number two to Hue-Williams, had previously departed the formation over Wilhelmshaven in a spectacular dive to sea level after inadvertently applying full flap. 'Christ, we've lost everything now. We're on our own,' thought Greaves, the front gunner. At that moment the rear gunner, Corporal Kidd, shouted: '109s!' Lemon clung desperately to the waves as the gunner called out the attacks. 'They're coming in... now... left! Now, right, right! He's overshooting.' They were hit repeatedly in the fuselage, the Wellington still streaking along with the spray breaking on the perspex of the front turret where Greaves tried in vain to bring his guns to bear. 'If we go down now, we've had it,' he thought, struck by the ghastly vision of the aircraft plunging unhesitatingly to the bottom of the sea if Lemon lost control for a moment. The observer in the astrodome was commenting on the German attacks. Suddenly, as one of the fighters closed again, there was a cry of choked astonishment from the rear turret: 'Christ! He's gone straight in!' Leutnant Roman Stiegler of II/JG77 was in

hot pursuit of Lemon's Wellington as it skimmed across the water when suddenly he found himself just a few feet above the waves. His wing tip touched the surface and his Me 109 cartwheeled and disappeared in a cloud of spray. Stiegler's wing man thought better of it and broke away. They were alone. There was an outburst of nervous hilarity on the intercom about the German's collision with the North Sea. Then Lemon cut in: 'Come on, cut the chatter, we've got to get home.'

Silent, exhausted by fear, they settled down for the long run back to Feltwell, flying all the way almost at sea level. In the front turret, Greaves swore he could taste the salt. At 3.40 p.m., N2903 landed back at Feltwell. After a half-hearted debriefing, they waited for the next Feltwell aircraft to return, yet by evening none had come.

After dropping his bombs over the Schillig Roads, Herbie Ruse, who was 37 Squadron's 'tail-end-charlie', was concentrating on holding formation on his leader. Herbie's only concern was to keep station on Thompson, to bomb when he did, to change course when he did. At the briefing the previous evening he had been surprised to learn that they were to bomb above 10,000 feet, for he could never remember any crew scoring hits in bombing practise on a target as small as a ship from that height. On exercises they had trained to attack in succession in pairs, making a series of runs over the target to judge their own errors. Before take-off that morning, it had been pre-arranged that, when a German naval vessel was sighted, the leader's pair would attack on the original course, the second pair would move out to port then attack and bomb from that quarter whilst the third pair, Thompson and Ruse, would move out to starboard and attack from there. This scheme was devised by the pilots of 37 Squadron themselves after several training sessions with fighter squadrons. It was to have been just as they practised in training but without the refinement of going round again to judge their errors. Now, however, their leader, Hue-Williams, was a mile or so ahead going flat out to try and catch up on Kellett, and 'Cheese' had made his unexpected and spectacular departure from the formation over Wilhelmshaven.

According to plan, Wimberley and Lewis broke away to port

and Thompson put his nose down and dived steeply to starboard followed closely by Herbie who watched his airspeed indicator going 'literally off the clock'. Just at that moment Herbie spotted a German fighter underneath them 'climbing like a lift'. In November they had carried out fighter affiliation exercises with Spitfires from Tangmere, and the fighter pilots had reported that they could have wiped out 37 Squadron in ten minutes. Then, nobody believed them. Tangmere could save its line-shoots for the Luftwaffe; Wellington bombers could take care of themselves. Now, it wasn't the friendly Spitfires that were climbing to make a mock attack but Messerschmitts, and the Tangmere boys were about to be proved dead right.

Oberleutnant Helmut Lent had just landed at Jever after an observation patrol along the coast. No sooner had he finished refuelling than he impatiently opened the throttles of his Me 110 and started to taxi towards the runway. Paul Mahle, his armourer, had just finished changing a drum of 20 mm ammunition and clung desperately to the wing as they bumped along the ground. As the Me 110 gathered speed, Mahle slid off the wing and hurled himself to the side to avoid being struck by the tail-plane.

Herbie Ruse's Wellington was by now racing downwards at an incredible 300mph, shaking in every rivet. Harry Jones in the rear turret was irrelevantly startled to see red roofs on the coast to the port of them. 'The roofs can't be red!' he muttered. 'Those are German houses, we have red roofs in England.'

Down the runway at Jever, Lent's fighter gathered speed. The joystick was eased back and it climbed swiftly to do battle. The visibility was so good that Lent could see fighters buzzing round the Wellingtons. 'Ah, that will be von Bülow's crowd,' he thought as he headed for the fray. Just at that moment he spotted a couple of Wellingtons sneaking off westwards in an effort to make a low-level escape over the sandbanks. He banked steeply and fell in behind the rear one. Harry Jones watched as the 110 streaked towards him at a closing speed of more than 100 mph. 'My God, isn't it small,' he thought, as so many thousands of air-gunners would think in their turn, in the next five years as the slim silhouette of the fighter swung in, guns winking. The first attack came on the Wellington's blind spot on the beam. With all guns blazing, the 110 streaked past but such deflection shooting was not easy and the stream of bullets seemed to have no effect. Lent swung round again but this time came in dead astern. At 600 yards Harry squeezed the triggers. His guns fired a single round and stopped. They were frozen up. He tried to traverse the turret. It was jammed by the cold. Lent thought he had knocked out the rear turret as there was no answering fire. Harry was still wrestling with his guns when the 110 came round again. There was a violent explosion in the turret and a savage pain in his ankle and back. 'Skip, I've been hit!' he called down the intercom. 'Can you do anything back there? No? Then for God's sake get out of the turret,' answered Ruse. Harry dragged himself up the fuselage towards the rest bed, half conscious with his back scored by one bullet, his ankle shattered by a second.

Tom Holley, the observer, was manning the dustbin and struggled to bring it to bear as the Messerschmitt raked the Wellington yet again. Morphia in hand, Fred Taylor, the wireless operator, bent over Harry Jones, trying to lift his wounded leg on to the rest bed. A burst of machine-gun fire smashed through the port side of the fuselage, shattering Taylor's head and back. Harry had persuaded the quiet northern boy to put aside his wartime scruples and get married only a few weeks before. Taylor collapsed on him, dying. The next burst caught Tom Holley as he struggled to pull himself up out of the dustbin turret, now jammed and useless. Hit in the face and side, Holley fell dead, draped half-in, half-out of his gun turret. By now N2936 was gushing a trail of dense black smoke and was clearly doomed. Helmut Lent broke away and set off in pursuit of Thompson's Wellington. When he caught up with it he attacked from astern once again. Later, when filling in his combat report, he wrote: 'Both the enemy's engines began burning brightly. As the plane hit the water the impact broke it apart and it sank.' Out of the side window, Harry Jones glimpsed Thompson's Wellington with its tail shot to pieces. Its rear gun turret had simply disappeared and with it Harry's friend, Len Stock, an instrument repairer from north London. It crashed into the sea beyond Borkum and the waves closed over the last resting place of N2935 as the body of

Sergeant Tilley, its observer, floated to the surface, to be recovered later by the Germans.

Herbie Ruse could smell the cordite from the explosions in the fuselage as he laboured to keep N2936 in the air, his revolution counter gone mad and his propellers in coarse pitch. Calmly he wound back the actuating wheel controlling the aircraft's trim so that if he himself was hit and fell from the controls, the Wellington should automatically seek to recover from the dive. Then the elevator controls collapsed and he knew his aircraft was finished. Beside him Tom May fought to help pull back the control column. Harry Jones, lying on the rest bunk, was astounded to see a burst of fire tear up the floor between May's legs as he stood straddled in the cockpit. May was hit only once, slightly wounded in the buttock. They saw the sand dunes of an island rushing up to meet them. It was Borkum, just a few miles east of neutral Dutch waters. With a grinding, wrenching, protracted shriek of metal and a whirlwind of sparks from the frozen ground beneath, Herbie brought the Wellington to rest. There were just a few seconds of merciful silence. May jettisoned the canopy and jumped down. Ruse was about to follow when he heard Jones's painful cry: 'I'm trapped!' As flames began to seep up the fuselage, Herbie hoisted Harry off the floor. 'My God, you're heavy, Jonah,' he complained. Then he half-dragged, half-carried the gunner out of the wrecked aircraft. The three men lay silent, exhausted and in pain, behind a dune in the sandy, frozen waste as their aircraft burned. At last a German patrol arrived to greet them with the time-honoured cliché: 'For you the war is over.'

Wimberley and Lewis had likewise broken away westwards over the Schillig Roads. Oberstleutnant Carl Schumacher, the geschwader commander, dispatched Lewis over the island of Wangerooge. For several days afterwards the wreck of N2889 could be seen sticking up out of the mud-flats off Spiekeroog. Only the body of the tail gunner, Aircraftman Geddes, was recovered.

'Pete' Wimberley battled his way westward through a succession of attacks but finally he too could no longer keep his battered and beaten up aircraft in the air. He was forced to ditch in the sea close to the island of Borkum. Shortly a

German patrol boat arrived and picked Wimberley out of the water. He was the only survivor from N2888. In his book, *Angriffshone 4000*, Cajus Bekker affirms that Helmut Lent 'brought down a third Wellington which had already been shot up. This plunged into the sea 15 miles north-west of Borkum.' It could only have been N2888. Because he had simply delivered the *coup de grâce*, Lent was credited with only his previous two kills. So, for five of 37 Squadron's six Wellingtons, their first encounter with the Luftwaffe had also been their last. As Wimberley's Wimpy crashed into the sea at 1.45 p.m., the rear formation of the big diamond ceased to exist.

Out over the sea, having passed directly over a flak ship ten miles south-west of Heligoland, Kellett's tightly knit band fought doggedly for its life. It is a measure of the fierceness of the struggle that continued for almost half an hour that, from those that survived, 149 Squadron was credited with six kills, three possibles and five doubtfuls. 9 Squadron claimed five kills, two possibles and five doubtfuls. 37 Squadron's lone survivor was credited with two doubtfuls.

Quite suddenly things quietened down. Paul looked at his watch and noted that it was just after 1.50 p.m. At the astrodome, Sandy, scanning the skies for fighters, found to his immense relief that they were on their own. Behind, Peter Grant glanced up for a moment and 'quite suddenly, there were just a few Wellingtons flying alone in a clear sky'. Schumacher's fighters had reached the limit of their endurance. Sandy glanced around again to make sure and spotted Briden just behind, staggering resolutely onward in his badly shot-up machine, petrol streaming from his riddled tanks. Ramshaw was still tucked underneath but he too was losing fuel fast. In 'R for Robert' there was subdued elation at their timely deliverance but little outward sign of celebration as they relaxed, all utterly exhausted by their exertions. 'Everyone pouring with sweat and throats so dry we could only croak,' wrote Sandy in his notebook next morning. Just at that moment, a very stern captain's voice came over the intercom: 'Navigator, remove the body from the front turret and attend to him.' Bunny Austin extricated himself from the dustbin and made his way forward to help young Doxsey out of the front gun turret and back to the rest bed. Bunny enquired, 'What's wrong boy? Where are you hit?' 'It's my flying boot, I'm hit in my foot,' came the reply. On examination it was found that the bullet had taken the sole clean off young Doxsey's flying boot. The lad was greatly concerned, not because he'd been hit but because he might be asked to pay for a new pair. At that, the tension evaporated completely. Paul put his hand into the depths of his flying jacket and produced a flask of rum. He handed it round. 'We had one damn good swig and it put new life into us,' wrote Sandy later. Over the intercom came a request for help from Jimmy Mullineaux. Thinking he had been wounded, Paul ordered Sandy to pass the rum down to the rear gunner. Opening the turret doors, Jimmy shouted to Sandy to give him a hand reloading the guns but Sandy didn't seem to understand. He passed the rum flask into the outstretched hand of the gunner who grasped it and closed the turret doors. The rum flask was not seen again until they all climbed down at Coltishall aerodrome, two hours later. Paul shook it but there wasn't a drop left. Jimmy smiled sheepishly.

> The route out was almost due north to north-west about 20 miles west of Heligoland, for as long as the attacks continued. As soon as they were abandoned, a course was set about west for the base. There were then only 10 aircraft in the formation, two of these gradually dropping back.[xiv]

In his report, Richard Kellett also went on to say: 'The enemy pressed home their attacks in a splendid manner,' striking a curiously gallant note in describing an ill-matched slaughter.

The battle over, JG1's initial tally of downed British bombers stood at 38. Their 'bag' is listed in Table 1 on page 84. Clearly this initial claim was grossly exaggerated. In reality, Bomber Command lost ten aircraft in the actual battle while two later ditched in the sea on their way home and three made emergency landings back in Britain. The losses that day are given in Table 2. The large discrepancy is hard to explain. It is important to stress that German fighter pilots were not permitted to make unsubstantiated claims. Their reporting procedure was very rigid and had to be strictly adhered to.

Before any claim could be confirmed it had to pass through many bureaucratic channels. Questions such as type of aircraft, nationality, exact position, altitude and time of engagement had to be meticulously answered. The fighter pilot had to complete a combat report that described in detail how the engagement progressed until the final kill. If possible, witnesses on the ground had to be found to corroborate the claim. On top of all that, another fighter pilot had to be cited as a witness and testify in writing that he had observed the combat and could vouch for the fact that the enemy aircraft had crashed. To back up their claim of 38 aircraft shot down, the Luftwaffe insisted that there had been a force of 44 Wellingtons (later increased by the German High Command to a force of 52 Wellingtons). A couple of hours later, the initial score was modified by XI Air Administrative Region in Hamburg to 34 bombers destroyed. Months later, once all the reports had been carefully sifted and analysed, the Reich Air Ministry in Berlin issued a statement confirming 27 of the claims. This was still more than double the true figure and five more than Kellett's entire force. For many years, even long after the war, German historians have disputed the official British figures in the belief that they had been originally issued to conceal the enormity of the disaster. Careful examination of the operations record books of all squadrons equipped with Wellingtons at that time reveal no deception. Obituaries from the Commonwealth War Graves Commission record the identity of all service personnel who died during the war and have no known grave, as would be the case for aircraft shot down over the sea. None of the airmen reported missing on that day belonged to any squadron other than 149, 9 and 37. Reference to other RAF squadrons operating twin-engined bombers indicate no other type of bomber being involved. Finally, personal discussions with Air Commodore Kellett, Group Captain Harris and Wing Commander Austin confirm *without a shadow of doubt* that only 22 Wellingtons took on the might of the Luftwaffe that day.

The Germans were not alone, however, in over-estimating their score. British newspapers headlined the fact that 12 enemy fighters had been destroyed and no fewer than six of them were Göring's new and much vaunted Messerschmitt

84 THE BATTLE OF HELIGOLAND BIGHT 1939

Table 1

1	14h 30	Uffz Heilmayr	II.JG 77	30 km SSW Heligoland
2	14h 30	Stfk J. Steinhoff	10. (N)/JG 26	30 km SSW Heligoland
3	14h 30	Fw W. Szuggar	10. (N)/JG 26	30 km SSW Heligoland
4	14h 30	Uffz Niemeyer	II./JG 77	NNW Wangerooge
5	14h 30	Uffz Niemeyer	II./JG 77	NNW Wangerooge
6	14h 30	Oblt Henz	II./JG 77	NNW Wangerooge
7	14h 30	Lt Schirmböck	II./JG 77	NNW Wangerooge
8	14h 35	Obstlt Schumacher	Stab/JG 1	N Spiekeroog
9	14h 35	Stfk J. Steinhoff	10.(N)/JG 26	35 km SSW Heligoland
10	14h 35	Uffz Gerhardt	10.(N)/JG 26	35 km SSW Heligoland
11	14h 35	Uffz Wilke	10.(N)/JG 26	35 km SSW Heligoland
12	14h 35	Uffz Portz	10.(N)/JG 26	35 km SSW Heligoland
13	14h 35	Stfk W. Falck	I./ZG 76	20 km SW Heligoland
14	14h 35	Uffz Fresia	I./ZG 76	20 km SW Heligoland
15	14h 40	Fw Gröning	I./ZG 76	E Langeoog
16	14h 42	Lt H. Lent	I./ZG 76	5 km N Borkum
17	14h 45	Stfk W. Falck	I./ZG 76	20 km SW Heligoland
18	14h 45	Uffz Fresia	I./ZG 76	20 km SW Heligoland
19	14h 45	Oblt Jäger	I./ZG 76	NW Borkum
20	14h 45	Oblt G. Gollob	I./ZG 76	NW Langeoog
21	14h 45	Ofw Fleischmann	I./ZG 76	NW Spiekeroog
22	14h 50	Oblt O. Robitzsch	JGr. 101	SW Heligoland
23	14h 50	Oblt R. Kaldrack	JGr. 101	SW Heligoland
24	14h 50	Oblt Poitner	II./JG 77	NW Norderney
25	14h 50	Fw Troitsch	II./JG 77	NW Norderney
26	14h 50	Fw Troitsch	II./JG 77	NW Norderney
27	14h 50	Oblt Lang	II./JG 77	NW Norderney
28	14h 50	Oblt Peters	II./JG 77	NW Norderney
29	14h 50	Lt Schmidt	II./JG 77	NW Norderney
30	14h 50	Oblt Jung	II./JG 77	NW Norderney
31	14h 50	Ofw Droste	II./JG 77	NW Norderney
32	14h 50	Uffz Holck	II./JG 77	NW Norderney
33	14h 50	Lt H. Lent	I./ZG 76	10 km WNW Borkum
34	15h 00	Oblt Gresens	I./ZG 76	25 km NW Borkum
35	15h 00	Lt Graeff	I./ZG 76	25 km WNW Borkum
36	15h 00	Uffz Kalinowski	l./ZG 76	25 km WNW Borkum
37	15h 00	Lt Uellenbeck	I./ZG 76	50 km N Ameland
38	15h 05	Lt Uellenbeck	I./ZG 76	50 km N Ameland

Totals:
- Stab/JG 1 = 1
- 10.(N)/JG 26 = 6
- JGr. 101 = 2
- II./JG 77 = 14
- I./ZG 76 = 15

  38

Les Aiglons, Combats Aeriens de la Drôle de Guerre by C.J. Ehrengardt; C.F. Shores; H. Weisse; J. Foreman. Published by Charles Lavauzelle, Paris-Limoges, 1983. Page 91.

Table 2 (See Appendix D)

Aircraft	Captain	Squadron	Credited to:
N2962	F/O Speirs	149	Ofw Fleischmann or Fw. Gröning
N2872	S/Ldr Guthrie	9	Stfk Falck
N2939	P/O Lines	9	Stfk Falck
N2941	F/O Allison	9	Uffz Fresia
N2940	F/O Challes	9	Uffz Fresia
N2904	S/Ldr Hue-Williams	37	Oblt Gollob
N2935	F/O Thompson	37	Lt Lent
N2936	Sgt Ruse	37	Lt Lent
N2888	F/O Wimberley	37	Lt Lent (*Coup de Grâce*)
N2889	F/O Lewis	37	Obstlt Schumacher
Me 109D	Oblt Fuhrmann	10.(N)/JG 26	N2866 F/O Riddlesworth (+ Turner & Speirs?)
Me 109E	Lt Stiegler	6/JG 77	N2903 F/O Lemon

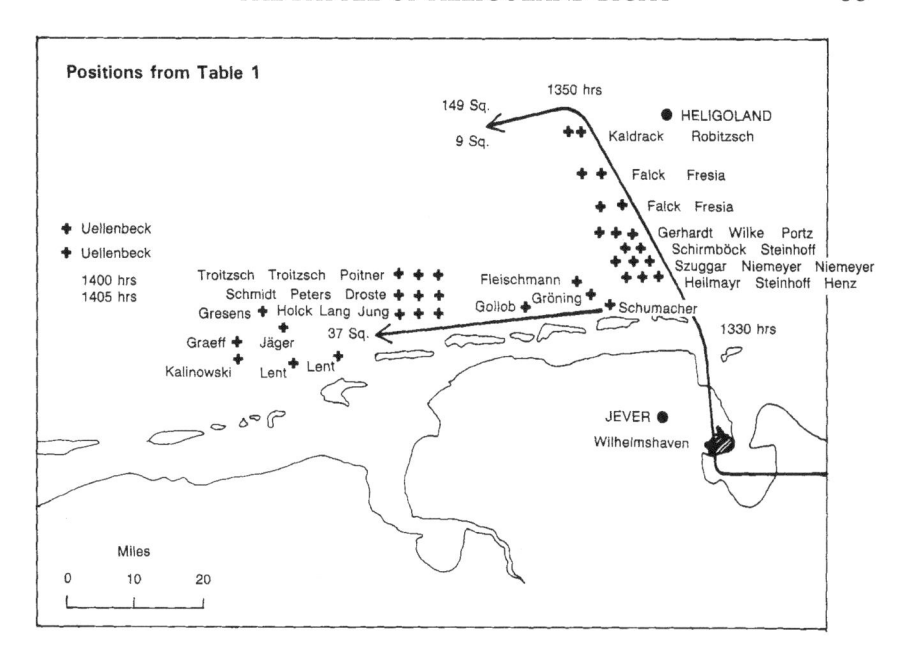

THE BATTLE OF HELIGOLAND BIGHT 85

Positions from Table 1

- Uellenbeck
- Uellenbeck
  1400 hrs
  1405 hrs

149 Sq.
9 Sq.
1350 hrs

Kaldrack Robitzsch
● HELIGOLAND
Falck Fresia
Falck Fresia
Gerhardt Wilke Portz
Schirmböck Steinhoff
Szuggar Niemeyer Niemeyer
Heilmayr Steinhoff Henz

Troitzsch Troitzsch Poitner
Schmidt Peters Droste
Gresens Holck Lang Jung
Graeff Jäger
Kalinowski Lent Lent

Fleischmann
Gollob Gröning
Schumacher
37 Sq.

1330 hrs

JEVER ●
Wilhelmshaven

Miles
0   10   20

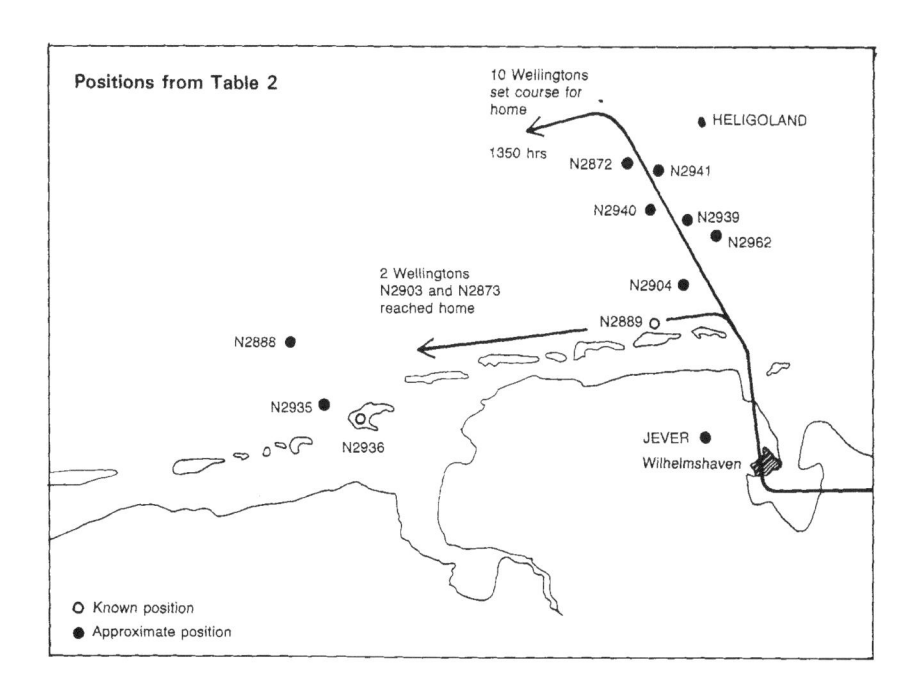

Positions from Table 2

10 Wellingtons set course for home
1350 hrs

● HELIGOLAND
N2872 ● ● N2941
N2940 ●   ● N2939
              ● N2962
         N2904 ●
2 Wellingtons N2903 and N2873 reached home
N2889 ○

N2888 ●

N2935 ●
     ○
   N2936

JEVER ●
Wilhelmshaven

○ Known position
● Approximate position

Bf110s. In reality, no Me 110 was reported missing. JG1 confirmed the loss of two Me 109s and a further one written off after crash-landing. Two 109s and two 110s were very severely damaged while seven 110s and one 109 suffered slight damage. In all, the Luftwaffe put up 25 109s and 19 110s. Forty-four fighters against 22 bombers gave odds of exactly two to one. It is significant that the surviving British aircrews estimated that there had been between 60 and 80 fighters in the sky over the Heligoland Bight. This over-estimation of aircraft numbers engaged in combat would crop up many times in later conflicts as the war progressed.

Bomber Command's true score was seven German fighters downed. II/JG77's commanding officer, Major Harry von Bülow-Bothkamp (a World War I ace), was forced to return to base early when his Me 109 developed engine trouble shortly after take-off. The two Me 109s of Fuhrmann and Stiegler crashed into the sea. A third, piloted by Leutnant Dietrich Robitzsch from Jagdgruppe 101 at Neumünster, was forced down when his engine was hit. With glycol all over his windscreen and his vision obscured, Robitszch broke off his attack on a Wellington to return to base. Just short of Neumünster his engine overheated and seized up. He forced-landed among the trenches and dugouts of a troop-training ground. The right tyre burst causing the Me 109 to slew round in a circle before coming to rest. Robitszch opened the cockpit hatch, climbed out on to the wing and jumped clear without a scratch. His machine was a write-off. Feldwebel Hans Troitsch, who shot down the first British bomber of the war on 4th September 1939, was hit and wounded. He managed to bring his Me 109 down on Wangerooge where it suffered extensive damage. Even the geschwader commander, Carl Schumacher, had to retire from the fray and nurse his Me 109 back to Jever. Not one of the Me 110s deployed, however, failed to get back home. Wolfgang Falck just made it back to Wangerooge by dint of skilful piloting. The circumstances surrounding the other Me 110 that was badly damaged that day are totally baffling. Oberfeldwebel Dombrowski, the radio operator/rear gunner in an Me 110 piloted by Leutnant Uellenbeck, relates in his personal recollections of the battle that his pilot spotted a flight of *three* Vickers Wellingtons 'flying extremely low'.

THE BATTLE OF HELIGOLAND BIGHT 87

The position of the encounter is recorded as having taken place 50km north of the Dutch island of Ameland. The time was 2.00 p.m. (GMT).[18] At precisely that time Kellett's surviving force of ten bombers was more than 100km away to the east, flying above 10,000 feet and, by then, clear of attacking fighters. Only one of 37 Squadron's aircraft survived past the island of Borkum and that was Flying Officer Lemon. His last encounter with the Luftwaffe was observing Roman Stiegler cartwheel into the drink. The only other Wellington that sought the safety of the waves and made it past Borkum was 9 Squadron's Sergeant Petts. There is a strange similarity between the accounts of Petts and Dombrowski (see Appendix A).

Sergeant Petts was flying 'just above the water', and Oberfeldwebel Dombrowski confirms that 'they are flying extremely low', when referring to the Wellingtons engaged by Leutnant Uellenbeck and his rottenflieger.

Throttles wide open and heading due west from Wangerooge, Sergeant Petts would certainly have managed to reach Ameland by 2 p.m. The question is where Dombrowski's other two Wellingtons came from. Likewise, where did the Me 110 spring from that Sergeant Robertson jubilantly claimed had 'gone in'?

Question marks notwithstanding, somebody shot 33 bullet holes in Uellenbeck's fighter, wounded the pilot and rear gunner and forced them to break off their attacks. But by 2 p.m. there simply weren't enough Wellingtons left for Uellenbeck to claim one, let alone two, victories. Kellett reported that he counted ten Wellingtons in his formation after the battle. This means that Flying Officer Macrae must have caught up with and joined the nine survivors from Kellett's and Harris's formations. This leaves only one Wellington that could have been in the right place at the right time to shoot down Uellenbeck, and that was N2873 piloted by Sergeant Petts.

By dint of careful scrutiny of all the available records and reports on the action[19], it is possible to account for the ten Wimpys shot down and allocate them to just seven of the

---

[18]3.00 p.m. (15h 00) German time.
[19]See Appendix D.

Luftwaffe fighter pilots. Apart from Falck, Fresia, and Gollob, there were only two other Me 110s of I/ZG76 that reported their position as being anywhere within 25km of Kellett's main formation. All the other Me 110s reported their engagements as having taken place in the vicinity of Borkum, over 80km away. In Uellenbeck's case, the distance was over 120km. Paul Harris confirmed that Flying Officer Speirs was shot down by an Me 110, and the only two candidates left are Oberfeldwebel Fleischmann or Feldwebel Gröning. What happened to the other 17 official German claims will probably remain a mystery.

The geschwader commander, Carl Schumacher, had been forced to retire early from the battle because of damage to his Me 109E-1. On returning to fighter HQ at Jever he was presented with reports coming in thick and fast from his fighter squadrons. None it seemed had returned empty-handed, except III/JG7 at Nordholz. From Captain Seliger there were no reports of any victories. How could that be? Then his adjutant owned up. In all the excitement, the headquarters staff had clean forgotten all about the gruppe at Nordholz. They had never been sent the order to scramble. Next day, at a briefing for the international press in Berlin, Schumacher was quoted as saying that things had all gone according to plan; he had even been able to hold squadrons 'in reserve'. That sounded so much better.

Shortly after 3.00 p.m (German time), the last fighter returned to base and the Luftwaffe was able to take stock of the day's events. By chance, Generalleutnant Wolff, who was in charge of XI Air Administrative Region, happened to be visiting the island of Borkum that day. He watched Herbie Ruse crash-land his Wimpy. Afterwards he examined the wreckage carefully and made a surprising discovery. Straight away he made for Jever where he took Carl Schumacher aside. 'We examined the wreck minutely and believe you me, Schumacher, there wasn't a single bomb on board,' he confided. Added to this, the information extracted from the surviving British pilots, Wimberley and Ruse, had the Germans completely mystified. Not only had the British dropped no bombs on Wilhelmshaven but it now appeared that they hadn't been carrying any in the first place. The explanation offered by

THE BATTLE OF HELIGOLAND BIGHT 89

the two British pilots seemed to confirm that the RAF had taken leave of its senses.

'No attack was ever intended'; 'The Wellingtons were only on a navigation training exercise'; 'It was a training flight for new pilots and navigators'; 'Instead of bombs, the aircraft had been carrying extra trainees' – thus affirmed Wimberley and Ruse. To this day, all the German accounts of the battle seek to comprehend why Bomber Command should have been so foolhardy. Lengthy explanations have been proffered to account for the large discrepancy in numbers and the seemingly irrational behaviour of the British. The explanation is quite simple. The Germans miscounted and the British pilots lied to their captors.

When I put the question to Paul Harris he laughed aloud and, with a grin from ear to ear, he said, 'Well old chap, it's like this. Wimberley and Ruse told them a great big fib, didn't they, and the Jerries swallowed it, hook, line and sinker.'

The Germans did concede, however, that the British had put up a good fight and the geschwaderkommodore noted in his report the 'tight formation and excellent rear-gunners of the Wellington bombers'.

While Schumacher and Wolff were scratching their heads over the seemingly eccentric behaviour of the 'Tommies', Richard Kellett was shepherding the remnants of his battered flock homeward. Paul Harris handed round his precious rum flask as he assessed the situation.

> Flying number three on my port side was Flying Officer Michael Briden with his second pilot Billy Brown. As soon as we were clear of the fighters I was able to take stock of my flight. All seemed OK, except one, poor Briden; I could see petrol streaming from his port tank. Our tanks were not self-sealing. He called me up on the R/T to say that he was running short of petrol and could they take the shortest possible route home. Sandy looked back and confirmed that there was a plume of gas spraying out of Briden's port wing. Finally, some 50 miles off our coast his engines failed. I followed him down and he ditched successfully. I got a DF fix on him and I did a run over the aircraft low down and released my dinghy which was

situated at the rear of the starboard engine nacelle. I did this in case his had failed. The aircraft was still floating. However, it was not intended that the dinghy should be released in the air, only after ditching, so, to my horror, it stuck on my tail-plane, and for a moment I thought I was going to join Briden. However, apart from severe vibration all was well so, having done all I could, I tottered home and landed at the first aerodrome I could find. N2980 was but little damaged; it had acquitted itself well but poor Briden and Brown were not found, the whole crew was lost. I fear their dinghy must have been holed by a bullet and the sea was cold.

Bunny Austin vividly remembers the battle and the return journey home.

During the raid itself, the most striking thing was, perhaps a little in retrospect, the vision of sitting there in the turret watching one's own aircraft being shot out of the sky and being quite helpless to do anything about it. There is no doubt as Paul says, the losses in the other squadrons were due very largely to loose flying and, if you have to fly in daylight at that sort of height with very poor armament you must make the most of it and keep tight formation. The .303 inch gun turrets were pretty useless against 20mm cannon. The German fighters should in fact have done probably better than they did. On the way back we formated on Briden. We kept with him because he was losing fuel from his wing tanks and it was clear that he was in difficulty. Ultimately he ditched about 30 miles off Cromer. He made a very good ditching and all his crew got out into the dinghy. It was at this time that Paul decided that the thing to do would be to drop our dinghy to give them an additional dinghy in the sea. There was some protest because they were not designed to be loosened in the air and there was always the risk that it would catch around one's own tail-plane. Indeed this is what happened. We circled and tried to get a fix. Jock Watson transmitted the position and we then flew as accurate a course as we could back to the English coast. I kept the most careful

THE BATTLE OF HELIGOLAND BIGHT

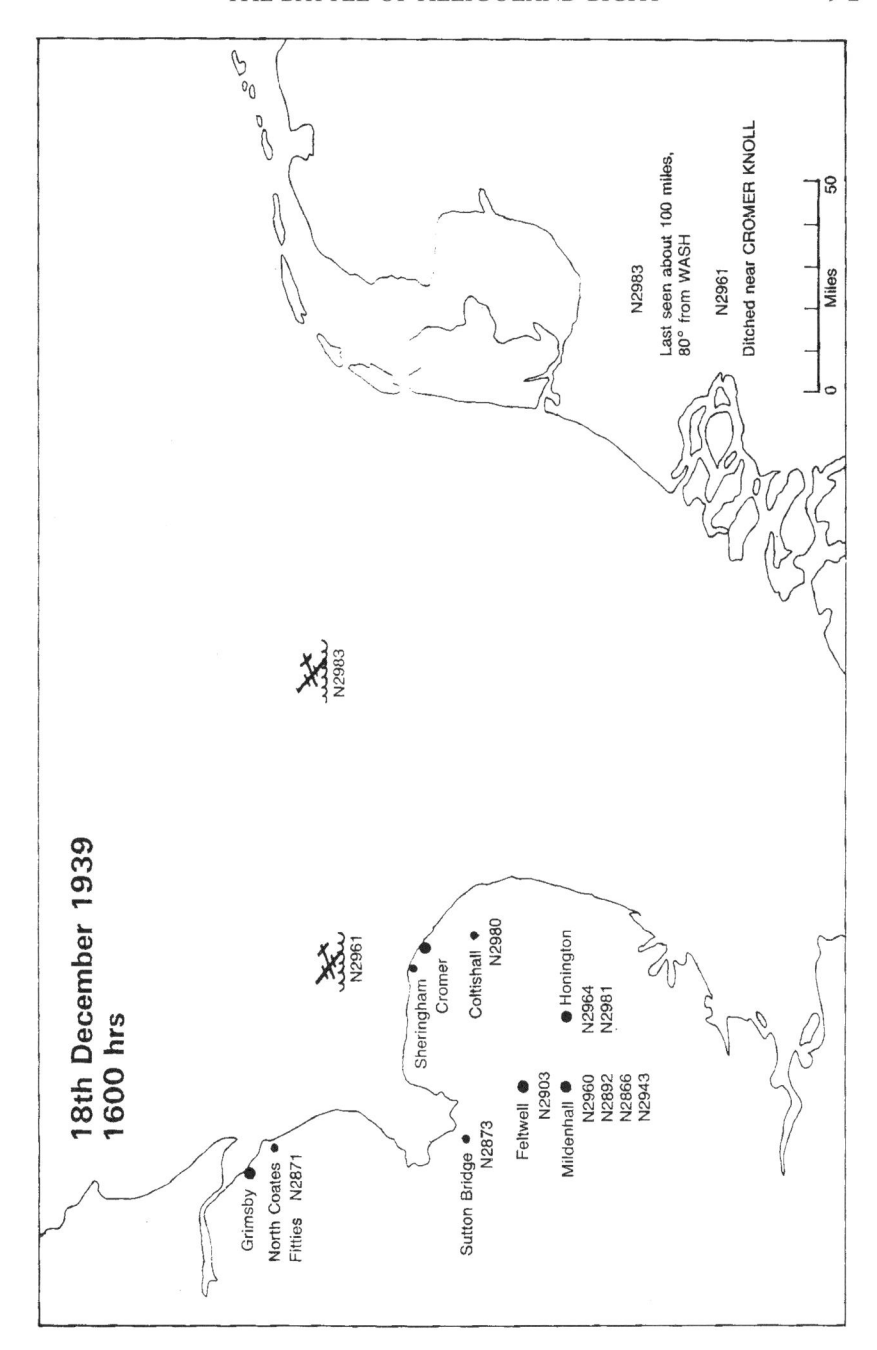

navigation fix that I could bearing in mind that in those days we were entirely without radar and working almost solely on dead reckoning navigation.

From Cromer and Sheringham the lifeboats put out and headed at full speed for the position given by Jock Watson to join a destroyer, a high speed launch and another lifeboat in the search, but the North Sea in December was just as implacable a foe as the Luftwaffe. They had been warned in training that they might expect to survive for 15 minutes under such conditions. Michael Briden and his crew were never seen again.

9 Squadron's N2983 was more fortunate. Sergeant Ramshaw spotted a trawler about 100 miles out from the Wash and ditched as close to it as he could. Less than 15 minutes later the *Erillas*, skippered by S. Sinclair, reached the scene and rescued the survivors. The rear gunner, Leading Aircraftman Lilley, had been killed during the battle but the other four crew members were hauled from their dinghy and that night were safely in Grimsby Hospital. Ironically, on the same day that Briden and Ramshaw ditched in the North Sea due to lack of fuel from their holed tanks, the Air Ministry in London issued an order that Bomber Command should desist from further attacks in the Heligoland Bight area until Wellington bombers had been fitted with armour plating on *all* their fuel tanks.

With the dinghy stuck firmly on the tail-plane, the elevator holed and ready to break at any moment, the fuel tanks dangerously low and the starboard engine feathered to cut down the awful juddering on the controls, N2980 sought a safe haven. The first available aerodrome was Coltishall close by Norwich. Having spent over six-and-a-half hours in the air and endured the undivided attention of the Luftwaffe during the biggest air battle of the war to date, they were met by a highly irate engineering superintendent who roared up in his big car and greeted them with the words: 'You can't land here, this airfield is not completed.' As Bunny Austin said, 'I won't give you the words that were used back to him.' Sandy commandeered a push-bike and headed for the nearest phone to inform Operations of Briden's predicament: 'Had awful trouble getting on for some fool of a girl in the exchange was behaving with bureaucratic efficiency in spite of it being a priority call. Ticked me off for my language and said she would report me just because I said: "for Christ's sake get a bloody move on."'

After the little misunderstanding with the site engineer had been amicably settled, Mr Bowles ran them the 50 miles back to Mildenhall in his big Rover, 'which was a damned good show,' noted Sandy.

Meanwhile, the rest of 149 Squadron were landing at Mildenhall. Kellett, Turner, Riddlesworth and Bulloch all touched down safely. Apart from a collection of assorted bullet holes and the odd chunk of missing geodetics they had all survived the battle virtually unscathed. Likewise, Grant and Purdy returned to Honington with only superficial damage. Had the Air Ministry fitted self-sealing tanks and armour plating to the port wing, then Briden and Ramshaw would undoubtedly have made it back as well. Grant told his tale to the CO and the adjutant in the officers' mess, then went exhausted to bed. An officer who put his head into the mess a little later found it deserted but for the CO, who sat bowed and old, alone by the fireplace.

Macrae forced-landed at North Coates Fitties in an aircraft that had been shot to pieces. By chance, Sandy Innes happened to see the aircraft some days later: 'Flew photographer up to North Coates in Magister. Coldest trip I remember. Below freezing and landed in a snow storm. At North Coates is Macrae's Wellington where he forced-landed after Monday's affair. God knows how he got back and how no one was hit. Plane was riddled with bullets and they had even gone through armour plating. Three petrol tanks at least were holed. Rear turret was riddled.' Petts could not make it back to Honington either and burst a tyre on landing at Sutton Bridge. N2873's starboard wing had been on fire but the armour plating had kept the fire away from the fuel tanks. The starboard side of the fuselage had more holes in it than a sieve. Lemon was the only survivor from 37 Squadron to make it back to Feltwell. N2903 landed safe and sound.

That night there was a party at the Bird in Hand. Paul Harris's wife, Kit, had pints of beer all lined up along the bar and, as Sandy later noted, 'I can't remember anything being so good as my first pint of beer that night and did I need it.' As they drank their pints, they listened to 'Lord Haw-Haw' on the wireless telling them that the Luftwaffe had just shot down 38 of their 22 Wimpys. That raised a great laugh.

Next day, both sides were hailing the 'Battle of Heligoland Bight' as a major victory. The Germans had a special reason for going to town on the story. In his *Berlin Diary* William L. Shirer relates:

> *Berlin, 18th December 1939.*
> The populace is still a little bit puzzled about how the big victory of the *Graf Spee* suddenly ended by the pocket-battleship scuttling itself off Montevideo yesterday afternoon. But Goebbels and Göring have pulled a neat one to make them forget it as soon as possible. The attention of the German people tomorrow morning will be concentrated by the press and radio on something else, an alleged victory – this time in the air – off Heligoland. An official statement which the papers and radio have been told to bang for all it's worth says that 34 out of 44 British bombers were shot down this afternoon north of Heligoland. A very *timely* victory. We had just left the evening press conference after firing embarrassing questions about the *Graf Spee* and were putting on our overcoats downstairs when Dr Boehmer rushed in breathlessly and said he had some big news and would we please return upstairs to the conference room. Then he read us in breathless tones the communiqué about the 34 British planes being shot down. Suspect it is eyewash.

Oberstleutnant Carl Schumacher, Staffelkapitän 'Mäcki' Steinhoff, Staffelkapitän Wolfgang Falck, Oberleutnant Pointner, Leutnant Lent, Oberfeldwebel Fleischmann and Unteroffizier Niemeyer were summoned to Berlin to be interviewed by the German and international press on the events of 18th December. Over the Christmas and New Year period, newspapers round the world regaled their readers with the heroic exploits of the Royal Air Force or the Luftwaffe depending on their particular sympathies.

> 'WILL ANOTHER FILM BE MADE?' trumpeted *Der Angriff*.
> *The Lion has Wings*. A film bearing this title was made using mock-ups and models and all that sort of paraphernalia – when English politicians dreamed up the first successful attacks on Kiel and Wilhelmshaven. And British cinema audiences will soon be able to see the lion rampant stretching its wings on the screen.
>
> Outside, in the cold light of day, the old lion was already looking rather toothless. But today, if they wish to make another film – this time about the 18th of December operation, they will not have any difficulty thinking of a title. 'The wings the lion once had' is all they need to call it.
>
> *Der Angriff*, 19th December 1939

The Germans were not alone however in embellishing the facts. That following Thursday, newspaper reporters descended on Mildenhall, as Sandy recorded in his little notebook.

> The press came down to take our photos going off on the raid and returning, exactly three days late but that didn't worry them. So we all had to get into our full flying kit, Mae Wests, parachutes, etc., and perform the most ridiculous antics, very nearly running to our planes. Then pictures of the Wellingtons flying and crews getting out. The mere fact that some of those were never on the raid is nothing of course to them. Then finally they picked on me to pose for them and God was that a performance... And finally my photo in the papers. Splashed all over. Enormous affair in the *Scotsman* – and in the *Sunday Graphic* – I will never be able to live that down!

'HEROES OF THE BIGHT' HOME: NAZI ACES ROUTED: RAF ROUT NAZI SUPER-FIGHTERS: RAF GETS BEST OF BIGGEST AIR BATTLE OF THE WAR – 12 NAZI PLANES SHOT DOWN: SEVEN OF OUR MACHINES WERE LAST NIGHT UNACCOUNTED FOR.

These were but a few of the front page headlines that filled the papers over that festive season. As morale boosters they were just what the doctor ordered but as a true record of the events that day, they painted a picture viewed through rose-coloured spectacles. The Air Ministry indulged in a little verbal subterfuge to conceal the truth about the British losses but Sandy Innes had his suspicions.

> We lost ten aircraft over Wilhelmshaven and two came down near England and one crew was saved. Air Ministry said that 'seven of our aircraft are not accounted for' because three were seen going towards Germany under some control but no power. So only seven are unaccounted for. True of course, but it is juggling with the truth which is a pity and tends to sap confidence in the veracity of our reports. However it's a damn good show that we got so many of them!

Slaughter of these proportions at this still squeamish moment of the war provoked an unprecedented upheaval and *post mortem* at 3 Group and at Bomber Command. Ludlow-Hewitt, a C-in-C already well known for his sensitivity to casualties, flew in person to Norfolk to hear first-hand accounts of the operation. Group Captain Hugh Pughe-Lloyd, a 3 Group staff officer who had commanded 9 Squadron until a few weeks before, said in one of a mass of reports inspired by the disaster, 'I dislike the course taken to the target. On this occasion we made landfall near the German-Dutch frontier and ran the whole way down it, giving the enemy all the warning he can get.' This was almost the only instance of open criticism of the planning of the operation.

Most senior officers studied the events of 18th December and drew much more hopeful and face-saving conclusions. They readily accepted that the Wellingtons had to be provided with beam guns and self-sealing tanks. But, granted these measures, it seemed to them that the elements of Kellett's formation which had stuck rigidly together as ordered had fared astonishingly well. Only one of Kellett's own section of four aircraft had been lost, and an impressive list of enemy fighters destroyed had been accepted. Of the six aircraft on the starboard side, all would have survived the battle had they

Top left: Paul Harris photographed just after the 3rd December raid on Heligoland. Snap taken by Sandy Innes.

Top centre: Acting Flight Lieutenant K.C. Doran.

Top right: Flying Officer A. McPherson.

Middle: A crowd, including women and children carrying their gas masks, watch as the coffins of two German airmen who were shot down in the raid on the Firth of Forth are escorted to the cemetery by men of the RAF.

Bottom: Wing Commander Griffiths photographed with Corporals Pettitt (right) and Bickerstaff (left). Two days after the raid, His Majesty King George VI conferred the DFC on Griffiths and the DFM on Pettitt and Bickerstaff.

Top left: Oberstleutnant Carl Schumacher survived the war as a Generalmajor with the Ritterkreuz (Knight's Cross of the Iron Cross).

Top right: Major Harry von Bülow-Bothkamp was awarded the Ritterkreuz for his leadership in the West.

Bottom left: Staffelkapitän Johannes 'Macki' Steinhoff went on to become one of the great leader personalities of the Luftwaffe. He was awarded the Ritterkreuz and achieved the remarkable total of 176 victories. He was seriously wounded on 18th April 1945 during take-off in a Me 262 but survived the war to become inspector general of the German air force.

Bottom right: Staffelkapitän Wolfgang Falck later rose to command the Luftwaffe's premier nightfighter force, Nachtjagdgeschwader 1 (NJG1). He became a key figure in the development of radar-guided interception and was awarded the Ritterkreuz.

Top: Pilots of 2/ZG76 in their hut waiting for the next scramble. Second from the left, sitting, is Unteroffizier Fresia, the Rottenflieger or 'Kaczmarek' of Hauptmann Falck.

Middle: The 'well camouflaged aerodrome at Shillig Point' was called Jever, shown here with an Me 109 and an Me 110 during the winter of 1939.

Bottom left: Me 109E of II/JG77 being readied for combat.

Bottom right: Oberleutnant Gordon Gollob went on to become one of the Luftwaffe's top fighter aces with 150 victories to his credit. He was one of only 12 Luftwaffe pilots to add the much coveted 'Diamonds' to his Ritterkreuz.

Top left: Pilot: Squadron Leader Harris.

Top centre: Second Pilot: Pilot Officer Innes.

Top right: Navigator: Sergeant Austin.

Middle left: Wireless Operator: Aircraftman Second Class Watson.

Middle centre: Front Gunner: Aircraftman First Class Doxsey.

Middle right: Rear Gunner: Aircraftman First Class Mullineaux.

Bottom: Sandy's record of the stations kept by 149 Squadron and the three aircraft of 9 Squadron during the Battle of Heligoland Bight.

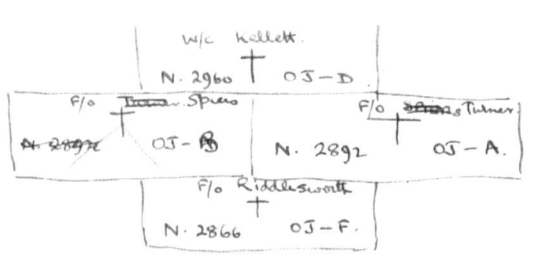

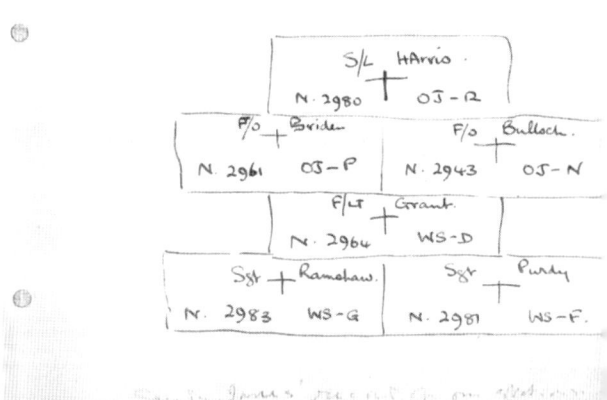

Top: Here the second pilot of a Wellington bomber is taking a message from the wireless operator who is located in a tiny compartment behind the pilot.

Middle: Photograph taken by Wellington A OJ (Flying Officer Turner) of 149 Squadron while flying over Wilhelmshaven on 18th December 1939.

Bottom: The pilots of the Marienkäfer Squadron (2/ZG76) with a Me 110C.

Top left: Air Vice-Marshal Baldwin and Air Chief Marshal Sir Ludlow-Hewitt (left).

Top centre: Air Commodore Bottomley (shown here later as an Air Vice-Marshal).

Top right: Richard Kellett.

Middle: Wellington Mk 1s of 149 Squadron over Paris, 14th July 1939 (Bastille Day). Wellington G-LY (L4272) was Flight Lieutenant Duguid's aircraft on 4th September 1939 raid on Brunsbüttel.

Bottom: A rare photograph showing a Mk 1A Wellington of 9 Squadron, with its 'dustbin' turret lowered for action (*photo: T. Mason via Chaz Bowyer*).

op: A tantalising glimpse of 'R for Robert' in the background.   *Bottom:* 149 Squadron's B Flight crew room.

Top: Sergeant Herbert Ruse (pointing) of 37 Squadron being briefed for an operation. On the far right is the squadron CO, Wing Commander Joe Fogarty with Flying Officer Vaughan-Williams. On the left is Flying Officer Lewis.

Middle: Oberleutnant Helmut Lent went on to become one of the outstanding personalities of the Luftwaffe. He was one of their top aces with 110 victories to his credit. Like Gordon Gollob, he too succeeded in adding the 'Diamonds' to his Ritterkreuz. During a daylight landing on 5th October 1944 one of his engines failed and his aircraft touched a high tension wire and crashed. Lent was critically injured and died two days later.

Bottom: The remains of N2936's forward section, Herbie Ruse's Wimpy.

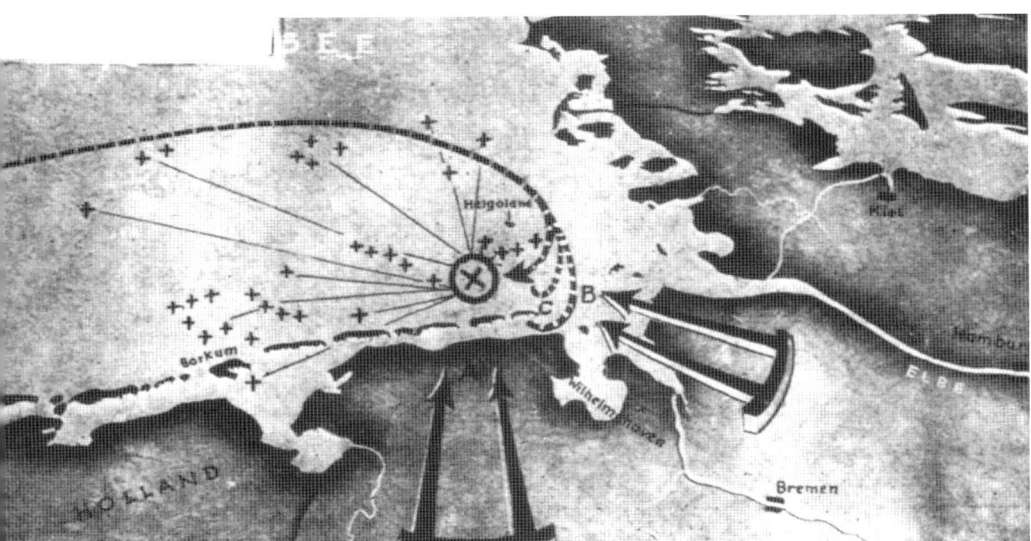

Top: Aircraft wreckage burning on the sea after the Battle of Heligoland Bight.

Middle: German newspaper photograph and caption detailing where the 34 Wellingtons were shot down:

> "In order to avoid the fire from the Heligoland batteries the English flew in a broad arc round the island and then turned south (dotted line). The German fighter squadrons attacked the enemy from both sides (A & B), broke up their closed formations (C) and then pursued the individual Vickers Wellingtons until they ended up in the 'drink' (see crosses). Individual aircraft which managed to evade the fighters came under fire from flak batteries on the islands and on the coast. They had to turn back without managing to release their bombs."

Bottom: International press conference in Berlin to report on the 36 bombers shot down on 18th December 1939.

Top: Robert MacFarlane, Rhiannon Naismith, Naomi Leech and Robert Duncan (left to right) presenting the Marwood-Eltons with souvenirs of their visit to Loch Ness.

Middle: The old warrior poses for a very historic photograph, right under the office window of its creator, Barnes Wallis.

Bottom left: Barnes Wallis.

Bottom right: Loch Ness Wellington Association Ltd. Executive Committee members. Left to right: Don Storer; Ken Crichton; Robin Holmes (Chairman); Richard Kellett; Morag Barton and Bob Allwood.

Top left: Morag Barton, the co-ordinator of the Brooklands Museum, presents Air Commodore Richard Kellett with the alarm clock, marked off in 'Vickers Time' that the RAF Long Range Development Flight presented to Mr Gordon Montgomery in 1938. Standing between Morag and Richard is Jeff Montgomery, Gordon's son.

Top right: At long last Paul Harris is reunited with the old Wimpy in which he won his DFC at the Battle of Heligoland Bight. Assisted by Squadron Leader John Rootes, Paul visited Brooklands Museum in November 1985. Less than two months later he died peacefully at his home.

Bottom: Volunteers at work on the Wellington fuselage. Brooklands Museum 1st August 1991.

Top: To the accompaniment of cracks and bangs from stress members within the geodetics that had not experienced loads for 45 years, the old bomber finally emerges, dripping wet, from Loch Ness. Many of the spectators were taken by surprise when they saw just how big the Wellington really was.

Bottom left: Only when the tail section was lifted clear of the water to reveal the gun turret, did the real significance of the aircraft dawn on the majority of the spectators. 'R for Robert' was a war machine from a bygone era.

Bottom right: For a few brief moments 'R for Robert' is airborne again.

Top: The author with his two sons, Drew (left) and Keith (right) who helped to dismantle the Wimpy.

Middle: Peter Grant, over from Canada for the recovery of 'R for Robert', handles the old Wimpy's control column. It was with this control column that Paul Harris held his bomber in tight formation under the Luftwaffe's onslaught and with which Nigel Marwood-Elton struggled while ditching on Loch Ness.

Bottom: Aerial view of 'R for Robert' photographed by Peter Grant as he flew over it in a light plane piloted by the crane's owner, Mr James Jack. By a remarkable coincidence, this is exactly the same view Peter Grant would have had of N2980 as he flew above and behind Paul Harris in formation during the Battle of Heligoland Bight.

No. 1,290. SUNDAY, DECEMBER 24, 1939. TWOPENCE.

Inside Story of War's Biggest Air Battle

Won 'Great Glory'

MEMBERS of the Royal Air Force who took part in the dramatic fighting over the Heligoland Bight.

In a "Sunday Graphic" picture they are seen at their base "somewhere in England," discussing plans of attack before a flight.

Top: Paul Harris and his men on the front page of the *Sunday Graphic*.

Middle left: Sergeant Herbie Ruse at the start of six years as a prisoner of war.

Middle right: Harry 'Jonah' Jones in a German hospital after being rescued by Herbie Ruse from his burning aircraft on the island of Borkum.

Bottom: The bodies of Sergeant Holley, Sergeant Tilley, Corporal Taylor and Aircraftman Geddes were buried on Borkum with full military honours.

Il sergente inglese Herbert Ruse prigioniero della battaglia aerea di Helgoland del 18 dicembre. Il Ruse, benchè con l'apparecchio colpito e incendiato potette atterrare in un'isoletta del Mar del Nord.

HE ENGLISH SERGEANT HERBERT RUSE, A PRISONER ROM THE AIR BATTLE OF HELICOLAND ON 18 DEC RUSE ALTHOUGH WITH HIS AIRCRAFT DAMAGED AND FLAMES WAS ABLE TO LAND ON AN ISLET IN THE NORTH SEA.

Top: Paul Harris and Wolfgang Falck enjoying one another's company at the 1984 Farnborough Airshow.

Bottom: 'R for Robert' reaches for the sky after 45 years on the bottom of Loch Ness. A close up of the starboard wing clearly shows the 1940 RAF roundel.

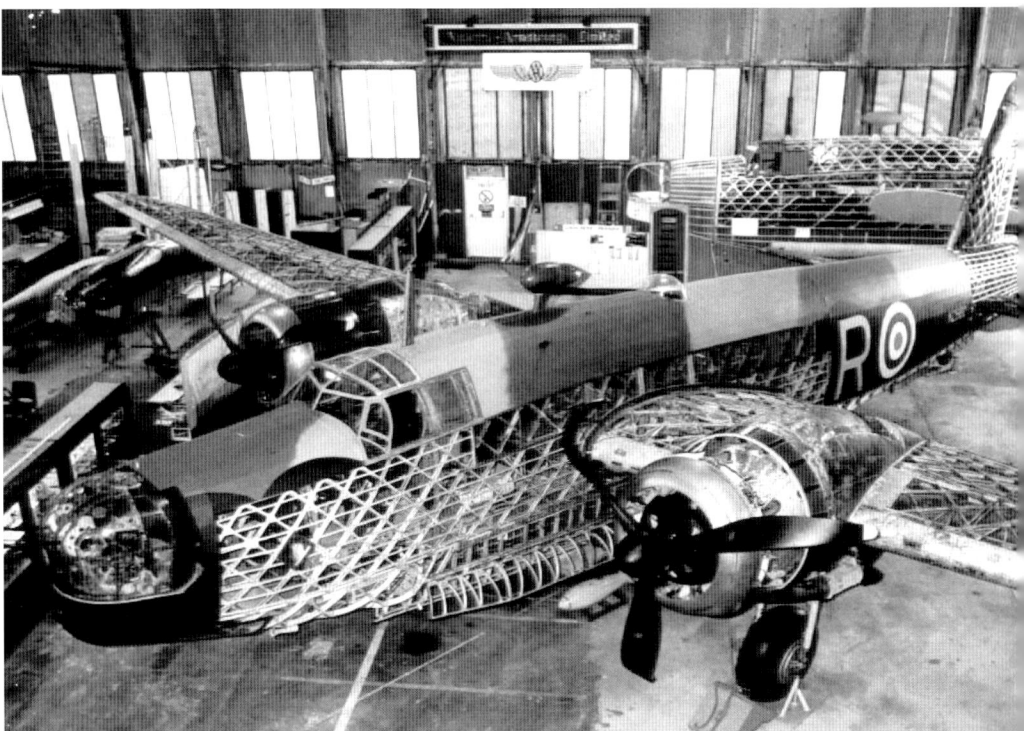

Top: 'Only another thousand miles, Charlie, and we'll be home.'

Bottom: 'R for Robert' has now been restored and is on display to the public at Brooklands Museum in Weybridge

been fitted with self-sealing tanks.

Why therefore had the port and rear sections of the formation fared so badly? Air Vice-Marshal Baldwin's report[xv] to Ludlow-Hewitt on the 19th contained no breath of criticism of the strategic and tactical concepts underlying the operation.

> I am afraid [he wrote firmly on 23rd December] there is no doubt that the heavy casualties experienced by 9 and 37 Squadrons were due to poor leadership and consequent poor formation flying. Squadron Leader Guthrie is reported as being almost a mile ahead of his formation. For some unknown reason Hue-Williams, who I thought was a very sound leader, appears to have done the same thing… I have not by any means given up hope of being able to drive home the lessons learnt… I have already taken steps to prevent a repetition, but I was allowing a certain period to elapse before pinning results on to individual actions, although instances of bad leadership have already been pointed out to all units.

In his reply to Baldwin's letter of 19th December 1939, Ludlow-Hewitt acknowledged the importance of good formation flying.[xvi]

> I do not think you can do more than get your unit and flight commanders together and rub into them the vital importance of good formation flying. The maintenance of tight unshaken formations in the face of the most powerful enemy action is the test of bomber-force fighting efficiency and morale. It is the Air Force equivalent of the old 'thin red line' in the army, or if you like, of the Greek phalanx or of Cromwell's Ironsides, and it is that aspect which should be brought home to all captains of aircraft. The great and unforgivable crime is for the leader of the formation to fly away from his followers.

In truth, the blame for the heavy losses cannot be laid at the door of the 'captains of aircraft'. Guthrie and Hue-Williams had never faced the enemy before and paid the ultimate price for their inexperience; Kellett, Harris and Grant had, and survived. There had been no prior planning or liaison between the participating squadrons. The ultimate blame must rest squarely on 3 Group headquarters. As Paul Harris points out, 'There is no doubt that the two squadrons (9 and 37) left us because they were untrained. One cannot blame them for this because we had been given no previous opportunity to fly together. Group headquarters laid on no group formation training – a fatal error.'

In conclusion, 3 Group's summary of the lessons to be derived from the events of 18th December stated, 'There is every reason to believe that a very close formation of six Wellington aircraft will emerge from a long and heavy attack by enemy fighters with very few, if any, casualties to its own aircraft.' 3 Group's operational instruction No. 21 of 23rd December stated: 'With the intention of combining useful training and operations, sweeps will continue to be carried out... If enemy aircraft are encountered, gunners will be able to practise shooting at real targets instead of drogues...' 'The gist of all these comments seemed to display a surviving if somewhat chastened confidence in the principle of the self-defending formation.'[xvii]

Some senior RAF officers still persisted with the notion that self-defending bomber formations could take care of themselves. Air Commodore Norman Bottomley issued a tactical memorandum on 29th December in which he continued to refer to the 'inviolability of a tight bomber formation', and he put the losses of the 14th and 18th down to straggling.

> Even more instructive was the difference in tone between what Sir Edgar Ludlow-Hewitt said in December 1939 to his group commander, Air Vice-Marshal Baldwin, and what he said in January 1940 to the Air Staff. On the former occasion most of his remarks were concerned with the need for better formation flying, better gunnery and greater crew efficiency as the means of successful daylight bombing. On the latter occasion he pointed to the December actions as strong evidence against carrying out the Ruhr plan. In fact, the actions in December 1939 were taken as a powerful warning of the superiority of the day-

fighter over the day-bomber, and the series of formation attacks was not continued after 18th December.[xviii]

Cajus Bekker[xix] considers that the British decision to abandon daylight raids after 18th December 'was to have a decisive influence on the future conduct of the war'.

JG1's summary of the lessons learned on 18th December was altogether more realistic and their report concluded:

> The British seemed to regard a tightly closed formation as the best method of defence, but the greater speed of the Me 109 and Me 110 enabled them to select their position of attack. Rigid retention of course and formation considerably facilitated the attack …It was criminal folly on the part of the enemy to fly at 4,000 to 5,000 metres in a cloudless sky with perfect visibility… After such losses it is assumed that the enemy will not give the geschwader any more opportunities of practise shooting at Wellingtons.

Having found that the crashed Wellington on Borkum had no bombs on board and believing the stories told by Wimberley and Ruse, the Germans reached the logical conclusion that the British had been indulging in some form of suicidal exercise, which was indeed not far from the truth.

Paul Harris was now in no doubt as to where he stood on that issue. 'After 18th December I hoisted the warning flag and let it be known that I would not go on any more raids unless they were competently led, and I named only two people I would follow, one of whom was of course Kellett.'

Richard Kellett was later accused by the survivors of the other squadrons of flying too fast for them to keep up. This is totally refuted by Paul Harris. Indeed it had never been intended that the four formations of the big diamond should stick rigidly together. This is clear from the conclusions drawn from the operation.[xx]

THE SIZE OF FORMATIONS

6. Although 24 aircraft were sent out on the reconnaissance on 18th December, this formation was not necessarily meant to keep any particular disposition except

> for convenience in approaching the target area and bearing in mind that the formations should not be in line astern, or all at one height. The instructions issued on the evening of 17th December, during the conference held at headquarters and attended by leaders, were that, whilst the four formations of six aircraft should proceed in company, each one was a self-contained unit for defensive purposes.
> 7. It has always been considered that a formation greater than 12 aircraft is unwieldy and therefore unmanageable by one leader, and that the largest possible defensive formation where mutual support is possible is probably one of six aircraft.
> 8. The only object therefore in sending more than six or 12 aircraft on any operation is in order to achieve concentration in time over the target area, and thus split the defences. Unless leaders of formations will understand this principle and not endeavour to follow the leader of the whole formation to the detriment of their followers' station-keeping, the formation is bound to suffer.

Sadly, Squadron Leader Guthrie and Squadron Leader Hue-Williams seem to have failed to take those instructions on board and suffered the consequences. Squadron Leader Paul Harris kept his head and his formation of six Wimpys survived the battle intact. Wing Commander Richard Kellett lost only one aircraft, and that might have survived if his formation had had the extra 12 guns that turned back early.

A couple of days after the raid, Air Chief Marshal Sir Edgar Ludlow-Hewitt, C-in-C Bomber Command, arrived at Mildenhall with his retinue, to hear the story first hand. Paul Harris well remembers the occasion.

> A few days later the C-in-C Bomber Command Ludlow-Hewitt, came to see our squadron in person. This was quite an occasion. Our AOC, Baldwin, the station commander, Franky Coleman, Kellett, and others all crowded into Kellett's office while Ludlow-Hewitt, surrounded by a galaxy of staff officers, asked questions. Star turn, aircraftman first class, Jimmy Mullineaux, was

brought in so that the C-in-C, Ludlow-Hewitt, could talk to this hero, which indeed he was (I was very proud of him), but after a time it was all too much for him; the eminent 'brass hats', the questioning and the braid so affected him that my highly strung, modest, little Jimmy suddenly said, full of courtesy and respect to the last, 'May I faint please', which he promptly did, into the arms of Sandy Innes, who carried him out. He was but an AC1 and very young, one of the first DFMs of the war.

Ludlow-Hewitt later put his finger on the problem when he said, 'All our previous experience had indicated that the fighter defences of north-west Germany were weak and apparently half-hearted. The tremendous opposition encountered on the 14th and 18th did, therefore, come as a surprise to us, and there is no doubt in my mind that it was due to strong reinforcements by crack squadrons from elsewhere.'[xxi] How right he was.

The day before the battle, I/ZG76 arrived at Jever. Their Me 110s probably accounted for eight of the ten Wellingtons shot down. Two of the pilots, Lent and Gollob, went on to become top aces with 260 victories between them. Of the fighter pilots who took part in the action, eight later won the Knight's Cross of the Iron Cross; four added the Oakleaves, three the Swords, and two the Diamonds, to their Ritterkreuz. 'Mäcki' Steinhoff achieved the incredible total of 176 victories (six in the jet-propelled Me 262). Surprisingly enough, the official British history of the battle states: 'There was nothing to suggest that any "crack" squadrons had been brought into the area before the engagement.'[xxii] With a combined total of approximately 500 confirmed victories when the war ended, Schumacher's pilots that day can only be described as 'crack'. Kellett on the other hand referred to his pilots and crews with typical service understatement: the RAF raiders are described by their leader as 'just a normal team'. The Germans, he says, 'were worthy opponents'. But to have fought their way through the combined strength of *four* Luftwaffe fighter squadrons, *in daylight*, Kellett and his crews were every bit as 'crack' as their adversaries.

Notwithstanding JG1's actual score of 12 bombers shot

down, it had not been altogether an impressive performance by the German fighter pilots. Even after their belated interception, they made repeated ineffectual long-range attacks. Had they then possessed the experience they went on to gain over the fields of Kent and on the Russian Front, it would have been remarkable if any of Kellett's Wimpys had survived at all. Nevertheless, 12 Wellingtons lost out of a force of 22 was a disaster on a scale hitherto unprecedented. A 50 per cent loss was ten times the casualty rate which Bomber Command could ever hope to sustain. 'From 18th December onward we tacitly abandoned the belief that our Wellingtons and Hampdens could operate by day in the face of German fighter opposition.'[xxiii] 3 Group's Wimpys were sent off to be fitted with armour-plating in their port wings and French self-sealing coverings for their petrol tanks.

The Battle of Heligoland Bight was Bomber Command's rude awakening to the facts of life as they pertain to modern technological warfare. Kellett's casualties were just 12 of the 8,325 aircraft they lost, and the 57 men who died that day would be followed by more than 55,500 as the war pursued its relentless course. Few of those who survived that raid on Wilhelmshaven lived to enjoy the celebrations of VE Day.[20]

Wing Commander Kellett was shot down in a Wellington bomber during a combined operation to take Tobruk early in 1942. He was captured by the Germans and spent the remainder of the war as a prisoner of war, eventually landing up at the famous Stalag Luft III of *Wooden Horse* and *Great Escape* fame. He was repatriated after Germany was defeated in 1945. He died on 3rd January 1990.

Flying Officer Turner was the captain of Halifax KK645 of 76 Squadron which was reported missing from operations against Hanover on the night of 22nd/23rd September 1943.

Flying Officer Riddlesworth was killed in a flying accident on 25th February 1941 when Wellington L4276, of 11 OTU, crashed.

Flying Officer Bulloch was killed two weeks later while leading a flight of three Wellingtons on a daylight armed reconnaissance sweep into the German Bight on 2nd January 1940.

---

[20]VE Day – Victory in Europe Day, Tuesday, 8th May 1945.

Flight Lieutenant Grant was sent off to give a lecture to a Bomber Command gunnery school on the realities of facing fighter attacks in daylight. On his return he was severely reprimanded for having given 'an unpatriotic talk likely to cause dismay and demoralisation'. He retired from the RAF in 1945 as a wing commander.

Sergeant Ramshaw retired from the RAF in December 1966 as a wing commander. He died in May 1972.

Of Sergeant Purdy no trace can be found.

Flying Officer Lemon was shot down by nightfighters whilst attacking Duisburg on the night of 25th/26th July 1942. His Wellington bomber caught fire and he and his crew were forced to bale out over Holland. He was captured and spent the rest of the war as a prisoner of war. After repatriation he later commanded 53 Squadron during the whole of the Berlin Airlift.

Sergeant Petts was commissioned in November 1941 and took part in the first two 1,000 bomber raids on Cologne and Essen. He was awarded the DFC and Bar in 1944, having taken part in over 100 missions. He survived the war and died in 1969.

Flying Officer Macrae died most pathetically. He collected his Distinguished Flying Cross from the King at Buckingham Palace on the 5th March 1940. After a celebration party with his crew, he took off from Weybridge to fly home to Norfolk, and crashed.

Sergeant 'Herbie' Ruse spent the next six years as a prisoner of war in the company of Tom May, 'Jonah' Jones and Pete Wimberley. They were the only survivors from the aircraft that were shot down during the battle.

Sergeant Holley, Sergeant Tilley, Corporal Taylor and Aircraftman Geddes were all buried with full military honours in the cemetery on Borkum.

As for the crew of old 'R for Robert', they collected no fewer than three medals that day. Paul Harris and Sandy Innes each received the DFC while Jimmy Mullineaux was awarded one of the first DFMs of the war.

Squadron Leader Harris was hospitalised with a bad case of pneumonia shortly after the raid and did not fly again until 5th March 1940. He was promoted to commanding officer of 7

Squadron with the task of reforming with Stirling bombers. Later, he was given a mobile Wellington wing in the Western Desert which he took over just after the battle of El Alamein and, with a short break of four months as a staff officer in Algiers, remained with 205 Group until the end of the war. He died on 29th December 1985.

Sergeant Austin was transferred with Paul Harris to help re-arm 7 Squadron with Stirlings, and he took part in the first operational raid with Stirlings to bomb oil tanks at Rotterdam. He was later promoted to squadron leader and after the war was chosen for a permanent commission, being only the second navigator to be so selected.

Aircraftman Second Class Watson was later promoted to sergeant and it is believed that 'Jock' was shot down over East Anglia by an intruder when returning from a raid on Germany in a Stirling.

Aircraftman First Class Doxsey was later promoted to sergeant and is thought to have been 'reported missing' over Germany.

Aircraftman First Class Mullineaux was later commissioned and subsequently shot down over Germany in 1942 and captured. He escaped three times and was once adrift for three months, passing himself off as a Walloon. He was eventually captured by the Gestapo who beat him so severely that finally he shouted in German, 'Stop it. I'm a British officer'. Instantly the Gestapo interrogators snapped to attention and saluted him. He was repatriated after the war in very poor health and subsequently suffered a series of nervous breakdowns resulting from the treatment he had received as a prisoner of war.

Pilot Officer Innes was perhaps the saddest case of all. While on an astro-navigation cross-country practice on 4th April 1940, Wellington bomber P9267 approached too low looking as if it was going to overshoot the runway. At 200 feet it turned to port, crashed into the ground and burst into flames, one mile south-east of Mildenhall. Of the seven crew aboard, five were killed and two were badly injured. Pilot Officer Sandy Innes, DFC, was one of those who perished. He had been home on leave over the festive season and the entry in his diary for Christmas Day reads:

25.12.39 Betts told me how much the family have been worrying over me. What on earth can I do to stop them except ring up every time there is a raid... Why can't they realise that I love the life in the air and even if I do pass out I will do it while I am doing something I love like life itself and in the middle of the most amazing thrills it is possible to imagine. I mentioned it to them and I could see the tears forming. God knows, I am lucky to have a family like that. I think I am heartless not to feel the same except I probably do, but am too dense to realise it unless it actually happened, which God forbid.

Three months later he made the last entry in his notebook:

2.4.40 More night flying – this time searchlight co-operation. The first time I had done it and it was very interesting. We were caught properly several times sometimes with eight or ten lights, violent manoeuvering and also desynchronising motors and also climbing and diving threw them off. Most of the time they never got us at all which promises ill if the blitzkrieg comes. Again had trouble landing. This time my landing light was unserviceable. Made a dud approach and had to go round again. Hair-raising for Strachan took the flap off too quick and we must have dropped to within 50-100 feet of the ground. Gardiner brushed a tree-top coming in and Griffith-Jones hit a post after landing. Quite definitely we need a lot more practise. Every time we night fly something exciting happens, which is not bloody good enough.

Thereafter, the pages of the little hardback notebook are blank.

Sandy was not the pilot of P9267 when it crashed. But if it had not been a training exercise at Mildenhall, the odds were overwhelming that it would have been Cologne, Hanover, Berlin, Frankfurt or perhaps even Wilhelmshaven some night in the next five years. Likewise, most of the Luftwaffe fighter pilots who took part in the Battle of Heligoland Bight lost their lives eight months later in the Battle of Britain or on the

Russian Front or defending 'The Fatherland' against the armada of Allied bombers that followed in the wake of our old warrior N2980 from Weybridge.

5
Blood, toil, tears and sweat

Two weeks after the disaster of the Battle of Heligoland Bight, as a new year dawned, Air Vice-Marshal Arthur Harris, then serving as AOC 5 Group, (later to become famous as 'Bomber' Harris commander-in-chief Bomber Command), told his commander-in-chief at High Wycombe that so long as three bombers were in company in daylight the pilots 'considered themselves capable of taking on anything'.

That very same morning of 2nd January 1940, Squadron Leader Paul Harris was instructed to send three aircraft out on a daylight sweep into the Heligoland Bight. He selected Flying Officer Bulloch to lead the formation and gave Pilot Officer Innes his first captaincy as number two aircraft. Sergeant Morrice was detailed to fly number three position. Eighty nautical miles north-west of Heligoland the three Wellingtons were jumped by a 'schwarm' of Me 110s led by Leutnant Herget from Schumacher's I/ZG 76. Two of the Wellingtons were shot down and only Pilot Officer Innes succeeded in escaping. It was this sweep that really marked the end of daylight operations for Bomber Command. It brought home very forcibly to every pilot that, in daylight, they were most decidedly *not* 'capable of taking on anything'. All the Wellingtons had been fitted with armour plating in both wings and self-sealing fuel tanks. Now there were no excuses. Even the top brass could no longer delude themselves and were forced to accept that the lessons of 18th December and 2nd January were conclusive. Bomber Command's heavy bombers were thereafter confined to the hours of darkness. Sandy Innes escaped by the skin of his teeth, and that night he recorded his experience in his notebook:

2.1.40 And what a sweep. A/B at noon. Bulloch leading. Me number two and Morrice number three, first time I had captained an aircraft on operational trip. Our own crew but Swift as second pilot. We were on an offensive patrol looking for German fleet and when about 80 miles from Germany damned if we didn't run into fighters. First thing I knew was a stream of tracer apparently just missing my left ear. Intercom had more or less packed up. I was in fairly tight formation on Bull. And then everything happened. I saw Me 110s on every side. All I did was to press myself into my seat so that no bits were outside and formate and hope like hell. I heard our gunners firing and more tracers came along then an Me suddenly appeared underneath going forward and Doxsey gave it the gun – behind it to start with but then the tracer went in, and apparently it went down. Next thing I saw was a small fire in Bull's plane on port wing – this spread and I just stared at this wondering what he was going to do and then wondering what I was going to do. Soon it spread to about half the wing and I thought this is no good, formating on a thing which might blow up at any moment and as he was going down I went up to formate on Morrice. He however was behaving oddly and proceeded to dive very steeply in an erratic manner from side to side. I tried to formate on him but though I was at full boost and touching 300 mph at 10,000 feet, i.e. 350 mph, he was still gaining. But then he went underneath me so I pulled level and saw him no more.

Bull meantime had been seen to hit the sea, so I was left alone with all 12-15 Messerschmitts. So yours truly put his nose down and seawards. This was at suggestion of Swift who came forward at intervals from fire control to tell me in dumb show what was toward. Intercom unserviceable so I was left wondering what the hell was happening. He turned up once waving a Colt six shooter. I had visions of him (a) shooting the petrol tanks (b) shooting himself. Actually all he wanted to do was to take pot shots at the enemy. So I said OK not knowing what he wanted. Don't think he did. Eventually got down to sea level at 20 feet and carried on there for some 80 miles and then climbed and handed over to Swift. Aircraft seemed to be in bad way but all lads OK, bullet holes all round but see more tomorrow.

Got back at 4 p.m. everyone very sympathetic for it was a damned pointless sort of show not having dropped any bombs. Went along to see Mrs Bulloch. She was with Stewart and taking it marvellously – even laughing over the baby – I couldn't understand it but women are amazing things. It was forced good humour so the sooner she broke down the better. She apparently knew when I came back alone that Bull was dead. Difficult business though. I came along to comfort her if possible and all I could do was sit around and talk of everything else. After that went back to Bird in Hand for farewell party to Lieutenant Commander Chapman. Bed at 2 a.m.

3.1.40 Not feeling so hot this morning after last night's party, though slept very well. Funny business this going out and some of us not coming back.

Casualties have been high in this group and the North Sea must be piled high with bits of Wellingtons. Yet it doesn't seem to affect anyone. We talk about them and how they were shot down and it is so impersonal. A good thing really for it would be really bad if you were to get a close up. And in any case you don't consider it a human loss so much as the loss of an aeroplane. Perhaps it's callous but it makes it easier to put up with. Anyhow be that as it may. I was busy this a.m. writing out reports, signing them, questioning gunners and crew. Went along and saw aircraft U. Sure was shot about a bit, though surprisingly little damage is done. We were very lucky for the big burst went bang through fuselage in the only part where there is nothing. After lunch we (all the crew) were interviewed by AOC in his office with short-haired WAAF in attendance. We each told our story and many more details came out. Wing Commander Kellett came back from leave so I had to tell him. He had his DFC up and it looks very good.

4.1.40 This morning was interviewed with crew by three

wing commanders and two squadron leaders from command or Air Ministry. Wanted to know all about Me 110s and their tactics. Lasted 1½ hours. Our crew have had more experience of these Me 110s and fighters generally than any other in command I expect. We also have quite a respect for them and their pilots. It appears it was Leutnant Schumacher and his squadron again. Probably best in German Air Force and a budding Richthofen – that is unless we put a stop to him. I gather 149 are going to be given a rest for a bit for we have been in every action bar one since war began (in North Sea) and our crew most. In fact Sergeant Austin said we must be bloody lucky – but maybe also with all the practise our gunners are better than most.

30.1.40 Large interval due to getting a very bad go of flu and tonsillitis at home, bed for ten days and only just back.

31.1.40 No flying with fog around. Started to thaw and everything mucky. Paul Harris is away having had gastric or bronchial pneumonia; saw him yesterday but he won't be back for weeks. My aircraft from last raid is still being repaired, nearly four weeks on it. This evening saw wing commander and was informed that as we were the most experienced crew in operations we were to be used to train new people coming in and also to experiment in different methods of bombing and attacks. All very interesting and should put the family in a more easy frame of mind.

Wing Commander Bunny Austin's account of 2nd January 1940

I would like to say something about this raid because it had a far greater impact on many people in the squadron than indeed 18th December which was much more publicised. It's often thought that the 18th December raid was the last major daylight operation; indeed it was in numbers but on 2nd January 1940 three aircraft from our squadron, 149 Squadron, were detailed to do a sweep of the North Sea down the islands and back, down the Dutch coast in a general circular pattern. The object of the exercise was to see if there was any enemy shipping. I recall that at briefing we were specifically told: 'Don't worry there is not likely to be any attacks from enemy aircraft.' Originally Paul was due to lead this flight of three but at the last moment he came along to the crew room and said that he wouldn't in fact be flying and Flying Officer Bulloch would lead and that Sandy Innes with Pilot Officer Swift as second pilot would take the aeroplane and we would fly number two to Flying Officer Bulloch. Sergeant Morrice would be the third captain. We in fact duly set off and that's all we knew when we went; we learned a lot more about what it was all about when we came back. We were attacked by a Lieutenant Schumacher and his squadron of Me 110s and the first thing we heard about the attack was Mullineaux shouting out: 'Fighters, fighters, fighters'. I went back to man the dustbin turret and as I let it down things were disintegrating all around. I remember almost the beauty of the situation, of seeing things in mid-air from bits of geodetic to bits of the catwalk. Anyway, getting into the turret, I saw that the other two aeroplanes were already going down, one in flames and the other one I lost sight of. Quite clearly there would have been no survivors and no parachutes. Anyway we fought as best we could all over the sky and I remember that I personally fired some 1,500 rounds from each of my guns and during the activity I called for some more ammunition and Pilot Officer Swift came running back. In the excitement he had his revolver out and I thought he was going to shoot me for mutiny or something. Afterwards I said: 'What the hell have you got your revolver going for?' – and he said: 'Well I was standing in the astrodome and I felt I had to do something, I felt so helpless.'

Anyway the object of mentioning this raid is not to specifically highlight that event but it's perhaps stemming from that raid that I realised the great guts of the wives of the people living in the area. That evening Flight Sergeant Bill Kelly came along and said that Mrs Wakeham, whose husband had been in one of the aeroplanes, would like to see me. It wasn't something I relished doing but I knew her and we're all friends anyhow so I went down and the first thing she said was 'Oh do come in Bunny you must be very, very tired'. She had another woman, one of the sergeant pilot's wives, with her, but insisted that she made coffee and I always recall how calm she was and she wanted to know really if there was any hope at all. I had to say that there must be very little indeed. I was deeply touched by the concern she felt for me, having just lost her husband, and this typified the spirit appertaining at that time. Later, I'm afraid, we were to lose Jock Watson, and Doxsey, I'm pretty certain, was killed later in the war as well. Jimmy Mullineaux was shot down and made a prisoner of war.

New Year's Eve 1940 saw the end of 'R for Robert'. It also marked the end of the most momentous year in British history. It was the year in which a third of a million men were spirited off the beaches at Dunkirk by a fleet of little ships. It was the year in which a handful of Spitfires and Hurricanes drove back the full might of the Luftwaffe. It was the year of 'blood, toil, tears and sweat'. The war went on for another five long years, but the British did not have to endure another year of struggling on alone. Deprived of his prey, Hitler turned east towards Russia just as Napoleon had done many years before. Japan too made an equally monumental blunder when it 'awakened a sleeping giant' at Pearl Harbor. Russia, with the unconquerable 'General Midwinter', and America, the 'great arsenal of democracy', joined forces with the little island that had firmly stood its ground. Together, they eventually crushed the tyrants Hitler, Mussolini and Tojo. But the struggle was long, hard and bloody.

By 1944 however, technology had stepped in to give a helping hand with the Mosquito as the 'speed bomber' and the Mustang as the 'long-range fighter escort' that were so sadly lacking in 1939. Now it became possible to sweep the sky over Germany clear of its defending fighters. Göring later said, 'When I saw the Mustangs over Berlin, I knew the war was lost.' The Führer came to power with a promise to the German people: 'Give me four years and, I promise you, you won't recognise your cities.' With the help of Wellingtons, Stirlings,

2nd January 1940
Time 1400 hrs (approximately)

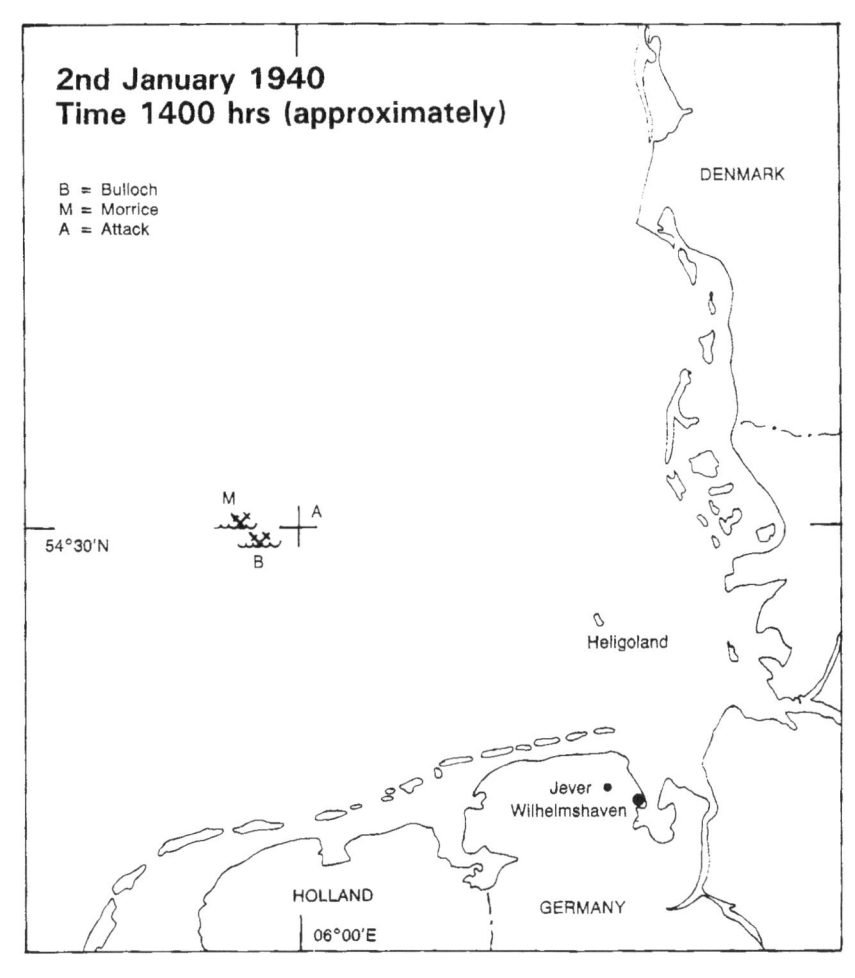

B = Bulloch
M = Morrice
A = Attack

DENMARK

54°30'N

Heligoland

Jever •
Wilhelmshaven

HOLLAND
06°00'E
GERMANY

149 Squadron
N2943 F/O Bulloch   Shot down in flames 54° 27'N, 5° 47'E.
N2868 P/O Innes   Claimed to have shot down two Me 110s.
N2946 Sgt Morrice   Last seen 54° 34'N, 5° 40'E pursued by several Me 110s.

The three aircraft from 149 Squadron formed one of several flights of Wellingtons carrying out armed reconnaissance sweeps in the German Bight that day. (3 from 9 Sqn; 6 from 38 Sqn; 2 from 115 Sqn; 3 from 99 Sqn and 3 from 149 Sqn.) The Wellingtons were fitted with new armour plating and self-sealing fuel tanks.

Luftwaffe[xxiv]
Four Me 110s of 1/ZG76 led by Lt Herget attacked 149 Squadron's three Wellingtons.
Ofw. Fleischmann attacked N2943 and shot it down in flames.
Lt Habben attacked N2946 which released its bombs before crashing into the sea with its right wing on fire.
Uffz. Grams pursued a Wellington which dived towards the sea trailing black smoke (possibly N2943 or N2946).
Two Me 110s were damaged but both got back to base on one engine (one gunner was wounded).

N2943
F/O Bulloch

N2946
Sgt Morrice

N2868
P/O Innes

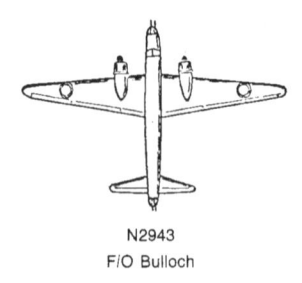

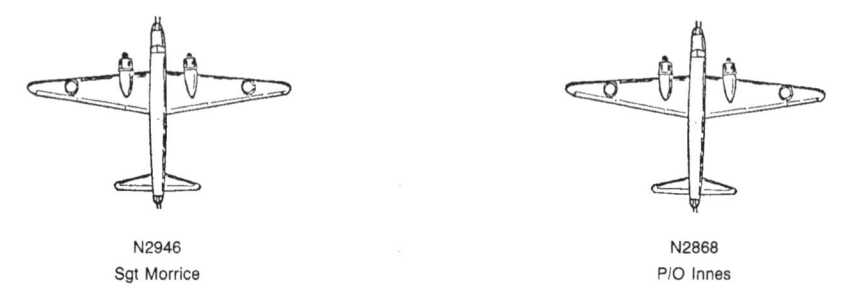

149 Squadron, 2nd January 1940.

Lancasters, Halifaxes, Mosquitoes, Fortresses, Liberators and many other kinds of bomber, this was one of the few promises he was able to keep.

Eventually the Germans were brought to a halt at Stalingrad, the Italians threw in the towel and the Japanese suffered the trauma of the atomic bomb. The war ended in 1945 with everyone worn out. Sickened by the carnage and appalled by the revelations of the concentration camps, we turned away from all the instruments of war. Historical preservation was the last thing on our minds as we picked ourselves up, dusted ourselves down and looked round at the ruins all about us. Away with all the impedimenta of war. Away with all the aeroplanes that had served us so faithfully. Away with them *all* to the scrap yards. Not one single battle-scarred Wimpy was set aside for posterity to gaze upon and help commemorate the courage and bravery of all those who flew in them. Group Captain Marwood-Elton unwittingly did us a great favour when he ditched N2980 on Loch Ness. Later in the war, on the

'R for Robert' flew fourteen operational missions to Germany.
In those days, the average life expectancy of a Wimpy was about six missions.

20 November 1939	N2980 Taken on charge of Number 149 Squadron at MILDENHALL	
Date	*Target*	*Pilot*
3 December 1939	Heligoland	F/Lt J.B. Stewart
18 December 1939	Wilhelmshaven	S/Ldr P.I. Harris
20 February 1940	Heligoland	F/O G.P. Miers
15/16 March 1940	Hanover (Nickel raid)	F/O G.P. Miers
31 March 1940	Special Sweep (Training)	P/O H.A. Innes
16 April 1940	Special Sweep (Training)	F/O J.S. Douglas-Cooper
17 April 1940	Special Sweep (Training)	F/O J.S. Douglas-Cooper
25 April 1940	Special Sweep (Training)	F/O J.S. Douglas-Cooper
5/6 May 1940	Sylt and Borkum (Security Patrol)	F/O J.S. Douglas-Cooper
14/15 May 1940	Aachen (start of Strategic Bombing 15th May 1940)	F/O J.S. Douglas-Cooper
17/18 May 1940	Namur	F/O J.S. Douglas-Cooper

30 May 1940	N2980 Taken on charge of Number 37 Squadron at FELTWELL	
Date	*Target*	*Pilot*
5/6 June 1940	Cambrai and München-Gladbach	F/O Perioli
9/10 June 1940	Rocroi, Charlesville, Meziers	Sgt Watt
11/12 June 1940	Furnay-Guspunsant, Nousonville	F/O Griffiths
14/15 July 1940	Marshalling Yards at Hamm	W/Cdr Merton
6/7 August 1940	Synthetic Oil Plant at Mors	P/O Watt
15/16 August 1940	Marshalling Yards at Hamm	P/O Dingle
26/27 August 1940	Frankfurt, Stokum, Hamm, and Brussels Aerodrome	F/O Griffiths

6 October 1940	N2980 Taken on charge of Number 20 O.T.U. at LOSSIEMOUTH	
Date		*Pilot*
31 December 1940	N2980 Ditched on Loch Ness	S/Ldr N. Marwood-Elton

night of 22nd/23rd March 1944, his Halifax was shot down over Giesen by a nightfighter. He bailed out at 16,000 feet and landed in a snow-covered forest. He was repatriated on VE Day.

It is also worth relating the subsequent fate of other 149 and 37 Squadron aircrew associated with N2980. It helps to gauge the terrible losses suffered by Bomber Command. 'R for Robert' was only one of over 100,000 military aircraft produced by British industry during the war. Of the twenty-one officers who flew in her, only five are known to have survived the war.

Wing Commander J.B. Stewart (Canadian)	Retired
Group Captain P.I. Harris DFC	Retired
Flying Officer H.A. Innes DFC	Deceased
Wing Commander G.P. Miers DFC	Deceased
Flying Officer C.G. Birch DFC	Deceased
Squadron Leader A.J. Strachan	Deceased
Squadron Leader M. Bryan-Smith DFC	Deceased
Flying Officer J.S. Douglas-Cooper	Deceased
Pilot Officer M.B. Dawson	Deceased
Pilot Officer J.R. Swift	Deceased
Flying Officer Griffiths	No Trace
Wing Commander W.N. Perioli OBE, DFC	Retired
Pilot Officer G.H. Muirhead	Deceased
Squadron Leader D.F. Benbow DFC	Retired
Flying Officer A. A. Scott	Deceased
Air Chief Marshal Sir W.H. Merton KCB, CBE, OBE, CB	Retired
Pilot Officer Watt	No Trace
Flying Officer A.C. Dingle	Deceased
Pilot Officer Hayes	No Trace
Pilot Officer Turner	No Trace
Pilot Officer Littlejohn	Deceased

As for all the other thousands of Wellington bombers, they soldiered on with Bomber Command right into 1944. Their final mission was laying mines off Lorient on the night of 3rd/4th March with 300 (Polish) Squadron. By then they had also become the mainstays of Coastal Command and the

Operational Training Units (OTUs). The last Wellington ever built was RP590, a Mk X which was handed over from its Blackpool factory to the RAF on 25th October 1945, two months after the Japanese surrendered. The Wellington was the only Allied bomber to fly first line operations from the day the war started to the day it finished. It completed its last mission for the RAF (a training flight) in March 1953. During its service career it served everywhere, with everyone and was universally loved by all who flew in it or spent their time servicing it. It bombed, laid mines, swept mines, hunted submarines, dropped torpedoes, towed gliders, transported troops, acted as an air ambulance, dropped the first 4,000lb Blockbuster, helped Barnes Wallis test his bouncing bomb, developed the first high-altitude pressure chamber, assisted with early electronic counter-measures and acted as a test-bed for the first jet engines. Perhaps it was because of this incredible versatility that it never acquired a specific pinnacle of achievement on which to hang its own claim to fame. The Lancaster has the Dam Busters, the Mosquito has the breaching of the walls of Amiens prison, maybe 'R for Robert' and the Battle of Heligoland Bight can accord the old Wimpy a similar place in our affections. Surprisingly perhaps, the Wellington was built in greater numbers than any other multi-engined aircraft in Britain, a staggering 11,461.

It is outside the scope of this book to elaborate on the history of the Vickers Wellington bomber because it has been done so much more ably elsewhere.[xxv] It is sufficient to say that it did the job for which it was designed (and a lot more besides) most efficiently but, like all the other 1930s aircraft, it was overtaken by the ever growing pace of wartime technology. It was a unique aircraft that evolved from the previous age of giant airships. It could never exist today. Metal fatigue showed up after prolonged use as cracks and fractures in the structure, a malady well understood today but unheard of in the 1930s. As a 'cloth bomber', its further development was limited by its fabric covering, which peeled off at the increased air speeds demanded of later bombers. But it was there when we needed it. It could be repaired like a meccano set with new pieces of geodetic or spare bits scrounged from wrecked aircraft, with the joins hidden under fabric patches. On more than one occasion a Wimpy returned from Germany to confront a team of astonished erks[21] with great chunks shot out of its wings or fuselage. On more than one occasion those same erks worked round the clock and had it flying again in a few days, ready for its next trip back to Germany.

The official historians of the British air offensive against Germany, Webster and Frankland, view the three actions which were fought on the 3rd, 14th and 18th December 1939 as 'among the most important of the war'. This is certainly true as regards the effect they had upon Air Ministry thinking. It was from these three raids that their policy of daylight operations by self-defending bomber formations was found to be, quite simply, 'not on'. Surprisingly enough the Luftwaffe did not grasp the fact that this lesson also applied to them. It is true that they were able to provide their bombers with strong fighter escorts from conveniently based airfields in France. But the lesson was exactly the same; it just took longer and was much more painful to learn. The Americans on the other hand, were confident that once they had fitted their bombers with power-operated gun turrets[22] and protected them with armour plating, they would succeed where the British and Germans had failed. With their thirteen 0.5 in. Browning machine guns bristling all over the place and flying at 30,000 feet, the US Eighth Airforce's B17s embarked on deep-penetration raids into Germany in daylight. In an incredible feat of arms, the Luftwaffe fought them to a standstill. On 17th August 1943, 376 Flying Fortresses set out on precision attacks on ball-bearing factories at Schweinfurt, Regensburg and Wiener Neustadt. Sixty of these huge machines were shot down. The Americans tried Schweinfurt again a few months later only to suffer a further paralysing loss of sixty more B17s out of a force of 291. After 'Black Thursday', 14th October 1943, the US Eighth Airforce was forced to abandon, temporarily, its deep-penetration raids into Germany.

The theory of the invincible bomber subjugating an entire enemy nation was first mooted in 1921 by the Italian General Guilo Douhet in his book *The Command of the Air*. Guilo

---

[21] Erk, a slang term used in the RAF for an aircraftman.
[22] As originally conceived, the B17 had no power-operated gun turrets.

Douhet had not reckoned with the then unheard of invention called radar. Eventually the British and American air forces triumphed by sheer weight of numbers, the arrival of the long-range escort fighter, the Luftwaffe's chronic shortage of fuel and its rapidly diminishing stock of trained pilots. Three dates are engraved on the tombstone of the 'bomber will always get through' philosophy – 18th December 1939, the Battle of Heligoland Bight; 15th September 1940, Battle of Britain Sunday; and 14th October 1943, Black Thursday. Each represents a decisive defeat of intruding enemy bombers by defending fighters. The British and the Germans switched to night bombing. The combat wings of the US Eighth Airforce in Britain received their first North American P51 Mustangs on 1st December 1943.

Battle of Britain Sunday and Black Thursday are well documented and analysed in numerous official and popular publications. While the importance of the Battle of Heligoland Bight is acknowledged by Webster and Frankland in the official history[xxvi], it is conspicuous by its absence in most popular accounts of World War II. This may be due to the not unnatural tendency to play down a defeat, but is more likely caused by the obscurity of the events that occurred during the Phoney War. To most people in Britain, the war really only started on 10th May 1940 when Hitler invaded Holland, Belgium and Luxembourg. But to those servicemen who fought between 3rd September 1939 and 10th May 1940 there was nothing phoney about the war. Another reason for the obscurity of the December 1939 raids on the German navy may be the fact that, even to the people who took part in them, their real purpose was unclear. The official reason given at the time was to mount 'a major operation with the object of destroying an enemy battle-cruiser or pocket-battleship'. Though goaded into action by a hard-pressed Winston Churchill, Bomber Command had no traditional interest in battleships, nor for that matter had they the foggiest idea how to sink them.

Battleships were the province of the Royal Navy, and, as relations between the two organisations were particularly strained at this time, so co-operation between the two services was strictly limited. At the time there were really only two ways to sink a battleship using aircraft. The first called for the use of torpedoes dropped from a very low level and the other required *precisely* placed bombs released from dive bombers. Only by these two specialist methods could the overriding constraint of the Phoney War be met: no German civilian must be hurt. In the opening months of the war Bomber Command knew next to nothing about torpedoes and for many years had set its face firmly against the use of dive-bombers. By far the riskiest method of trying to hit a battleship was to drop bombs on it from a great height, a notoriously random process at the best of times. If the ship happened to be in dock at the time, the chances of avoiding civilian casualties were indeed slim. In the contemporary Bomber Command reports on the three December 1939 raids, it is significant that there is a total lack of concern at the highest level in Bomber Command regarding the failure of these raids even to dent let alone sink a German battleship with a bomb. After being shot down and captured on 18th December, Flying Officer Wimberley and Sergeant Ruse attempted to mislead their captors by saying that no attack had been intended and that they were only on a 'navigation flight' over Heligoland Bight[xxvii]. While Wimberley and Ruse thought they were giving false information to the enemy, they were, in point of fact, not far from the truth.

In a letter from 'Jackie' Baldwin, the AOC No. 3 Group, to his C-in-C, Sir Edgar Ludlow-Hewitt[xxviii], the following extracts are significant.

> 18. *Tactics*. Now to return to tactics, and the question of how to improve formation flying under AA fire. I am afraid I can only hark back to the experience of the last war when carrying out long raids into Germany.
> 22. The other lesson we learnt was that in order to 'blood' the formations, it was necessary to give them a short raid to some appropriately placed enemy aerodrome or other suitably placed target, in order to subject them to anti-aircraft fire and a limited attack by enemy aircraft, but giving them a chance to return across our lines before straggling became too pronounced.
> 23. At the present moment, we are pushing out these formations unaccustomed to the war issues, almost to the

limit of the aircraft's endurance, and into heavily defended areas, and exposing them to a somewhat lengthy attack during which there is no possibility of assistance or respite, should straggling become apparent.

In his reply to this letter[xxix], Sir Edgar Ludlow-Hewitt made the following point:

> 3 ...I had welcomed an opportunity to carry out high-altitude bombing operations on the north-west coast of Germany for the very reason which you gave in paras 22 and 23 of your letter, namely in order to give our formations experience under conditions in which enemy opposition was unlikely to be severe. In this, of course, we were disappointed and admittedly surprised, the opposition being far stronger than anything we had expected. Actually, as you suggest, there is no other means by which we can get our formations this experience except by operations against the fringe of the enemy's defences on the north-west coast.

It emerges from this correspondence between Air Vice-Marshal Baldwin and Sir Edgar-Ludlow Hewitt that the two sweeps on 3rd December and 18th December 1939 were most probably conceived as a 'test of bomber-force fighting efficiency and morale'. Put more simply, they were to 'blood the formations'. The sweep by 99 Squadron on 14th December was slightly different in that it was called for by Coastal Command for the express purpose of finishing off the *Nürnberg* and the *Leipzig*. Jackie Baldwin likened 99 Squadron's experience to the 'Charge of the Light Brigade', but nevertheless he telephoned Air Commodore Bottomley at Bomber Command HQ at High Wycombe at 3 p.m. on 17th December to urge a further operation against Wilhelmshaven.

Wing Commander Kellett and his captains were of course unaware that their missions were primarily intended to probe the enemy's defences and find out how bomber formations would fare in modern combat. This they discovered, but at the same time they unwittingly revealed an infinitely more profound truth about the new form of aerial warfare. Stanley

Baldwin had been dead wrong in his assertion that 'the bomber will always get through'. For the first time in warfare, radiolocation, later known as radar, picked up Kellett's Wellingtons as they approached Heligoland, thereby making 'R for Robert' one of the first hostile aircraft to be so detected. The defending anti-aircraft guns and fighters were given eight minutes' warning of the attack. On that occasion Kellett's formation just escaped by the skin of its teeth because the bulk of the defending fighters took off that little bit too late to intercept the intruders. Gone forever were the days when you could nip over the trenches to drop a few surprise bombs on an enemy airfield or ammunition dump and then race back to the safety of your own lines. Formations could no longer be 'blooded' by this simple World War I tactic. For quite a different reason to that intended, the three December raids by the Wellingtons into the Deutsche Bucht were an unqualified success. They jolted most senior officers in the RAF out of the past and into the present, into the sudden realisation that they were not engaged in a simple continuation of World War I as so many of the top brass had expected. Ludlow-Hewitt quickly recognised 'that penetration into enemy territory was practically nil, and it is the amount of penetration which is the real criterion of the severity and difficulty of the operation'. On the 14th and 18th December raids, Bomber Command lost half their aircraft just skirting the fringes of the German defences.

It was just conceivable that the 50 per cent loss suffered by 99 Squadron could have been a fluke, but for 149, 9 and 37 Squadrons to suffer a 55 per cent loss was conclusive evidence that there had been a dramatic change in aerial warfare since 1918. It is not known if Ludlow-Hewitt was aware that the Germans had been using radar, because he attributed the heavy losses to 'strong reinforcements by crack squadrons from elsewhere'. Throughout Bomber Command there was now a general realisation that pushing ahead with the Ruhr plan, deep into Germany in daylight with no defence other than gun turrets, would be suicidal. Bomber Command could not risk having its meagre resources completely wiped out. On the other hand, the Whitley's of 4 Group had been penetrating deep into Germany on Nickel[23] raids and returning

---

[23]Nickels; propaganda leaflets.

unscathed *night* after *night*. For the price of 22 Wellington bombers, the Royal Air Force discovered they were in a different war from the one they had been expecting and acted accordingly. At a cost of 1,733 aircraft shot down in the Battle of Britain, Göring was forced to the same conclusion.

But the final word on the outcome of the early raids into the Heligoland Bight must be left to the professional historian. In his book[xxx] *The Fight at Odds 1939-1941*, Denis Richards has this to say:

> The offensive (if such it may be called) against enemy warships during the long months of inactivity on land was singularly unimpressive in its immediate results. In the course of 861 sorties Bomber Command dropped only 61 tons of bombs; and the material achievement – some slight damage to the *Emden* and the *Scheer*, the sinking of a U-boat and a minesweeeper, and the destruction of ten fighters – was not worth the loss of 41 bombers. But the lessons learned in the process – learned, that is to say, not in some disastrous major campaign, but in the course of a few minor operations – were of the highest value to our cause. The improvement of operational technique; the fitting of self-sealing petrol tanks; the policy of using the 'heavies' of the time only by night – these were the real consequences of our failure. And, as lessons, they were learnt not only at little cost but in full time for the days of stress that were to come. Had this not been so, had the Air Staff been less sensitive to the early promptings of experience, the bomber force might well have been exposed, in the catastrophic days of May 1940, to losses that would have blunted its power at the moment of our greatest need.

Five-and-a-half years after Richard Kellett with his 24 Wimpys first spotted Heligoland through a gap in the clouds one mile away to the east, Bomber Command returned.

> The island fortress of Heligoland and the Dune airfield were attacked by more than 900 bombers on April 18. There were three aiming points, the main island, the naval

base and the airfield. Whole areas were laid waste – only photographs could convey the utter devastation. Marking, from the initial *Oboe* TIs to the last backer-up, was of a high standard and the master bombers kept a tight rein on an enthusiastic main force. The next day, 33 Lancasters of 5 Group, six carrying Grand Slams[24] and the remainder Tallboys[25], sent to flatten anything left standing, reported that the centre of the island was still ablaze.[xxxi]

Nine hundred bombers was a force big enough to have levelled Brunsbüttel, Heligoland and Wilhelmshaven in one go. The intervening years had changed Bomber Command from a puny token force to the instrument of Armageddon. The aircraft, the bombs, the radio navigation equipment, the tactics and the sheer professionalism of the organisation had transformed those young, eager and naïve faces first seen in *The Lion has Wings* into 'the most highly trained front-line soldiers in the history of warfare'. The day before Heligoland took its final pasting, the chiefs-of-staff of the Allied war effort issued a communiqué to the effect that 'area' bombing was to end. Two weeks later Hitler shot himself and a week after that the British Prime Minister Winston Churchill, stood up in the House of Commons to say that Germany had surrendered unconditionally. Japan held out for another three months before the world entered the atomic age.

Richard Kellett flew a little slower and Peter Grant stuck close to Paul Harris so they lived to tell the tale. Thereafter, Bomber Command switched to night-time operations and survived to grow into a mighty force of retribution. Knowing this, it now seems inappropriate to compare the early raids of December 1939 with that futile escapade of the Light Brigade. So, to what can we compare Bomber Command's first hesitant steps? In an age when our sensibilities have been blunted by lavish films and spectacular television sagas, it is not easy to find a modern epic that adequately conveys the simpler sentiments and emotions of 1939. To compare like with like we must turn the clock back to those less sophisticated days when

---

[24] 22,000 lb penetrating bomb.
[25] 12,000 lb penetrating bomb.

it was easy to tell the 'good guy' by his white hat and the 'bad guy' by his black one.

In 1939, as 149 Squadron was being marched down to the Comet cinema in Mildenhall to see a preview of *The Lion has Wings*, another film was packing them in round the country. *Gunga Din* provided a splendid piece of escapism with the swashbuckling adventures of Douglas Fairbanks Jnr., Cary Grant and Victor McLaglen. In it, the peace and stability of the British Raj were being threatened by a bunch of murderous Thuggees led by an evil Guru. Our three heroes, accompanied by Sam Jaffe as the faithful water bearer Gunga Din, had tracked the Thugs to their lair in the mountains, only to be captured and held prisoner in their stronghold called the Golden Temple. As the regiment marched to the rescue, pipes playing and banners waving, little did they know that they were heading straight into an ambush set up by the scheming Guru. The film reached its climax with the four prisoners escaping to the roof of the Temple, only to watch helplessly as the Regiment marched unsuspectingly towards the valley where the Guru had concealed his massive forces poised in readiness to spring the trap. Courageously, the frail Gunga Din climbed painfully up to the dome of the Golden Temple, stood up in full view of the enemy, put his beloved old bugle to his lips and blew a warning call. Alerted, the regiment formed up into battle order and, after a mighty punch-up, defeated the Thugs – their evil Guru committing suicide. After saving the Regiment, Gunga Din fell from the dome mortally wounded. For his bravery he was made a posthumous corporal in the regiment and buried with full military honours to the time honoured words, 'You're a better man than I am, Gunga Din'. This was hilariously corny stuff by today's standards but, to the uncritical eye of a wee schoolboy in 1939, pure magic. So it is with those hazy recollections of a film from the days of the Phoney War that I see the Battle of Heligoland Bight helping to blow the bugle call that alerted an unsuspecting Bomber Command and saved it from charging headlong into the Ruhr Valley – to almost certain annihilation.

6
Hidden away for all time

Just after 3 p.m. on New Year's Eve 1940, Squadron Leader David Marwood-Elton, his co-pilot, Pilot Officer Slatter, and six young trainee navigators took off from RAF Lossiemouth on the Moray Firth in a battle-weary Wellington bomber, just retired from active service to 20 Operational Training Unit. Their route took them south-west to Fort Augustus when they encountered heavy snow squalls at 8,000 feet over the Monadhliath Mountains. Suddenly the starboard engine spluttered and failed. The aircraft began to lose height, and all around were cloud covered peaks. The pilot gave the order to bail out and the six young trainees jumped from the stricken aircraft. One pulled his ripcord too soon; his 'chute was damaged on striking the aircraft and failed to open. The other five landed safely. The Wellington continued to lose height and, through a break in the cloud, the pilot spotted a long stretch of water and decided to ditch. As the plane came down the port propeller sent up a great spray of water. Marwood-Elton and Slatter struggled out on to the starboard wing, released the dinghy from its housing behind the engine, clambered aboard and paddled to the shore. As he watched his aircraft sink the thought crossed Marwood-Elton's mind that his plane was 'hidden away for all time' at the bottom of Loch Ness. The incident was all over in 90 seconds. While the aircraft was settling peacefully on to the bottom of the loch, London was reeling under the impact of the Blitz. The city had just suffered its worst attack of the war so far with 30,000 incendiary bombs gutting the square mile, including the Guildhall and eight Wren churches.

The trauma of the Second World War passed into history and Loch Ness settled back into its peacetime role as host to legions of intrepid monster-hunters. At first they came armed only with binoculars and cameras. Slowly, as time passed and technology advanced, more sophisticated equipment started to appear around the shores of the loch. The breakthrough came in 1968 when Professor Tucker from Birmingham University caused a sensation by reporting large underwater moving objects in the vicinity of his experimental sonar equipment in Urquhart Bay.

Over the next eight years many different types of sonar were tried out in the loch and a variety of targets were found, including the infamous 'Flipper' and 'Head' photographs of a Long Necked Plesiosaur (Nessie?). In 1976 Marty Klein of Klein Associates Inc. of Salem, New Hampshire, arrived at Loch Ness with the very latest side-scan sonar and found many more intriguing targets, one of which was a Catalina aircraft that went down in the Second World War. In 1978 the Department of Electrical and Electronic Engineering at Heriot Watt University in Edinburgh went up to Loch Ness with their Remotely Operated Vehicle (ROV) called PK1. The objective was to test the vehicle and take photographs of the Catalina. To our complete surprise, the aircraft we found was not a Catalina but a Wellington. Upon returning to Edinburgh a letter was sent to the Ministry of Defence informing them of our find. In reply, the Air Historical Branch suggested that the aircraft could be a very early Mk 1A that had ditched on New Year's Eve 1940. This was subsequently confirmed when the Royal Navy Deep Diving Team from HMS *Vernon* in Portsmouth searched the wreck in 1979 and found the serial number N2980 on the fuselage fabric. This was the aircraft that Marwood-Elton thought he had 'hidden away for all time' – this was Paul Harris's old Wimpy 'R for Robert'.

Subsequent surveys by Heriot Watt's ROVs in 1980 and 1981 revealed the sad fact that the old aircraft had been seriously damaged since it was identified in 1978. A large fishing net from a trawler was draped round the front gun turret and the fuselage aft of the wings had been torn apart. Perhaps someone had been trying to grapple for souvenirs. As the location of the aircraft was now common knowledge, its survival was in jeopardy. In order to save the aircraft and hopefully recover it before the damage got too great, the author set up a charity called the Loch Ness Wellington Association Ltd. in 1984. With funds donated by the public and The National Heritage Memorial Fund a recovery operation was mounted in September 1985. The first attempt proved to be a total disaster when the lifting frame collapsed. Another lifting frame was hurriedly designed 'on the back of an envelope' and sent off to be built at an engineering company located on the Moray Firth. This time the recovery was successful and old 'R for Robert' was craned out of the water at Bona Lighthouse, up at the north end of Loch Ness, on the 21st September 1985 and donated to Brooklands Museum at Weybridge.

The crew of N2980 when it ditched on Loch Ness were:

Squadron Leader N.W.D. Marwood-Elton	Pilot	Survived the war.
Pilot Officer Slatter	Co-Pilot	Killed in action 5/2/44.
Pilot Officer Lucton	Trainee Navigator	No trace of his record.
Sergeant Wright	Wireless Operator/ Air Gunner	Survived the war.
Sergeant Chandler	Trainee Navigator	Killed in action 2/8/41.
Sergeant Little	Trainee Navigator	Killed in action 26/6/42.
Sergeant Ford	Trainee Navigator	Killed in action 31/5/42.
Sergeant Fensome	Rear Gunner	Killed 31/12/40 when N2980 ditched.

Appendix A

Personal recollections of the Battle of Heligoland Bight

Group Captain P.I. Harris, DFC. Flying Officer H.A. Innes, DFC, by permission of his sister, Mrs S. Richardson. Flight Lieutenant J.J. Mullineaux, DFM, by permission of his daughter, Mrs M. Vick. Flight Lieutenant F.C. Petts, DFC and Bar, by permission of his son, Mr J.B. Petts. Oberfeldwebel O.K. Dombrowski, Iron Cross 1st & 2nd Class, by permission of *Jaegerblatt*, Journal of the German Fighter Pilots Association.

GROUP CAPTAIN P.I. HARRIS DFC

149 Squadron Mildenhall was in 3 Group. This group, equipped with the latest and best armed bomber in the Royal Air Force, was earmarked for day bombing which included the task of attacking the German Navy as and when found at sea.

3 Group had, until immediately before the war, been a night bomber group armed with the Handley Page Harrow. Our training then had been totally different, with no formation flying, so vital to survival in daylight operations. Almost overnight we became a day bomber group, but formation flying was not our forte. This was apparent on long distance flights by the whole group, supposedly in formation, over France shortly before the war, with the idea of building up French morale. Only two squadrons, 214 and 9, formated well; otherwise it looked more like a race than a formation flight. I was then a flight commander in 214 Squadron. Our commanding officer was an old friend of mine, under whom I had served in Palestine in the mid-thirties. The group did three flights to Marseilles and one to Bordeaux. 214 Squadron was

129

on all of them, and in one case we led the whole group, but the other squadrons were scattered all over the sky with little semblance of any formation.

Until the invasion of France in 1940, we in the Royal Air Force suffered from what is known as the Phoney War. This is not fully understood today. Our directive was simple but silly. No civilian might be killed or injured and only naval ships attacked at sea. We were virtually not allowed to drop our bombs on land. Transgression could, and did, involve being taken off flying and put in an operations room. This was before Churchill came to power. A friend of mine was doing a sweep in the Heligoland Bight when he was fired at by minesweepers, he did a run up at 10,000 feet and dropped his bombs, fortunately missing his target. A few days later I happened to pass the AOC's office and I asked him what he was doing there; he said, 'I am waiting to get a rocket, actually,' and I said, 'What on earth for?' and he told me the story. He was taken off flying and put in an operations room as a punishment for attacking ships that had fired on him: apparently they were requisitioned trawlers and not, *ab initio* as it were, naval ships. This shows the extreme punishment that could be inflicted on people who transgressed.

I was posted to 149 Squadron about one week before the war. I brought with me my own crew and also another crew, Michael Briden as captain and Billy Brown as second pilot. I am bound to say that I was not happy with what I found. Looking back it seems that we were posted there to hot up the squadron's formation flying and prepare it for battle. Some squadrons actually had commanding officers of the 1914-18 War vintage, who did no flying whatever. I started the war with one, but fortunately he left shortly before we began our operations in December, when Wing Commander Kellett arrived and transformed the squadron – just in time. None of these non-flying types should have been commanding squadrons; our High Command was at fault. You cannot lead a squadron if you cannot fly the aeroplane with which it is armed. When this is clearly understood one realises why the other squadrons did not survive, and 149 Squadron did, on 18th December 1939.

Initially we were armed with Wellington Mk 1s but they had

Vickers turrets which were useless. Sights did not follow the guns and the ammunition belts stuck in the ducts. But soon Frazer-Nash turrets were fitted in the 1As including a Frazer-Nash retractable under-turret, a 'dustbin', which rotated through 360 degrees and when firing aft could fire 2 degrees above the horizontal which was very useful, backing up the rear gunner against stern attacks. All turrets, front, rear and mid-under, had two .303 Brownings firing 1,000 rounds per minute; and the 1,000 round belts, one to each gun, were fed efficiently. Our gunners were volunteer ground crew and not well trained: we had no gunnery leaders then and the only training they had was when they were able to come up with us when not working on the ground. We were particularly lucky in that Archie Frazer-Nash used to drive up fairly frequently in his Bentley and fly with me, testing his own turrets and guns. We also had a partner of his who came up and did much testing with us.

By 3rd December, when Kellett led 24 Wellingtons to Heligoland, we were in fairly good form. We bombed through heavy flak, but sank only one small ship. Our gunners were moderately trained, and with the turrets and guns working well, we were ready for battle. On this raid we saw but few fighters and Kellett led well but a little bit too fast, so I could not keep up with him and when we got back he asked me if he had led all right and I said, 'Go a little slower next time'. This is a particularly important point as, had we not gone on that raid together, and had he not realised the need to fly slower so that I could keep up with him, he might have led too fast on the Wilhelmshaven raid with the result that 149 Squadron and the three aircraft of 9 Squadron would have been annihilated.

On the Heligoland raid of 3rd December, N2980 was flown by Flight Lieutenant Stewart, a Canadian. Although the flak was heavy at Heligoland we all survived and we were not attacked by fighters. I see from my logbook that I took over N2980 on 10th December and flew it four times with my crew before 18th December, by which time my gunners were used to the guns, could fire them well and operate the turrets efficiently, thanks to Frazer-Nash, even if we were not particularly crack shots. Now we come to the big day.

On the evening of 17th December my commanding officer

and I were summoned to group headquarters together with the commanding officers of 37 and 9 Squadrons to be briefed for a group operation the next day, a sweep in the Heligoland Bight area searching for the German fleet. Kellett was to lead. A brilliant pilot, no better leader could have been chosen for this impossible task and our squadron, 149, had the honour of providing nine aircraft and leading the whole group, totalling 24 aircraft. Kellett had Lieutenant Commander Rotherham with him, a Fleet Air Arm officer, to identify enemy ships and aim the bombs provided the targets were not too close to land. In the event there was a battleship there, but moored in the dock. At the briefing I was told that Peter Grant was to fly with me; this was the first time that we had ever flown together and my parting words to him were: 'Stay close to me whatever happens' – and this, fortunately for us all, he did most ably.

Our 24 Wellingtons were divided into four flights of six aircraft each, Kellett leading with six of 149, and myself in N2980 on his starboard side with three of my own flight and three of 9 Squadron's led by Grant. We were in boxes of six stepped up in order not to mask our guns, not an easy position for Grant. On Kellett's port side were six aircraft of 9 Squadron and 37 Squadron were arse-end-charlies, obviously the most vulnerable position, unless they kept very close and flew above Kellett. To have flown underneath and behind him would have masked the fire of his rear gunners and been obviously dangerous. I cannot remember if there was any discussion on this matter but all I know is that 37 Squadron did not stay with us for long. 37 Squadron were flying in pairs, not in vic formations of three like the rest of us, but in line astern stepped down: it was more manoeuvrable but had obvious disadvantages since the rear guns could shoot down their own people. On the run out I saw 37 Squadron, as it seemed to me, almost on the skyline. They were a long way off, not practising close formation flying on Kellett – essential for survival. Only one aircraft of 37 Squadron returned home, 'Cheese' Lemon, who lowered his flaps by mistake over the target instead of opening his bomb doors and, having leapt suddenly into the air, descended at great speed to sea level and managed to weave his way home in spite of heavy fighter attacks. Had he not made this mistake he would probably have been wiped out with the rest of his squadron. He was lucky to get home, the only survivor of 37 Squadron. I kept very close to Kellett all the way out, and ensured that Grant kept close to me. Kellett flew at exactly the right speed so I had no difficulty in formating with him. The other squadrons seemed to be far away and running their own show in an independent but dangerous sort of way. The further they were away the nearer I kept to my leader.

Kellett led us over the Heligoland Bight but saw nothing and then he steered for Wilhelmshaven. On the run in at 15,000 feet there was heavy flak, accurate for height, but fortunately trailing behind us and as it kept catching up, my rear gunner, Jimmy Mullineaux, kept saying: 'Hurry up Sir, it's catching up on us.' Meanwhile, the fighters were collecting above us like flies waiting for us to clear the flak before they attacked. With my eyes glued on Kellett I saw nothing. He told me on our return that there was a pocket battleship in dock but we could not attack it because of explicit instructions to this effect: no risk of bombs on land – The Phoney War!

Once clear of the flak, Kellett and I were on our own with ten aeroplanes. There should have been 12 but two returned early about an hour out from England. The other two formations of 9 and 37 Squadrons had disappeared. One of Kellett's four aircraft went down in flames early on so the battle was finally joined for some 30 minutes between our nine aircraft and the Germans. We were entirely on our own and N2980 behaved immaculately, as did my crew. I kept as close to Kellett as possible and Grant clung to me like a limpet, flying really well. So our nine aircraft presented a concentrated but unattractive target with nine rear turrets and nine dustbins to contend with. The front turrets had, of course, very little shooting and, I think, fired only once.

The events inside N2980 were exciting. I, of course, saw almost nothing, my eyes being fixed on Kellett, survival depending on maintaining formation. My second pilot, Pilot Officer Sandy Innes, a splendid Scotsman, was at the astrodome to control our gunners. This he did magnificently, like a commentator at a football match, so I knew what was going on. My rear gunner, Aircraftman Jimmy Mullineaux, eventually fired all his ammunition, 1,000 rounds per gun, so

Sandy nipped down to him with short, spare belts of 300 rounds each so that Jimmy was able to keep firing one gun while loading the other in between attacks. Sergeant Austin, my navigator, manned the dustbin. Aircraftman Doxsey in the front turret had a dull time, except once.

While I could see nothing, I knew exactly what was happening from Innes's narrative. As far as I remember all our guns worked well, unlike those of some other squadrons which I believe froze at 15,000 feet. Those of N2980 worked perfectly in the Frazer-Nash turrets; we had tested them on the way out and I had done a lot of air firing with Frazer-Nash, to whose turrets we undoubtedly owed our lives.

I did, however, see one fighter, a Messerschmitt 110 which suddenly shot across my bows in a vertical turn doing a complicated and well executed attack on Kellett. It seemed to black out the sky and, considering how close I was to Kellett, his attack was brilliantly timed not to crash into me or any of my other aircraft. I do not know how he did it. Naturally, our front gunners, who had as yet fired no shots in anger, all let fly and he went down pouring out smoke. Aircraftman Doxsey in my front turret had his foot grazed by a bullet. Of course, all our front gunners claimed a victory and we were convinced of this. We now know from German records that no Me 110 was destroyed, although some were damaged, as ours certainly was. But that pilot certainly deserved to survive.

The crew of N2980 fought superbly. My navigator, Sergeant Austin, manned the mid-under dustbin retractable turret. My rear gunner, Jimmy Mullineaux, got an immediate and well merited DFM for his efforts. I enjoyed writing his citation. Sandy Innes was decorated later but sadly did not survive long. I was fortunate with my crew. Flying with them was a pleasure.

After the battle, Kellett was accused of flying too fast by the survivors of the other squadrons. This is nonsense. He flew perfectly; I stayed with him without difficulty. He did not go too fast for me. The fact is that the others were untrained in formation flying and were not led by their own commanding officers, who in turn had not discussed, or practised formation flying with Kellett. It was like trying to form a football team of people who had never met before and had never played together as a team, and had different ideas about the rules.

The leader of a flight must know the difficulties facing each individual in his flight. Leading my box of six stepped up I had to understand the feelings and difficulties of the other five pilots. Kellett leading his lot had the task of flying in such a way that I could keep in touch with him. Neither too fast nor too slow. In a turn, it is obvious that the aircraft on the inside of the turn are going slower than those on the outside. If the leader flies too slowly the aircraft on the inside may stall and fall out of the sky. If he turns too fast the aircraft on the outside cannot keep up, while the only aircraft that can follow him without much difficulty are the arse-end-charlies, who, of course, are going at the same speed as the leader. A large formation can obviously be turned only very slowly, and the bigger it is the slower must be the turn. Once formation was lost it was not easy to regain it. A single aircraft can do this by opening the throttle and belting ahead to catch up but the leader of a flight cannot easily do this; he has to keep his flight together and fly a bit faster, but not so fast that the formation disintegrates. Knowing this I kept close to Kellett from the moment we took off until we finally broke up after the engagement. Formation flying requires the highest discipline, skill and practice.

We survived simply because Kellett's leading was immaculate, we kept in close formation, our guns worked and two of our formation's three losses were almost certainly due to having no self-sealing tanks.

Our squadrons had their own ideas and whimsies about formation flying. There were basically two schools of thought: close formation relying on concentrated firepower and mutual support, and loose formation relying on manoeuvrability but at the sacrifice of firepower and mutual support. The latter school unfortunately ignored the immensely superior manoeuvrability and speed of the fighter. 149 Squadron adhered to the former school and had a commanding officer who was a brilliant leader and knew his job; the other squadrons did not. The result was that our formation was weakened and 149 Squadron, with three aircraft of 9 Squadron, ably led by Flight Lieutenant Peter Grant, were left alone to fight the ultimate battle. There is no doubt that the other two squadrons left us because they were untrained. One cannot blame them for this because we had been given no previous opportunity to fly together, and Kellett had no chance to discuss the matter with them and impose his will on them as a leader. Group headquarters laid on no group formation training. However, it laid on active operations in which squadrons which had never before flown together were sent into action. The lessons of the pre-war French flights were ignored – a fatal error.

FLYING OFFICER H.A. INNES, DFC

18.12.39 Well, bombing raid number two is completed, though not so successfully as last time. Started off with 24 aircraft. Led by Wing Commander Kellett. Two dropped out on way out and remainder came on. We went out toward Denmark and south-east to Heligoland. Height 15,000 – no cloud at all and Germany was stretched out below us for miles and miles. Very fine sight and the estuaries seemed to be half frozen over. We had one fighter attack us on run south, but it was probably there to get our height and air speed. We feinted toward Bremerhaven and Wessermünde and then west to Wilhelmshaven where we got the attack signal. By this time archies had opened up in great strength. At first they were up to 1,000 feet below us but improved to amazing accuracy later on. Some of them getting our height to within 10-12 feet though fortunately to one side. A fine sight watching them explode and enlarge. At first there is a jet black splodge which immediately widens out, then you get the bump if it is close. After that you look back and it is as though you have left a large wood with all the bursts hanging about in the sky like tree tops. Anyhow I dropped my bombs. Don't expect any good for we had no time at all and aimed at a boat in outer harbour. Anyhow when bombs went we cracked off and with a goodly attention of ack-ack we made the English coast – but not too easily. All the way from the target we were attacked by fighters. Fleets of them single-seater and twin-engine Me 110 attacks continued for 25 minutes during which they came in say 15 times from the rear.

19.12.39 I am always falling asleep writing this up. Hence rather involved account last night before I packed it up.

Anyhow we have got an hour longer lie in bed this morning so I can complete narrative.

Their fighters were damn good. The idea we had that they were windy of us turned out to be all bunk. We had Me 109 and 110, majority of latter. These seem to be bloody good. They were thrown all over the sky and seemed to be doing all of 400 mph. God knows how many of them there were. Anything up to 50-60 and they came in without ceasing – sometimes two and three at once all from different directions. I had moved straight to astrodome after bomb release and was controlling the turrets. It worked very well for I could see everything except underneath when I had to leave it to the centre gunner. Several times I directed the rear gun onto a target he had not seen – so I think it has justified itself. Anyhow it was not my idea of a picnic, for it was a horrible sight seeing these damned Messerschmitts coming straight for you and all you could do was to talk. Actually I had a camera and took numerous photos which relieved me of some of the jitters by having something active to do. I don't know how many times they came in – probably 30-40. Our formation of three kept up magnificently and also the three behind and above were pretty good and by that and that alone we made good. Our fire power was grand and I think we got quite five Messerschmitts between us. Several times I could see the tracer meeting the aircraft and then it would give a nasty jerk and it would crack off downwards. Never saw them right down for I always had to turn to more attacks, but rear gunner saw several into the drink. They were using cannon and also machine guns and the tracer was whipping around us. Halfway through front gunner called out he was hurt so wireless operator went forward to take his place. We expected to have to pull out a corpse but rather a white faced Doxsey came out under his own steam. It appeared the bullet had pierced his boot and given him a hell of a bruise in the instep before going out. Anyhow that left me to have to carry reserve ammunition. Which I did several times. Awful job for it kept falling out of the boxes and trailing behind and getting caught up in the geodetics and then quick back to fire control again. We were at 14,000 feet and the temp was minus 15 but by God I was running fit to beat records. Sweat pouring off – lack of oxygen and cold completely forgotten.

Meanwhile as it went on I saw fewer and fewer of our aircraft following us. Two of ours went down with port wings blazing and like bloody fools no one seemed to jump and then it was too late for they blew up. Suppose they thought they could get down to land. So again it is the idiocy of some bloody fool in not armouring both wings that has cost us several aircraft and many lives. Another aircraft of ours I saw hit almost at the end of the engagement. The starboard wing just blew off, the petrol appeared to pour out and ignite in one solid mass of flame about 100 feet thick and the fuselage and remaining wing went down in a sickening spin. I don't think anyone could have got out for they must have been thrown against the side by the spin and held there. It was a terrible sight and yet awe inspiring but I don't want to see it again.

Anyhow eventually the fighters broke off some 70-80 miles from the coast and we relaxed, everyone pouring with sweat and throats so dry we could only croak. Paul Harris handed round the brandy[26] and we had one damn good swig and it put new life into us. My God it was necessary. Our formation of six were all there, as well as the CO and his three, and there were one or two more further back. As it turned out we must have had seven shot down and probably two more came down in the drink on the way home. Feltwell lost five out of six. Poor 37. I wonder who they were. So their pet formation didn't work so well after all. We lost Jimmy Speirs and Norman Lines in one aircraft over Germany and then on the way home we heard Michael Briden calling CO to say he was losing petrol and could he take the shortest way home. Sure enough I could see the plume of gas coming out of his port wing. All went well till we were half an hour off England when I saw his engines coughing and he fell away in a glide towards the sea. I was flying then and I told the squadron leader and he told me to follow him down. I did this though it was a bit tricky for we were 10,000 feet and Mike went down behind us. Anyhow as luck would have it I just caught sight of him before he went through the clouds which were broken. I circled round again and then from about 1,000 feet saw him touch down. Must

---

[26]It was actually rum.

have been good landing or alighting, for although it was down wind and the splash went right over the aircraft it came to rest on an even keel having slewed round through 90 degrees. Floating nicely, I came down to 300-400 feet and came past several times. Next time round, the dinghy was open and floating aft of the engine. Next time round it was by the nose of aircraft which was settling down. I could see them by the dinghy. Next time round the plane had almost gone and the boys – three of them it seemed – were in the water with the dinghy on end and it was then that I had a horrible fear that it might be holed and was sinking also. Maybe though it was only because they are devils to get into. Anyhow it was then we thought of releasing our own dinghy for them. All this time we had been sending out SOS and trying to get a radio fix. Anyhow I came back once more and only by a silvery patch on water was I able to see them. I gave the signal and Sergeant Austin pulled the dinghy release, about 50 yards before them. But it was a tough break on us for it came back and burst on our tail-plane and remained there, setting up the most awful juddering in the controls. There was nothing more we could do for we hadn't much petrol ourselves and in addition the elevator was holed and liable to break at any moment.

So we turned straight for home on one engine to lower the drag on the starboard side. We were only making 120mph and got back in half an hour, landing at Coltishall, a new aerodrome under construction. Here I commandeered a push bike and beat it for a phone to inform operations... After seeing the operations and intelligence we were actually able to relax, this was about 6.15 p.m.

Went along to the Bird in Hand afterwards to talk it over with Paul and the boys and the group captain stood me supper there which was also much needed. Finally bed at 11 p.m. and I am glad to say deep sleep, possibly due to the beer. Never in my life have I ever had such a thrilling time – I wouldn't have missed it for anything but by God I don't want to go through it again. I have often heard people argue about their biggest thrill – fast run downhill on skis, 10 mile point hunting, pig sticking, but I know now quite well that I have had the biggest of the lot. And I am glad I had such a marvellous view of it all.

19.12.39 *Night*. Well today was been the anti-climax. Spent the morning wandering around, everyone feeling rather flat, doubtless because I suppose everyone was celebrating their safe return. I went along to intelligence office to see my films and what did I find? Of my own camera which I had used taking I thought some 10-12 snaps of Messerschmitts attacking us and flying near us, all were duds. Several into the sun, several of clear sky and others where I had simply not cocked the camera and no exposure was made. There was however one poor shot of the dinghy on the tail. After that I was busy writing out reports, reports, reports – pages of them – on fighter tactics, best formation, and finally on Michael and his landing. He was not picked up, though messages had come in saying he had been, but no-one could trace these, and he had not turned up. Boats and planes had been searching all day. Our aircraft R was brought over and we had a look at it – there were about six bullets through it, and one burst of AA. One bullet went through the port wing but just missed the tank – lucky. Doxsey's bullet was found, still in the front turret.

20.12.39 Still writing reports – the hangover from a raid is almost as bad as the real thing. Also today the commander-in-chief turned up to hear all about it. I was hauled up to the CO's office to say what I had seen, trying affair with one air chief marshal, one air-vice marshal, one group captain, one wing commander and one squadron leader – finally yours truly (one pilot officer). I had a bad cold and had to keep on blowing my nose to stop sniffing. Commander-in-chief was very pleasant. I was jawing for about 20 minutes then Mullineaux was called in and, poor lad, it was a bit scaring for an aircraftman. He talked very well for about five minutes and then said 'Please Sir, may I faint' – and fell slick over as cold as mutton. I caught him as he fell. Came round quick and continued sitting while he finished his story. After that the c-in-c had a few words to say to the crews. It appears that it is the biggest aerial battle that has ever taken place, over 100 aircraft being engaged and lasting for 40 minutes. Our total casualties were 12 aircraft and 11 crews. One crew of 9 Squadron were picked up in their dinghy out of the drink. Their losses were probably about 20. Quite likely many more for we don't know how many were shot by our boys who never came back.

In the evening I went over to Methwold and Paul and Captain Frazer-Nash came too. It was the Christmas party for B Flight and all the old faces were there and they gave us a cheer when we came into the pub which felt grand but we just blamed each other for having brought us out of the fight and then went into the more serious duty of drinking. I was then taken back to Methwold and we stayed there till 1.30 a.m. and so to bed. I left my car there and came back in Frazer-Nash's Rolls-Royce – more comfortable.

ACCOUNT BY FLIGHT LIEUTENANT J.J. MULLINEAUX OF RAID ON 18TH DECEMBER 1939

I had a false sense of security when Squadron Leader P.I. Harris told me we were going to attack shipping in Wilhelmshaven, as on our previous raid we were met by three Me 109s who soon broke off their attack when we returned fire. This instilled untold courage and made me look forward to our next engagement. Anyhow on the morning of 18th December we were briefed and our target was to be a daylight attack right into the heart of the German naval defences. The strength of the attack was the amazing number of 24 Wellington bombers Mark 1A. This formation was to be made up from the whole of 3 Group in which command I was serving. Our crew consisted of Squadron Leader P.I. Harris, pilot, Pilot Officer Innes, second pilot, Sergeant F. Austin, navigator, Aircraftman Second Class Watson, wireless operator, Aircraftman Second Class Doxsey, front gunner and myself rear gunner.

Bombs were loaded on the aircraft and guns and ammunition were checked, wireless and navigation tested, but during this time I am sure we were all wondering whether we should come back or not. I remember I did and was very nervous indeed.

We took off from Mildenhall and after about half an hour we joined up with other crews from the group. The leader of the attack was Wing Commander Kellett and my captain was the leader of the formation of six aircraft.

The weather was ideal, visibility about ten miles, no clouds. We pressed on until we passed over Heligoland when we were attacked by three Me 109s but with the concentration of fire they too immediately broke off the attack and we pressed on knowing full well that the alarm had been given and that a warm reception would be waiting for us when we approached our target.

About five minutes' flying time from the harbour we encountered heavy, accurate flak which soon forced the formation to open up. In we went straight and level for about ten minutes, the flak getting heavier and more accurate. I could feel the bursts and very soon the whole of the sky seemed full of black puffs. I was sure one would find its mark and blow us clean out of the air.

Luck was with us, we did not get hit and very soon we altered course and headed out to sea on a reciprocal course. This was our bombing run. It was during the run that I first saw little black specks on the horizon and within seconds, as it were, I recognized them as Me 109s and Me 110s. Our bombing run completed, the fighters came in to attack and very soon the whole sky seemed full of them. I estimated their strength to be about 100. I called frantically 'Fighters'. Immediately Austin took up position in the mid-under turret and Pilot Officer Innes went to the astrodome. We had not long to wait before the first fighter came in to attack our aircraft. It was an Me 110. Innes was the first to see it. In he came and I could see his machine guns blazing away. I opened fire at 300 yards and continued to fire until he broke away at 20 yards. No sooner had he broken than another attack took place and this continued throughout the engagement. During the short spells I looked around the sky and could see our bombers going down in flames. This had a great effect on me as I had been pumping bullets into the attacking aircraft and did not seem to get any results. Another fighter came up and no sooner had it attacked and I opened up than it seemed to blow up. My bullets had found their mark. The captain shouted, 'Good show, Mullineaux'. That was all I needed. I got stuck in with added zest and it was not long before the second went down. He came dead astern. I opened up at 400 yards. The mid-under gunner was also firing at him and between us we blew the aircraft out of the air. Other attacks came again and again. I could hear the front gunner firing over the intercom and he too shot one down. But after a while my ammunition ran out. I called frantically to the captain for more. He sent the second pilot down but in his excitement he opened the door of my turret and simply threw it at me. The result was that I had no assistance to load both guns. I did however manage to get one gun going after a while and throughout the rest of the engagement I kept it going and with the aid of the mid-under gunner kept most of the fighters from firing accurately at us, from astern.

During the latter part of the engagement I heard a blood-curdling scream from the front gunner. 'He has been shot,' I immediately thought. Then from the captain came, 'Wireless operator, drag the body out of the front turret and take over'. But after the engagement was over I looked back from my turret and saw the front gunner calmly sitting on the bed. A bullet had torn the sole of his boot from the upper.

Another amusing incident took place. It was when Innes had dumped the ammunition in my turret. I called to the captain for help but he thought I had stopped a bullet and immediately sent Innes back again with a bottle of his closely guarded rum. Innes opened the turret doors and asked if I was OK. I said I just wanted help with the ammunition but he did not seem to understand; all he did was to pass the bottle of rum into my hand and close the doors again. Needless to say my captain never saw his rum again.

After what seemed many hours the fighters broke off their attack but I regret to say we had many bombers missing and our only consolation was knowing we had destroyed an equal number of enemy fighters.

FLIGHT LIEUTENANT F.C. PETTS, DFC AND BAR OPERATION ON 18TH DECEMBER 1939

On a number of previous occasions reconnaissance Blenheims had found German warships off the German coast in the Heligoland area and had been followed by a bomber striking force. In the short days of mid-December it was decided to dispense with the preliminary reconnaissance and to despatch a bomber force in the morning to search for and attack German warships. It was established subsequently that security about the proposed operation on 18th December was extremely poor; certainly on the evening of the 17th it was widely known in Bury St. Edmunds that 9 Squadron crews had been recalled because of an operation planned for early the next day.

On reporting to the flights at 07.30 a.m. on 18th December we learned that 9 Squadron was to supply nine aircraft for a force of 24, with nine from 149 Squadron at Mildenhall and six from 37 Squadron at Feltwell. There were to be four groups of six aircraft: three of 149 and three of 9 in front, six of 149 to starboard, six of 9 to port and six of 37 in the rear. Targets were to be any German warships found in the area of Heligoland or the Schillig Roads.

To the best of my recollection bomb loads were four 500lb GPs[27] per aircraft. We were airborne from Honington about 09.00 a.m.; by 10.00 a.m. we were formed up with the other squadrons and were leaving the Norfolk coast. I was outside left of the whole formation, flying number three in a vic of three. Although the operation was planned for 24 aircraft, I believe that only 22 crossed the North Sea; I cannot now remember what happened to the other two but understand they turned back.

We climbed on course to 15,000 feet. Halfway across the North Sea we left all cloud cover behind; soon all aircraft manned and lowered the dustbin turrets. We continued without substantial change of course until we were within sight of low-lying land which must have been Sylt.

I was not sure how a large navigational error was involved but I was still surprised that we were so far north. The formation turned south, still at 15,000 feet in a clear sky. The coast was still in sight but there was no sign of enemy opposition until my rear gunner called, 'There's a fighter attacking behind – they've got him!' Then to starboard I saw an Me 109, with smoke pouring from it, change from level flight to a near vertical dive so abruptly that the pilot could hardly have been alive and conscious after the change of direction. I remember that at this stage I thought, rather prematurely, that encounters with German fighters were 'easy'.

We left Heligoland to port and shortly afterwards turned left towards the Schillig Roads where we had been told at briefing

---

[27]General Purpose bombs.

there was likely to be warship targets. We saw none but continued on a south-easterly course and I remember wondering how far up the river we were going in search of battleships and cruisers. I have vague recollections of ineffectual ack-ack fire at this stage and earlier as we passed Heligoland.

Next came a wide turn to starboard to take the formation over Wilhelmshaven and back seawards. In my situation at outside left of the whole formation I found it increasingly difficult to maintain my position. Repeated calls to my section leader to ask him to slow down brought no reply and in spite of opening up to full boost and increasing propeller revs to maximum I still could not keep up.

Over Wilhelmshaven we flew into intense ack-ack fire and trying to work out whether evasive manoeuvres were any use against the black puffs bursting all around. I was for a while less pre-occupied with the problem of staying in formation. The black puffs stopped quite suddenly and there in front were the fighters (thinking things over next day I decided there must have been about 40 of them), and still in spite of full throttle and full revs I was lagging behind. I dumped my bombs, and hoped to gain a little speed. About this time Balch on the front guns got his first fighter. An Me 109 away to port was turning in a wide sweep, possibly to attack the sections in front. I saw the tracer in Balch's first burst hit in the cockpit area and the canopy or part of it fly off; the second burst also hit and the Me 109 immediately went into a catastrophic dive with white smoke pouring from it.

About this time I decided that, in spite of my full throttle and full revs, I should never keep up. Ginger Heathcote pointed out the 37 Squadron six, forming the rear of the box of 24, and suggested that I dropped back to them. It was as well that I did not. 37 Squadron were flying in their own formation of three pairs stepped down in line astern. As the attacks developed, one of the six – I am not sure which but Pilot Officer Kydd was the rear gunner – went to dump his bombs. To open the bomb doors he first selected master hydraulic cock 'on', not realising that he had flaps selected down. The result was sudden lowering of full flap leading to an immediate gain of considerable extra height. Enemy fighters left this aircraft alone but shot down the other five of 37 Squadron. My account of this incident is, of course, second-hand but I heard it first a day or two after the event and later from Kydd when we were both instructing at 11 OTU.

Having decided that I could not catch up with my section leader I turned about 40 degrees to starboard, put my nose hard down and with the dustbin turret still in the lowered position screamed down to sea level. All the way down from 15,000 feet and then for some time just above the water I kept full throttle and full revs except when I reduced power for short periods in an evasive manoeuvre as fighters lined up to attack.

During the dive I was too pre-occupied with what was going on outside to pay much attention to my instruments; I did however notice my ASI[28] reaching the one o'clock position, second time round. It was not until we returned to the aircraft the next morning that I looked to see what that meant in terms of indicated air speed – it was 300mph! This was about twice normal cruising IAS[29] and I could not help wondering how much faster I could have gone before something broke.

I cannot remember just how many fighter attacks there were: the first came before I left cruising altitude, there were more on the way down with Me 110s passing us as they broke away, and finally we were chased along the water by three Me 110s. Robertson on the rear guns kept me informed as each attack developed and there were commentaries from the other two gunners.

We met each stern attack with a drill that we had agreed as a result of experience gained in fighter co-operation exercises. The usual sequence ran: 'There's one coming in, he's coming in. Get ready, get ready. Back, back.' Throttles slammed shut and pitch levers to full coarse. Bursts from our guns and enemy tracer past the windows. 'OK he's gone.' Open up again to full throttle and full revs.

Mostly the tracer was on the starboard side and it was not until some weeks later when we started taking aircraft back to Brooklands to have armour plate fitted behind the port wing

---

[28] Air Speed Indicator.
[29] Indicated Air Speed.

tanks that I realised that previously we had enjoyed this protection only on the starboard side.

Altogether that day my gunners claimed three 110s and two 109s, but I do not know that they were officially credited with any. I saw Balch's first 109 before we left formation and a 110 which also was his, and I have a clear recollection of Robertson's jubilant shout as he got the last 110. For the other two I could not offer much in confirmation even later the same day and there may have been some duplication of claims from other crews over hits before we started the descent. If I see Bob Kemp again I must ask him about this; I met him two years ago after an interval of 20 years but there were other things to talk about.

Balch's 110 deserves mention. The attack developed in the same way as others but immediately after the tracer ceased there was a shout from Robertson, the 110 came past close to our starboard wing; next there was a burst from my front guns and the 110 was gone. This was a fine example of the effectiveness of sudden throttling back at the right moment in causing a fighter to close more quickly than he intended to. Afterwards Robertson said that he had fired without apparent effect on this 110 as it closed, and then as it overshot and passed beyond his reach the enemy rear gunner put his fingers to his nose at Robertson before opening fire. At that moment Roberston saw Balch's tracer and that was that.

My recollection of what happened to the first of the three 110s which followed us down is now a little vague but I believe that it was hit by both Robertson and Kemp. I do remember quite clearly the end of the attacks: the drill had proceeded as before but Robertson's, 'Get ready, get ready; Back, Back,' was followed by a jubilant, 'I've got him, he's gone in!' The 110 had of course been obliged to get down to our level just above the water for his stern attack and there was no height in which to recover any loss of control. Robertson's next comment was, 'The other one's gone home, he's had enough!'

There had already been calls from Kemp and Balch that they had been hit and Heathcote had gone back to Kemp. Whilst I started checking at my end he helped Kemp (who was losing a lot of blood from a bad thigh wound) out of the dustbin and onto the rest bunk. Kemp in full kit was a tight fit in the dustbin and this move must have called for quite an effort from both. Heathcote next let Balch out of the front turret and went aft again. Balch had been hit in the sole of one foot but he was in urgent need of attention.

Roberston reported that he had emptied his guns into the last 110 and Kemp had called that the centre guns were out of action. Heathcote reported that there appeared to be no major damage to the aircraft, although it was a bit draughty as there were plenty of holes.

For my part I eased back to normal cruising throttle and propeller settings and checking round was shaken to find the starboard oil pressure gauge reading zero. The propellers on Wellington 1As did not feather so I had to be content with pulling the starboard engine right back as with that setting it would give less drag than if switched off, and if it did not seize it might be of some use if I wanted it. I opened up the port engine to 'climb power' and found that I was able to climb gently to 1,000 feet or so. During this time I had turned onto a course of 270. When Heathcote came forward again he agreed that 270 was as good as any because we did not know where we were and steering due west we ought to hit England somewhere.

Towards the western side of the North Sea we encountered some broken cloud which on first sighting raised false hopes that we were reaching land. We were finally sure that we were seeing land when we made out the shape of a Butlin's holiday camp ahead and knew we were approaching Clacton or Skegness. I had seen Skegness some months previously and when we reached the coast I was able to confirm that this was it.

I turned south-west to skirt the Wash as there was no point in crossing additional water on one engine. I first intended to carry on to Honington but in view of Kemp's condition and deteriorating weather ahead I decided instead to land at Sutton Bridge. Preliminary gentle checks of undercarriage and flaps, a slow approach and smooth landing and we stopped after a very short landing run – our damage included a burst starboard tyre. It was just 4 p.m.; we had been airborne for seven hours.

First concern was for an ambulance for our two wounded,

next a call to Honington – but no transport was available until morning – a preliminary debriefing and then something to eat. Next morning we went back to the aircraft to survey the damage and to collect various loose articles that we had left inside. The damage was mostly down the starboard side of the fuselage and on the starboard wing – the oil pressure had resulted from a holed oil tank. As a souvenir I took only a piece of wing fabric complete with cannon shell hole. Inside the aircraft we found that spare Irvin suits left on the rest bunk and the rear gunner's mascot had been stolen. This, I reflected, was how we were received on a Fighter Command station.

Next morning in the sergeant's mess at Honington I found that during the time we were thought to be missing I had lost the clean laundry which I had put to one side the morning of the 18th. I decided that no especial stigma attached to Fighter Command.

The operation on 18th December carrying, in search of warships, bombs quite unsuitable for such targets, cost 12 Wellingtons, 11 complete crews and several wounded. Among the 9 Squadron casualties was my flight commander and section leader, Squadron Leader Guthrie. Among the surviving crews were Sergeant Purdy and his section leader Flying Officer Grant, and Sergeant Ramshaw, who had ditched beside a fishing vessel off Hull.

OBERFELDWEBEL O.K. DOMBROWSKI, IRON CROSS 1ST & 2ND CLASS. THE 18TH DECEMBER 1939 – THE GREAT AERIAL BATTLE OVER THE GERMAN BIGHT

It was a 'ripping' day – to use air force slang. A superb day – blue sky, not a cloud to be seen. I can remember it just as if it was a few months ago, rather than 23 years.

There was something in the air that day. We were expecting the British to turn up – they had already penetrated airspace over Heligoland on 14th December and had lost six aircraft in the process.

Our briefing was to fly a pair of Me 110s on patrol along the East Friesian islands. We were at about 1,000m above sea level, engines throttles back, and if we hadn't been at war, one would have called it a brilliant flight.

Then – a radio message – enemy aircraft approaching the

German Bight at 4,000m.

So much for the nice flight. My leader, Lieutenant Uellenbeck, banks towards the German Bight. Let's hope we don't get there too late to engage them in combat – we're raring to go.

Soon we see small dots on the horizon in front of us – flak. We're going to make it!

Suddenly – what was that? Shadows – aircraft silhouettes below us – we bank steeply and immediately recognise a flight of Vickers Wellingtons with their typical shark fin tail. They are flying extremely low. The right-hand Wellington has lost formation and fallen behind. We'll go for this straggler. All systems go? Yes. The lights for the machine gun and cannons are red. The magazines are in place. Lieutenant Uellenbeck nods briefly.

From the right we build up a textbook attack. 400m... 300m... 200m... a hail of machine-gun bullets hits the target, our cannons bark. As our aircraft goes into a steep climb we see a ball of fire and the bomber hits the sea. Hurrah! (at that point) – a hit! Everything has gone perfectly.

The other two Wellingtons take a course for home, flying low in close formation. Uellenbeck tries the same attack again – it worked so well the first time round.

400m... 300m... the Wellington turns towards us. Our bullets miss. Another try. The two enemy aircraft have separated and their defensive fire is not so concentrated. Nevertheless, three further attacks are unsuccessful – taking quite a toll on our nerves! The pilot must be an old hand at this game. Every time we open fire he turns towards us and our shots pass over him.

Fourth attack. A brief exchange over the intercom: 'Dombrowski, shall we attack from behind?' I have no time to think or speak – our Me 110 is already on the attack!

600m... 500m... 400m... 300m... then a hammering noise followed by a hiss – we've been hit! I feel a blow to my left arm. Uellenbeck banks steeply up to a safe height. But at the same moment we can see that our attack has been successful. The Wellington catches fire and crashes into the sea. We see the splash and a burning oil slick.

The cabin is full of smoke. A smell of cordite fills the air. I can see splashes of blood. 'Uellenbeck (no time for titles) – you're hit – up on your left shoulder – clean through.'

Uellenbeck: 'So I am!'

Then, 'Dombrowski, I've lost our bearings. Get a QDM.'[30]

'How are you, lieutenant?'

'Never mind that – get a QDM!'

Ouch! My arm has gone heavy; my left hand suddenly begins to burn – blood – I'm hit too!

QDM! I slide from the receiver to the transmitter.

Pan from M8 EK QDM.

The beacon replies QDM 75.

It works smoothly – all credit to the beacon operators.

'How are you, lieutenant?'

'OK. We have the QDM. And why are you groaning?'

'QDM in operation. I have a wound in my left forearm.'

'Serious?'

'I'm losing a lot of blood.'

Then, on the horizon we see Me 109s and 110s. We've reached Jever. We breathe a sigh of relief. The aircraft rolls to a stop. Back to earth. Our squadron symbol, a ladybird with seven spots, has brought us luck yet again. We returned from engagement with the enemy with two shot down and the crew wounded. In the military hospital in Jever they discovered that the pilot and radio operator had been hit by one and the same shell – a phosphorus exploding shell. It had become bent and had therefore not exploded. We carefully split it in two and it served for a long time as a talisman for us. But we never again attacked another aircraft from behind.

Notes on documentation

The results of this, the first major air battle, are still a matter of controversy. British claims are that only 24 Wellingtons were involved, of which 12 failed to return and three were severely damaged. It was thought that 12 German fighters were shot down.

The OKM report speaks of 52 bombers of which 36 were shot down. Two German aircraft were shot down. It would seem clear that this is a considerable overestimation, probably

---

[30] A radio signal back to base requesting the compass heading to steer for home.

because of duplicated claims. What is clear is that the I/ZG 76 reported 15 aircraft shot down, of which 13 were confirmed while one aircraft shot down by each of Captain Falck and Lieutenant Gollob were returned.

Aircraft shot down were credited as follows:

Falck – one, Fresia – two, Lent – two, Gröning – one, Jäger – one, Fleischmann – one, Gresens – one, Uellenbeck – three, Graeff – one, Kalinowski – one.

Other units serving in Squadron 1 filed reports of aircraft shot down by Schumacher, Heilmayr, Steinhoff, Holck, Jung, Schmidt and Peters.

Appendix B

Memories of Peace

By C.G. Grey

A German communiqué was recently quoted in a London newspaper as stating that Squadron Leader Falck, a member of the Schumacher formation, had, with his command, particularly distinguished himself in recent fighting over Heligoland. The title of squadron leader is merely one of our usual newspaper inaccuracies. He is probably a captain in rank and commands a jagdstaffel of a gruppe commanded by Oberst-Leutnant Schumacher in a geschwader unnamed.

The German kette corresponds to our flight: a staffel is a squadron: a gruppe would be a wing if we had such a thing as a definite formation: and a geschwader would correspond to our group, but it is a single permanent entity like a regiment in our army, and its name is borne by all its gruppen and staffeln. The Richthofen Geschwader, purely a fighter organisation, was the first thing of the kind in the German Luftwaffe. Today, I believe, a geschwader may include bomber and fighter gruppen.

Those who were at the opening of the York Aerodrome and the festivities associated therewith will no doubt have recognised Captain Falck as the right-hand figure in the photograph of a cheerful group of German pilots with Lieutenant Colonel Schumacher and Dr Dietrich.

I met him first when he was ober-leutnant in a staffel of the Richthofen Geschwader at Damm, near Jüterbog, where there is a monument to record that the great Immelmann learned to fly there. Incidentally, an ober-leutnant is a full lieutenant and an oberst-leutnant is a lieutenant colonel. English people are liable to mix them just as they mix our adjutant, which is an appointment and not a rank, with the French adjutant, who is a non-commissioned officer, corresponding to our warrant officer, such as a sergeant major.

Afterwards various of our English sport flyers and officers of the RAF met Falck at Frankfort [sic] meetings and at York, to which meeting he flew with about half a dozen young German pilots in sporting aeroplanes. He was particularly well liked.

His name fits him well for he looks like a falcon. He is not big enough to be an eagle. But he has the aquiline features which artists and novelists love to ascribe to heroic bird-men.

He speaks excellent English and is a charming companion. He reminds me much of our great air fighter of the last war, Jimmy McCudden, VC, DSO, MC. He has the same boyish manner, the same straightforward look, and, I am sure, the same dispassionate attitude towards killing his official enemies, who might be his personal friends.

McCudden always described himself as a hired assassin, and never had any animosity against anybody. That sort is always the most dangerous fighter, for the coolness of his head is never disturbed by the heat of his emotions.

The day on which the great von Richthofen was killed McCudden came into my office really moved and said mournfully – 'And I did so want to talk it all over with him after the war'. I can only hope that Falck's English friends will be more fortunate.

McCudden was killed three days after he had finished writing that magnificent book, *Five Years in the R.F.C.*, which was republished not long ago under the misleading title, *Flying Fury*. Shortly after his death one of his best friends remarked – 'What a great argument McCudden and von Richthofen must be having.' – C.G.G.

The comparison in the last few paragraphs between Wolfgang Falck and Jimmy McCudden is strangely prophetic. The author had the great privilege of arranging a meeting between Oberst Falck a.D. and Group Captain Harris DFC, at the Royal Air Force Club in Piccadilly on the evening of Thursday 29th March 1984.

On being introduced that evening to Oberst Falck, Paul Harris smiled as they shook hands and said, with a twinkle in his eye: 'Well old chap, all I can say is you must have been one bloody awful shot, for which I am truly grateful.' Over dinner the talk was of Wellingtons and Messerschmitts. Forty-four years rolled away to reveal two real old professionals. There was no rancour, no animosity, but rather an instant rapport between two minds united in their common love of flying. As the evening wore on I would not have been at all surprised to have seen two shadowy figures in World War I uniforms, McCudden and von Richthofen, standing behind Paul Harris and Wolfgang Falck's chairs listening intently as the Battle of Heligoland Bight was fought all over again.

The two veteran airmen parted that evening with the promise to meet again at the forthcoming Farnborough Air Show, and Falck handed me an envelope containing a description of his Lady-Bug Squadron which he commanded on 18th December 1939.

Appendix C

The Marienkäfer (Lady-Bug) Squadron
by Wolfgang Falck

In the summer of 1939, Wing I of Destroyer Wing 76 was equipped with the Me 110. Before that date, we had been flying the Me 109. I was squadron leader of the 2nd Squadron at that time.

With the acquisition of the Me 110 a new era dawned for us, at least as far as flying was concerned: a transition from the single-engined to the twin-engined aircraft, from the single-seater to a plane that could carry a second man on board – a radio operator and gunner at the same time! In addition a reorganisation of our wing, even if in practice this was actually little more than a change of name, and the new Me 110 *Destroyer*, formally called *Heavy Hunter*, were further elements contributing to the initiation of a new chapter in the history of military aviation. Subsequently, and in order to make our wing appear as a homogeneous unit, a new squadron insignia had to be created.

Now, to design a squadron insignia has always been somewhat problematic. In the first place, the design has to be timeless and last for a long while. In the second place, it must be a true reflection of the spirit and the tasks of the unit and, in accordance with the circumstances prevailing at that particular moment, it had to reflect and symbolise the spirit of the times.

There were several things that had to be taken into account when designing our insignia, concerning the colours. As my convictions tended to be conservative, I preferred the colours of the old German 'Reich', which were black, white and red. Furthermore, as seven had always been my lucky number, I also wanted to have it included in some way. Then we needed a symbol of good fortune, so I selected the Marienkäfer or lady-bug, well known for this, and very much favoured by me. The outcome of this combination finally resulted in a red lady-bug with seven black spots on a white field in the shape of an escutcheon; our squadron insignia had been created.

This insignia was immediately adopted with great enthusiasm by all members of the squadron; the aircraft mechanics worked overtime, day and night, to affix it to all our aeroplanes as quickly as possible.

One day we had firing practice at ground targets. There were only a few planes operational and we had just received a new aircraft. Due to the last minute rush, the squadron insignia had not been affixed to it yet. However, being so short of planes, it also had to participate in the target practice even if the Marienkäfer was missing. As fate would have it, it was precisely that plane that flew too low when trying to fire at the targets. It hit the ground, and the pilot was killed. From that day on, no pilot or radio operator would ever even touch an aircraft that did not bear our insignia!

The war started on 1st September 1939, and we were based in Silesia from where we directed our first attacks against Poland. Without any casualties on our side, the Marienkäfer Squadron was highly successful, and press and radio mentioned it for the first time. In my capacity as squadron leader, I had a small square frame painted with a red lady-bug and its black spots on a white background. Whenever I landed, I used to open the cockpit window as soon as the aircraft touched down and fixed this frame to it in a special holder. In addition, we recorded every plane the squadron had shot down by marking a black stroke on the white field of the escutcheon.

After spending some time on the 'West Wall' over the winter, our squadron was transferred to Jever on 17th December. It was the first time we had flown over the sea in the west and we were issued with life jackets, rubber dinghies and emergency radio sets, all in the middle of that exceptionally cold winter.

On the next day, 18th December, we began our first preparatory flight, in groups of four each, to get acquainted with the sea, the coast, and the islands. I was flying in a north-westerly direction from the island of Borkum in the North Sea, when we suddenly heard, via the radio, that the British were heading for Wilhelmshaven and that we should fly to the Wilhelmshaven Heligoland area immediately. We could see the anti-aircraft bursts from far away, and shortly afterwards also the British bomber formation. They were Wellingtons, and our Me 109 hunters were circling around them. We were just approaching the British, when they deviated onto a north-westerly heading. We attacked at once and managed to shoot down a few planes in spite of the heavy fire from the British tail guns. My plane had been hit several times, the starboard engine had stopped functioning, fuel was running out of numerous holes on the surface, and the ammunition for the four machine guns contained in the fuselage, was in flames. To make things worse, I had to open the cabin window because of the dense smoke inside the cockpit. Shortly afterwards, the port engine packed up as well. Nevertheless, thanks to the altitude, the light weight resulting from the loss of fuel, the expended and burned-out ammunition, as well as a favourable wind, I was finally able to land smoothly with the accuracy of a glider, onto the aerodrome on the island of Wangerooge.

As it turned out after the battle, the Me 109 squadron led by First Lieutenant 'Mäcki' Steinhoff, who was to become German Air Force inspector later on, had been the most successful Me 109 squadron, and my own, the best among the Me 110s. The RAF had suffered terrible losses, although they were not quite as enormous as had been initially assumed by the Germans, although these claims had been made in good faith.

Now that the combat was over, on 19th December, the group commodores LTC Schumacher, First Lieutenant Steinhoff and I, as well as two more pilots, were summoned to Berlin to report on those events to the national and international press. Through the neutral countries, our reporting also reached England. This explains why, in my personal opinion, I was honoured with the greatest distinction that could ever have been attained during the war. Mr Grey, editor of the magazine, *The Aeroplane*, whom I had already met before the war, published an article about me! The fact that he should have described an 'enemy', who had victoriously fought against the air force of his own country, with so much fairness and objectivity has always flattered me much more than any piece of coloured ribbon or bit of engraved tin on my uniform.

Thus the lady-bug became famous and we could hardly cope with the multitude of letters and lady-bugs of all shapes and sizes and for all possible and impossible uses we received.

Appendix D

Claims and Losses

Only two claims can be confirmed with absolute certainty.

N2936 This Wellington was shot down by Helmut Lent. Records clearly state that the first aircraft he shot down crashed on the island of Borkum. Herbie Ruse stated, in correspondence with the author, that he was the pilot of the Wimpy that crash-landed on Borkum.

Me 109 piloted by Leutnant Stiegler. Records again state that it was his fighter that was lost when its wing tip touched the sea and it cartwheeled and disappeared. Peter Lemon has also been in contact with the author to say that it was his rear gunner, Corporal Kidd, who fired a long burst at a pursuing Me 109 and, as the fighter broke off the attack and turned clear, possibly because it had been hit, its wing tip just brushed the surface, and the fighter cartwheeled into the water.

All the other claims can only be supposition based on the evidence from:

The Operations Record Books of 149, 9 and 37 Squadrons
3 Group reports on the events of 18th December 1939.
The Luftwaffe War Diaries by Cajus Bekker.
Les Aiglons, combat aeriens de la Drôle de Guerre by
 C.J. Ehrengardt; C.F. Shores; H. Weisse and J. Foreman.
Personal account of the battle by Group Captain P. I. Harris,
 DFC.

N2935 Herbie Ruse also confirmed that he was flying as one of a pair with Flying Officer Thompson. They broke away westwards across the Friesian Islands and he and Thompson were still flying together as a pair when they were attacked by an Me 110. Bekker states that Lent spotted two Wellingtons and attacked and shot down the rear one which forced-landed on Borkum. Lent then went on to pursue the second Wellington and brought it down in the sea close by Borkum. Ruse confirms that Flying Officer Thompson's aircraft crashed into the sea just to the west of Borkum. Thompson probably fell to Helmut Lent.

N2889 Bekker relates that the Geschwader Commader, Carl Schumacher, shot down a bomber and: 'For days to come the wreck of the Wellington he had dispatched remained sticking out of the mud-flats off Spiekeroog.' This island is 20 kilometres to the west of the route taken by Kellett's main formation. A body was later washed ashore and identified as Aircraftman Geddes, the rear gunner from N2889. Ruse confirms that both Wimberley and Lewis broke away to port with the rest of 37 Squadron. It is therefore probable that N2889 was brought down by Schumacher.

N2888 Five aircraft from 37 Squadron took the course to the west over the Friesian Islands. N2903 was the sole survivor that made it back to Feltwell. This leaves only Wimberley's aircraft to be accounted for. Flying Officer Wimberley was picked up by a German patrol boat after he ditched his aircraft in the vicinity of Borkum. Bekker states that: 'Lent brought down a third Wellington which had already been shot up. This plunged into the sea 15 miles north-west of Borkum.' It could only have been N2888 as all the others have been accounted for. Because the Wellington had already been badly shot-up, Lent was not credited with this last victory, which was more than likely N2888.

N2904 Peter Grant observed Squadron Leader Hue-Williams racing far ahead of his formation in an attempt to catch up with Kellett's formation. At 2.45 p.m. (German time), according to Bekker, Oberleutnant Gordon Gollob attacked the rear left Wellington in a formation of seven. The only possible way in which seven Wellingtons could have been flying together at that particular time was if Hue-Williams had caught up with and joined Paul Harris's six Wimpys on the starboard side of the big diamond. The stated position of the encounter is however inconsistent with the known course of Harris's formation. It is impossible that seven Wellingtons were flying in formation to the north-west of Langeoog, 40 kilometres due west of Harris's flight-path. Ten minutes *before* that, Falck and Fresia had broken up the only other formation of six bombers, i.e. Flying Officer Guthrie's two flights, out on the port side of the big diamond. *If* Gollob did attack a formation of seven aircraft, then he must have mis-reported his position and it is possible that his victim was Hue-Williams.

N2962 Paul Harris was insistent that Flying Officer Speirs was shot down by an Me 110. There were only four other Me 110s that reported their position as being anywhere within 20 kilometres of Kellett's main formation. Two of these 110s were engaged in attacking 9 Squadron's formation out on the port side of the big diamond. This only leaves Oberfeldwebel Fleischmann or Feldwebel Gröning that could have been responsible for dispatching Speirs.

N2939 and N2940 Bekker relates how Wolfgang Falck and his number two, Fresia, ran into a close formation of returning Wellingtons at 2.35 p.m. (German time). In *Les Aiglons* it describes how Falck attacked the right-hand bomber in the last formation and watched it explode in mid-air. Fresia attacked the plane on the left-hand side of the same section and watched it crash into the sea with its port engine in flames. As Falck and Fresia raced in from the west, Guthrie's six aircraft would have been the first 'close formation' they encountered. In the 3 Group report it states that an aircraft in Flying Officer Allison's section appeared to explode and another was seen to go down with its port engine on fire. Sergeant Petts also reported that an aircraft in Allison's section was seen to receive a direct hit and fell to bits. Pilot Officer Lines was supposed to be in the number two position and Pilot Officer Challes in the number three position. However, Sergeant Murphy in Macrae's plane reported that the aircraft in Allison's section were changing position so it is not possible to be precise about Falck and Fresia's victims.

APPENDIX D 163

N2941 Fresia was credited with two victories and this would have been the remaining aircraft in Allison's section, possibly Allison himself.

N2872 Falck was shot down by the last aircraft he attacked. The 3 Group report states that Squadron Leader Guthrie was attacked by an Me 110 which he shot down in flames before he himself went down. If the aircraft of 9 Squadron were flying in their allotted positions then it is probable that Falck shot down Lines and Guthrie while Fresia put paid to Challes and Allison.

Me 109 piloted by Oberleutnant Fuhrmann. This fighter pilot attacked a flight of *four* Wellington bombers as related by Bekker. Paul Harris recalled watching an Me 109 attack Kellett's four Wimpys several times before it curled away seaward trailing a cloud of smoke. There was only one formation of four Wellingtons when the bombers cleared the flak over Wilhelmshaven and that was Kellett's four. Bekker states that Fuhrmann attacked a Wellington that flew on the left of a flight of four. As this was probably the position of Flying Officer Riddlesworth at the time, it is reasonable to presume that Fuhrmann fell to Aircraftman Second Class Gouldson, the rear gunner, assisted by the tail gunners in the adjacent Wimpys.

With JG1 claiming a total of 27 *confirmed* victories, it must be stressed that the above accounts are only the author's interpretation of the available evidence. It is not intended to be the final word on the battle as other records, not available to the author, may exist which would cast a different light on the events that day. What is known for certain is that *only ten* Wellingtons were shot down during the battle and logic dictates that a Wimpy can only be shot down once.

THE BATTLE OF HELIGOLAND BIGHT 1939

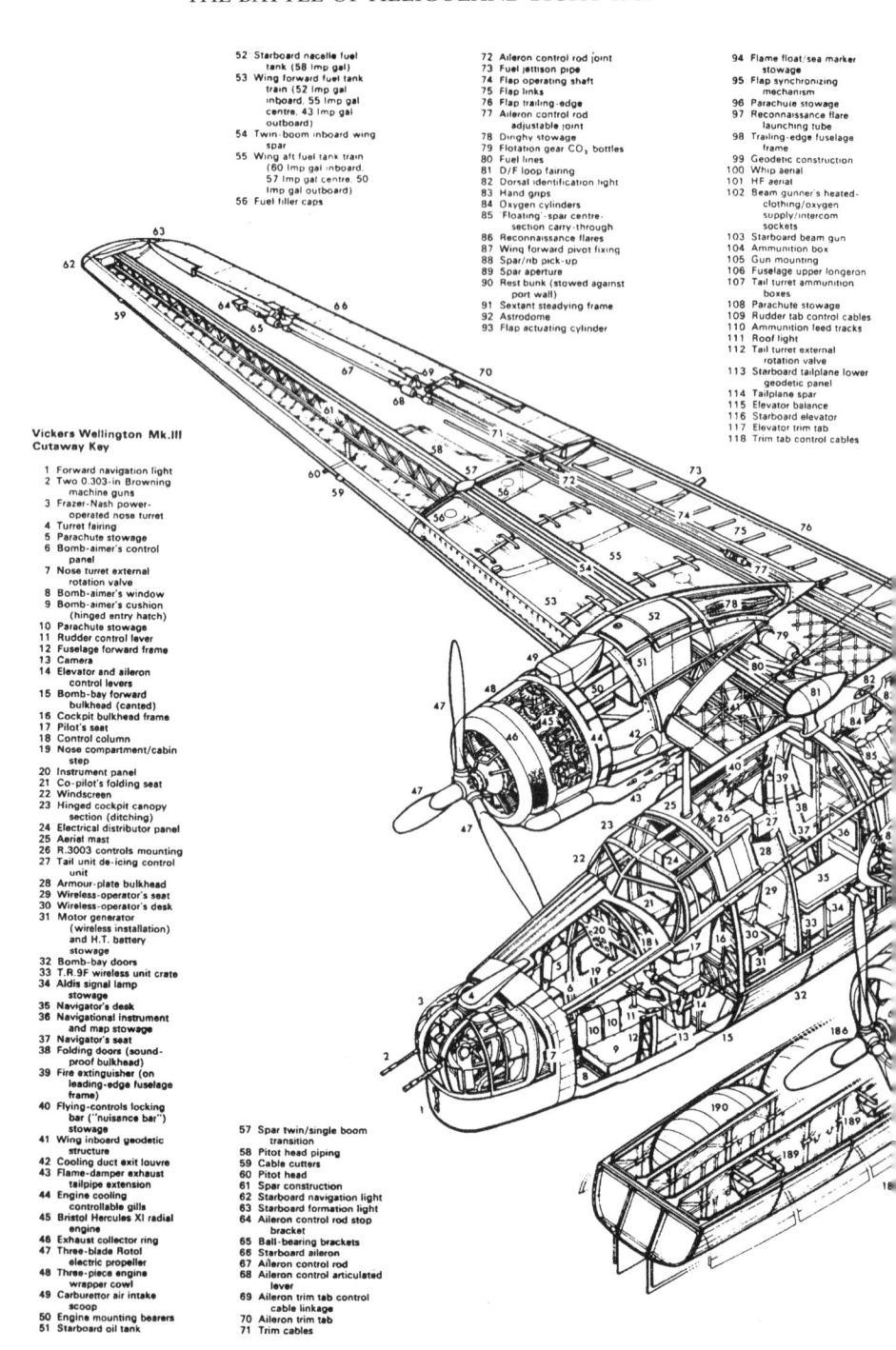

Vickers Wellington Mk.III Cutaway Key

1. Forward navigation light
2. Two 0.303-in Browning machine guns
3. Frazer-Nash power-operated nose turret
4. Turret fairing
5. Parachute stowage
6. Bomb-aimer's control panel
7. Nose turret external rotation valve
8. Bomb-aimer's window
9. Bomb-aimer's cushion (hinged entry hatch)
10. Parachute stowage
11. Rudder control lever
12. Fuselage forward frame
13. Camera
14. Elevator and aileron control levers
15. Bomb-bay forward bulkhead (canted)
16. Cockpit bulkhead frame
17. Pilot's seat
18. Control column
19. Nose compartment/cabin step
20. Instrument panel
21. Co-pilot's folding seat
22. Windscreen
23. Hinged cockpit canopy section (ditching)
24. Electrical distributor panel
25. Aerial mast
26. R.3003 controls mounting
27. Tail unit de-icing control unit
28. Armour-plate bulkhead
29. Wireless-operator's seat
30. Wireless-operator's desk
31. Motor generator (wireless installation) and H.T. battery stowage
32. Bomb-bay doors
33. T.R.9F wireless unit crate
34. Aldis signal lamp stowage
35. Navigator's desk
36. Navigational instrument and map stowage
37. Navigator's seat
38. Folding doors (sound-proof bulkhead)
39. Fire extinguisher (on leading-edge fuselage frame)
40. Flying-controls locking bar ("nuisance bar") stowage
41. Wing inboard geodetic structure
42. Cooling duct exit louvre
43. Flame-damper exhaust tailpipe extension
44. Engine cooling controllable gills
45. Bristol Hercules XI radial engine
46. Exhaust collector ring
47. Three-blade Rotol electric propeller
48. Three-piece engine wrapper cowl
49. Carburettor air intake scoop
50. Engine mounting bearers
51. Starboard oil tank
52. Starboard nacelle fuel tank (58 Imp gal)
53. Wing forward fuel tank train (52 Imp gal inboard, 55 Imp gal centre, 43 Imp gal outboard)
54. Twin-boom inboard wing spar
55. Wing aft fuel tank train (60 Imp gal inboard, 57 Imp gal centre, 50 Imp gal outboard)
56. Fuel filler caps
57. Spar twin/single boom transition
58. Pitot head piping
59. Cable cutters
60. Pitot head
61. Spar construction
62. Starboard navigation light
63. Starboard formation light
64. Aileron control rod stop bracket
65. Ball-bearing brackets
66. Starboard aileron
67. Aileron control rod
68. Aileron control articulated lever
69. Aileron trim tab control cable linkage
70. Aileron trim tab
71. Trim cables
72. Aileron control rod joint
73. Fuel jettison pipe
74. Flap operating shaft
75. Flap links
76. Flap trailing-edge
77. Aileron control rod adjustable joint
78. Dinghy stowage
79. Flotation gear CO_2 bottles
80. Fuel lines
81. D/F loop fairing
82. Dorsal identification light
83. Hand grips
84. Oxygen cylinders
85. Floating-spar centre-section carry-through
86. Reconnaissance flares
87. Wing forward pivot fixing
88. Spar/rib pick-up
89. Spar aperture
90. Rest bunk (stowed against port wall)
91. Sextant steadying frame
92. Astrodome
93. Flap actuating cylinder
94. Flame float/sea marker stowage
95. Flap synchronizing mechanism
96. Parachute stowage
97. Reconnaissance flare launching tube
98. Trailing-edge fuselage frame
99. Geodetic construction
100. Whip aerial
101. HF aerial
102. Beam gunner's heated-clothing/oxygen supply/intercom sockets
103. Starboard beam gun
104. Ammunition box
105. Gun mounting
106. Fuselage upper longeron
107. Tail turret ammunition boxes
108. Parachute stowage
109. Rudder tab control cables
110. Ammunition feed tracks
111. Roof light
112. Tail turret external rotation valve
113. Starboard tailplane lower geodetic panel
114. Tailplane spar
115. Elevator balance
116. Starboard elevator
117. Elevator trim tab
118. Trim tab control cables

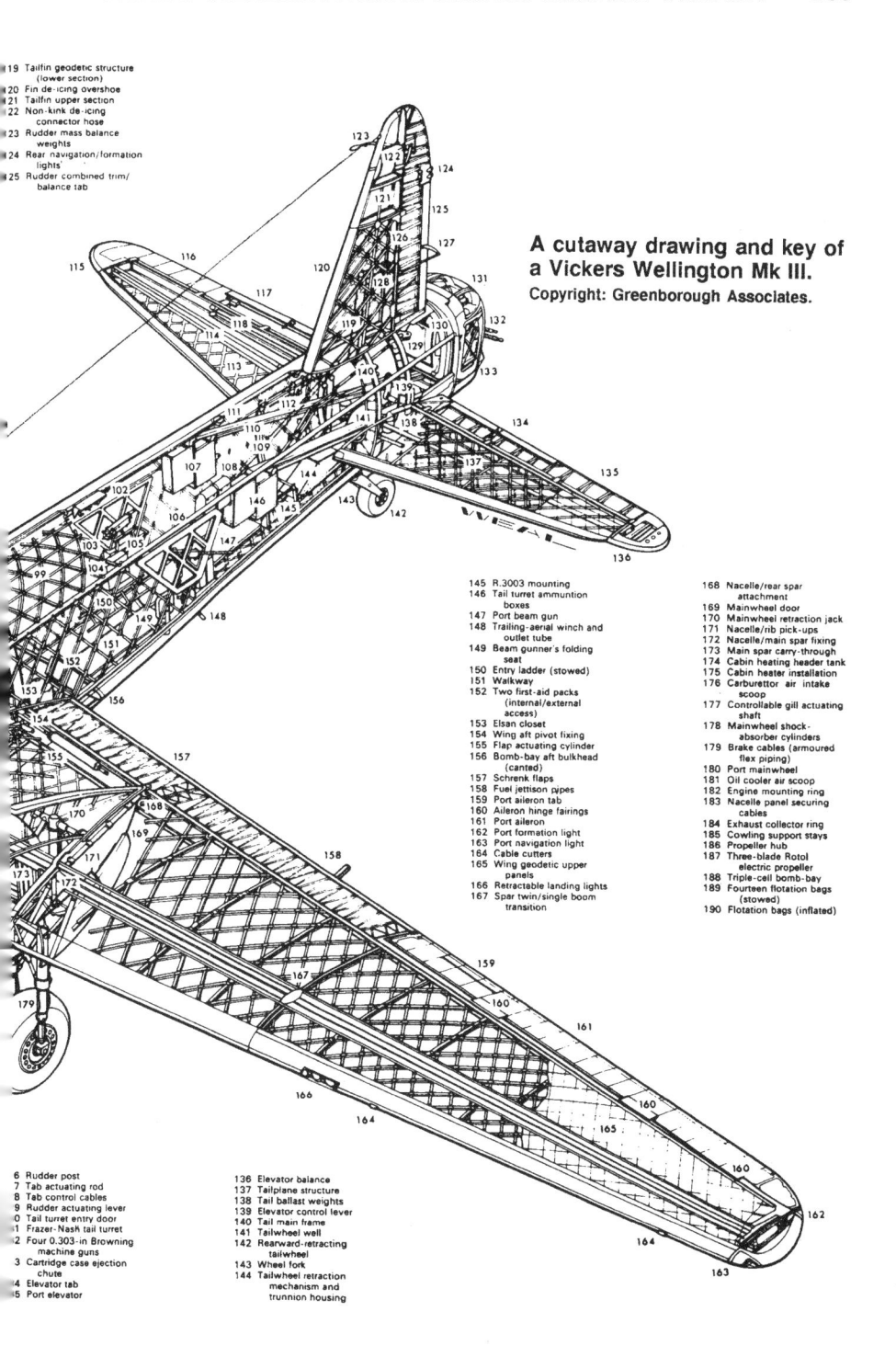

VICKERS WELLINGTON MK III CUTAWAY DRAWING WITH KEY 165

19 Tailfin geodetic structure (lower section)
20 Fin de-icing overshoe
21 Tailfin upper section
22 Non-kink de-icing connector hose
23 Rudder mass balance weights
24 Rear navigation/formation lights
25 Rudder combined trim/balance tab

A cutaway drawing and key of a Vickers Wellington Mk III.
Copyright: Greenborough Associates.

145 R.3003 mounting
146 Tail turret ammunition boxes
147 Port beam gun
148 Trailing-aerial winch and outlet tube
149 Beam gunner's folding seat
150 Entry ladder (stowed)
151 Walkway
152 Two first-aid packs (internal/external access)
153 Elsan closet
154 Wing aft pivot fixing
155 Flap actuating cylinder
156 Bomb-bay aft bulkhead (canted)
157 Schrenk flaps
158 Fuel jettison pipes
159 Port aileron tab
160 Aileron hinge fairings
161 Port aileron
162 Port formation light
163 Port navigation light
164 Cable cutters
165 Wing geodetic upper panels
166 Retractable landing lights
167 Spar twin/single boom transition

168 Nacelle/rear spar attachment
169 Mainwheel door
170 Mainwheel retraction jack
171 Nacelle/rib pick-ups
172 Nacelle/main spar fixing
173 Main spar carry-through
174 Cabin heating header tank
175 Cabin heater installation
176 Carburettor air intake scoop
177 Controllable gill actuating shaft
178 Mainwheel shock-absorber cylinders
179 Brake cables (armoured flex piping)
180 Port mainwheel
181 Oil cooler air scoop
182 Engine mounting ring
183 Nacelle panel securing cables
184 Exhaust collector ring
185 Cowling support stays
186 Propeller hub
187 Three-blade Rotol electric propeller
188 Triple-cell bomb-bay
189 Fourteen flotation bags (stowed)
190 Flotation bags (inflated)

6 Rudder post
7 Tab actuating rod
8 Tab control cables
9 Rudder actuating lever
0 Tail turret entry door
1 Frazer-Nash tail turret
2 Four 0.303-in Browning machine guns
3 Cartridge case ejection chute
4 Elevator tab
5 Port elevator

136 Elevator balance
137 Tailplane structure
138 Tail ballast weights
139 Elevator control lever
140 Tail main frame
141 Tailwheel well
142 Rearward-retracting tailwheel
143 Wheel fork
144 Tailwheel retraction mechanism and trunnion housing

Glossary

The list below gives equivalent wartime ranks in the Luftwaffe, RAF and USAAF.

Luftwaffe	Royal Air Force	US Army Air Force
1. Generalfeldmarschall	Marshal of the Royal Air Force	General (five star)
2. Generaloberst	Air Chief Marshal	General (four star)
3. General der Flieger	Air Marshal	Lieutenant General
4. Generalleutnant	Air Vice-Marshal	Major General
5. Generalmajor	Air Commodore	Brigadier General
6. Oberst	Group Captain	Colonel
7. Oberstleutnant (Obstlt)	Wing Commander (W/Cdr)	Lieutenant Colonel
8. Major	Squadron Leader (S/L & S/Ldr)	Major
9. Hauptmann	Flight Lieutenant (F/Lt)	Captain
10. Oberleutnant (Oblt)	Flying Officer (F/O)	First Lieutenant
11. Leutnant (Lt)	Pilot Officer (P/O)	Lieutenant
12. Stabsfeldwebel	Warrant Officer (W/O)	Warrant Officer
13. Oberfeldwebel (Ofw)	Flight Sergeant (F/Sgt)	Master Sergeant
14. Feldwebel (Fw)	Sergeant (Sgt)	Technical Sergeant
15. Unterfeldwebel	–	–
16. Unteroffizier (Uffz)	Corporal (Cpl)	Staff Sergeant
17. Hauptgefreiter	–	Sergeant
18. Obergefreiter	Leading Aircraftman (LAC)	Corporal
19. Gefreiter	Aircraftman First Class (AC1)	Private First Class
20. Flieger	Aircraftman Second Class (AC2)	Private

Luftwaffe Formations

Rotte	Two fighters working as a fighting pair.
Schwarm	Two Rotte.
Kette	A unit of three or four fighters.
Staffel	The nearest equivalent to an RAF squadron, 10-12 aircraft.
Gruppe	Three, occasionally four staffeln.
Geschwader	The Luftwaffe's largest formation; comprising approximately 100 aircraft, usually confined to one role; normally three gruppen.
Rottenflieger	Wing man, equivalent to the RAF's 'number two', also Rottenkamerad/Kaczmarek.
Rottenführer	Leader of a rotte.
Staffelkapitän	Luftwaffe officer commanding a staffel.

GLOSSARY

Geschwaderkommodore — Luftwaffe officer commanding a geschwader.
JG (Jagdgeschwader) — Fighter geschwader.
NJG (Nachtjagdge-schwader) — Nightfighter geschwader.
KG (Kampfgeschwader) — Bomber geschwader.
ZG (Zerstorergeschwader) — Literally 'Destroyer' and applied to bomber escorts, heavy fighters including the Me 110; thus ZG is a Heavy-Fighter Group.

For example, the designation I/ZG76 would refer to the first gruppe of Zerstorergeschwader 76, the Roman I indicating the gruppe. Individual staffeln within the gruppe would be designated with an Arabic numeral such as 2/ZG76.

Acknowledgements

I am greatly indebted to the following individuals for providing me with personal accounts, diaries and photographs from the period of the Second World War that is commonly referred to as the 'Phoney War'.

Paul Harris acquainted me with the historical significance of the Battle of Heligoland Bight after I had organised the recovery of his old Wimpy 'R for Robert' from Loch Ness in 1985. With Paul's help, I was able to locate Richard Kellet and 'Bunny' Austin. I was also able to track down David Marwood-Elton, Bill Wright, Peter Grant, Wolfgang Falck, 'Cheese' Lemon, Herbie Ruse and Harry Jones. Survivors from the very early days of the Phoney War who made it through to VJ Day (Victory over Japan, 15th August 1945), were few and far between. I was indeed fortunate to hear their personal stories and record their eye-witness accounts of the opening air battles of the war. From these accounts I was able to put a lot of meat on the bare bones of the official histories.

I am also indebted to Mrs J. Mullineaux; Tim Harris; Johannes Steinhoff; Joe Watts-Farmer (née Frazer-Nash); Joan Tarry; the Rev. Canon M.C.G. Sherwood and Ruth Stainforth (née Douglas-Cooper) for personal family details.

I would also like to thank the following organisations for permission to use extracts and photographs from their archives. The Imperial War Museum, London; Royal Air Force Museum, Hendon; Ministry of Defence, Air Historical Branch (Lacon House); The National Archive; London Film Productions Ltd; Bundesarchiv-Militararchiv, Freiburg; Gemeinschaft der Jagdflieger, Munich; British Libraries, Newspaper Library.

I am also indebted to the following for permission to quote from published works and private sources; Michael Joseph Ltd, for passages, particularly in Chapter 4, from *Bomber*

Command by Max Hastings; Octopus Books Ltd. for an extract from the *History of World War II* by A.J.P. Taylor; *Aeroplane Monthly* for an extract from a 1939/40 edition of *The Aeroplane*; the Controller of Her Majesty's Stationery Office for extracts from *The Strategic Air Offensive against Germany* by Webster and Frankland; *British Aviation, Ominous Skies* by H. Penrose; *Royal Air Force 1939-45* by D. Richards; Hansard; extracts from *Bomber Squadrons of the RAF and their Aircraft* by P.J.R. Moyes, published by MacDonald and Jane's 1976, reproduced by kind permission of Jane's Publishing Co. Ltd; Times Newspapers Ltd, for permission to reproduce extracts from 1939 copies of *The Times* and the *Sunday Times*; Jane's Publishing Co. Ltd, for extracts from *The Luftwaffe War Diaries* by Cajus Bekker; the Controller of Her Majesty's Stationery Office for transcripts of Crown-copyright records in The National Arhive, this includes material from the AIR files and the Operation Record Books of 149, 9 and 37 Squadrons; C.J. Ehrengardt for permission to reproduce Table 1 in Chapter 4; William Shirer © 1940, renewed 1968 by William Shirer, for an extract from *Berlin Diary*, Jane's Publishing Co. Ltd. for an extract from *Pathfinder Force* by G. Musgrove; *Jaegerblatt*, Journal of the German Fighter Pilots Association for an article by Oberfeldwebel O.K. Dombrowski; Jane's Publishing Co. Ltd. for the cutaway drawing of the Wellington Mk III.

In what can only be described as an incredible stroke of good luck, I located Mrs Sylvia Richardson, the sister of Flying Officer H.A. Innes DFC, and found that 'Sandy' had kept a *Diary of War 1939* which recorded the events during that period. I am also indebted to Mrs M. Vick for the article by her father, Flight Lieutenant J.J. Mullineaux DFM; Mr J.B. Petts for the article by his father, Flight Lieutenant F.C. Petts DFC and Bar, also Wolfgang Falck for the article on his Lady-Bug Squadron. The addition of all this first-hand material was greatly appreciated as it brought a close personal insight to these events and helped me to understand a little better the feelings and emotions of the combatants during those very early days of World War II. Above all, I am deeply indebted to Group Captain Paul Harris DFC for his recollections of events that took place such a long time ago. It could not have been an easy task to set down on paper such long forgotten memories. His notes, together with letters and personal discussions, were invaluable in helping me to piece together a picture of that period in our history that is sometimes overlooked.

While the recover of old 'R for Robert' from Loch Ness in 1985 was a unique and dramatic undertaking, the part played by a dedicated band of volunteers at Brooklands Museum must also be acknowledged and praised. It has been estimated that they spent over 100,000 man/woman hours, over a ten year period, restoring the aircraft to its present magnificent condition. The wonderful thing now is that you can go along to the museum and gaze at N2980 virtually as it was in 1939. You can touch it, look at its war wounds and then say a grateful thanks to Sir Barnes Wallis who gave us these superb aeroplanes at a time when we so desperately needed them. If your imagination is good enough, then you might even be able to see Paul Harris, Sandy Innes, 'Bunny' Austin, 'Jock' Watson, Jimmy Mullineaux and 'young' Doxsey climbing aboard their Wimpy to head off for their date with destiny at the 'Battle of Heligoland Bight'.

I consider myself privileged to have been part of an endeavour that helped to restore to the nation such a priceless part of our heritage.

Picture Acknowledgements

Plate section photographs courtesy of:
- Page 1: Top left: P.I. Harris
  Top centre, top right, middle: *The Second Great War: A Standard History*, published by Amalgamated Press Ltd. 1939-40
  Bottom: Imperial War Museum, C246
- Page 2: Top left, centre: Imperial War Museum, C1027, CH9856
  Top right: Richard Kellett
  Middle: *Wellington Special* by Alex Lumsden, Published by Ian Allan Ltd. 1974
  Bottom: T. Mason via Chaz Bowyer
- Page 3: Top and bottom: The Rev. Canon M. Sherwood
- Page 4: Top left: Imperial War Museum, C415
  Top centre: Mrs S. Richardson
  Top left: Imperial War Museum, C417
  Middle, left, centre and right: Imperial War Museum, C421, C426, C4280
  Bottom: Mrs S. Richardson
- Page 5: Top: Imperial War Museum, CH78
  Middle: The National Archives, Kew, Richmond, Surrey, CN5/15
  Bottom: Wolfgang Falck
- Page 6: All: *Die Ritterkreuztrager der Luftwaffe, Jagdflieger, 1939-1945*: by Ernst Obermaier, published by Verlag Dieter Hoffman, Mains, 1966
- Page 7: Top and middle: Wolfgang Falck
  Bottom left: Photo Cinema Video des Armées, Fort d'Ivry, Paris
  Bottom right: *Die Ritterkreuztrager der Luftwaffe, Jagdflieger, 1939-1945*: by Ernst Obermaier, published by Verlag Dieter Hoffman, Mains, 1966

Page 8:   Top: Harry Jones
          Middle: *Die Ritterkreuztrager der Luftwaffe, Jagdflieger, 1939-1945*: by Ernst Obermaier, published by Verlag Dieter Hoffman, Mains, 1966
          Bottom: Harry Jones
Page 9:   All: Wolfgang Falck
Page 10: Top: The British Library, Newspaper Library, Colindale, London
          Middle left: Wolfgang Falck
          Middle right and bottom: Harry Jones
Page 11: Top: Wolfgang Falck
          Bottom: Solo Syndication and Literary Agency
Page 12: Top and bottom right: BAE SYSTEMS
          Bottom left: Solo Syndication and Literary Agency
Page 13: Top: Author
          Middle: BAE SYSTEMS
          Bottom: Peter Grant
Page 14: Top: Aberdeen Journals Ltd.
          Middle: Brooklands Museum
          Bottom left: BAE SYSTEMS
          Bottom right: Brooklands Museum
Page 15: All: Brooklands Museum
Page 16: Top: Aeromodeller
          Bottom: Brooklands Museum

Images courtesy of:
Bomber Squadrons of the R.A.F. and their Aircraft by Philip Moyes. Janes Publishing Co Ltd. (Badges and Mottoes for 149, 9 and 37 Squadrons, Page 55)
Famous Bombers of the Second World War by William Green. Published in 1975 by Macdonald and Janes. Copyright: Greenborough Associates. (Vickers Wellington Mk III cutaway and key. Pages 164-165)

References

Chapter 1 A very good cottage on the foundations of a castle
i   Webster and Frankland, *The Strategic Air Offensive against Germany*, Volume 1, Trial and Error, p.191 (HMSO 1961).
ii   Penrose, H., *British Aviation Ominous Skies 1935-1939*, p.231 (HMSO 1980).
iii   *Hansard*, Volume 339, 1937-38, September 28th to October 6th, p.50.

Chapter 2 La Drôle de Guerre
iv   Armand van Ishoven, *Messerschmitt Bf 109 at war*, p.44-45 (Ian Allan Ltd 1977).
v   Ehrengardt, C.J. et al, *Les Aiglons*, p.26 (Charles-Lavauzelle, Paris-Limoges 1983).
vi   Richards, D., *Royal Air Force 1939-1945*, Volume 1, *The Fight at Odds*, Chapter II, p.44 (HMSO 1974).
vii   Letter to author from Bundesarchiv, Militärarchiv, Freiburg, 3 December 1986.
viii Bottomley, Air Commodore, Report on operation carried out by No. 99 Squadron on 14th December 1939 and covering letter dated 28th December 1939 (AIR files in The National Archives).
ix   Hastings, M., *Bomber Command*, Prologue, p.17 (Pan Books – 1981).
x   Webster and Frankland, *The Strategic Air Offensive against Germany*, Volume 1, Trial and Error, p.192 (HMSO 1961).

Chapter 4 The Battle of Heligoland Bight
xi   Kellett, R., Wing Commander, Narrative report dated 20th December, 1939 (AIR files PRO).
xii   Bekker, C. *The Luftwaffe War Diaries*, p.74

	(Macdonald 1967).
xiii	Bekker, C. *The Luftwaffe War Diaries*, p.77 (Macdonald 1967).
xiv	Kellett, R., Wing Commander, Narrative report dated 20th December, 1939 (AIR files PRO).
xv	Baldwin to Ludlow-Hewitt, letter dated 19th December, 1939 (AIR files PRO).
xvi	Ludlow-Hewitt to Baldwin, letter dated 24th December, 1939 (AIR files PRO).
xvii	Webster and Frankland, *The Strategic Air Offensive against Germany*, Volume 1, Trial and Error, p.198 (HMSO 1961).
xviii	Webster and Frankland, *The Strategic Air Offensive against Germany*, Volume 1, Trial and Error, p.201 (HMSO 1961).
xix	Bekker, C., *The Luftwaffe War Diaries*, p.79 (Macdonald 1967).
xx	HQ No. 3 Group report, 22nd December, 1939 (AIR files PRO).
xxi	Ludlow-Hewitt to Baldwin, 24th December, 1939 (AIR files PRO).
xxi	Webster and Frankland, *The Strategic Air Offensive against Germany*, Volume 1, Trial and Error, p.200 (HMSO 1961).
xxiii	Richards, D., *Royal Air Force 1939-1945*, Volume 1, *The Fight at Odds*, Chapter II, p. 47 (HMSO 1954).

Chapter 5 Blood, toil, tears and sweat

xxiv	Ehrengardt, C.J., Shores, C.F., Weisse, W. Foreman, J., *Les Aiglons, Combats Aériens de la Drôle de Guerre*, p.98 (Charles-Lavauzelle, Paris-Limoges 1983).
xxv	Lumsden, A., *Wellington Special* (Ian Allan Ltd 1974). Bowyer, C., *Wellington at War* (Ian Allan Ltd 1982).
.	Bowyer, C., *The Wellington Bomber* (William Kimber & Co. 1986). Andrews, C.F., *Vickers Aircraft Since 1908*, p.309 (Putnam 1969). Cooksley, P.G., *Wellington, Mainstay of Bomber Command* (Patrick Stephens 1987)

Chappel, F.R., *Wellington Wings* (William Kimber & Co. 1980).

xxvi Webster and Frankland, *The Strategic Air Offensive against Germany*, Volume 1, Trial and Error (HMSO 1961).

xxvii Bekker, C., *The Luftwaffe War Diaries*, p.76 (Macdonald 1967).

xxviii Baldwin to Ludlow-Hewitt, 19th December, 1939 (AIR files PRO).

xxix Ludlow-Hewitt to Baldwin, 24th December, 1939 (AIR files PRO).

xxx Richards, D., *Royal Air Force, 1939-1945*, Volume 1, *The Fight at Odds*, Chapter II, p. 47 (HMSO 1954).

xxxi Musgrove, G., *Pathfinder Force: A History of 8 Group*, p.181 (Macdonald and Janes 1976).

Index

A

Admiral Graf Spee, 53, 56, 94
Admiral von Scheer, 18, 20, 23
Allison, Flying Officer,
    Battle of Heligoland Bight 18.12.39, 60, 72, 84, 162-163
Anschluss, 14
Austin, Sergeant (later Wing Commander) Bunny
    navigator for 'R for Robert'
    background, 57-58
    account of Brunsbüttel raid, 21-23
    account of Heligoland Bight raid, 35-36
    at Battle of Heligoland Bight 18.12.39, 139, 141
    describes Battle of Heligoland Bight 18.12.39, 83, 90, 92
    lands, Coltishall, 81-82
    manned 'dustbin' under-turret, 52, 134, 142
    career after Battle of Heligoland Bight, 104
    account of 2nd January, 110-111
    on Paul Harris, 49-50
    Acknowledgements, 168

B

Baldwin, Jackie, (later Air Vice-Marshal) AOC
    No. 3 Group, comments on raid, 41-42
    Heligoland Bight raid de-brief, 100
    new attacks urged for 18.12.39, 44
    on formation flying, 97, 98
    on tactics, 120-122
Baldwin, Stanley, on aerial bombardment, 10
Battle of Britain Sunday 15.9.40, 46, 119, 123
Battle of Heligoland Bight 18.12.39, 56-106
Bekker, Cajus, 81
    claims and losses, 160-163
    on abandonment of daylight raids by British, 99
Belfrage, Bruce, radio announcer, 46
Benbow, Squadron Leader D.F. DFC, crew, 'R for Robert', 116
Berchtesgaden, 14
Berners Heath bombing range, 51
Bickerstaff, Corporal, 39, 40
Big Diamond formation, 61, 63, 71, 74, 81, 99, 162

INDEX

Birch, Flying Officer C.G. DFC, crew, 'R for Robert', 116
Black Thursday 14.10.43, 118, 119
Blenheim bombers, 8, 12, 16, 20, 23, 26, 143
Boeing B-29 bombers, at Japanese surrender ceremonies, 8
Bomber Command, 6-10, 13, 15, 17, 21, 26, 29, 30, 37, 41, 42, 44, 46, 47, 52, 53, 67, 69, 82, 86, 89, 92, 96, 100, 102, 103, 107, 116, 119, 120, 121, 122, 123, 124, 125
Bombing raid, RAF, first, 21, 50
Bona Lighthouse landing, 128
Bottomley, Air Commodore Norman, on formation flying, 42, 43, 44, 98, 121
Bowen, Sergeant, Wellington Pilot, 25
Brace, Sergeant, 39, 40
Brankmeier, Leutnant, 39
Briden, Flying Officer Michael F., pilot, N2961,
    Heligoland raid, 3.9.39, 32
    Battle of Heligoland Bight 18.12.39, 58, 60
    hit, 76, 81
    Paul Harris on Briden's ditching 89, 90
    Bunny Austin's recollection, 92
    at sea, 93
    Paul Harris's account, 130
    Sandy Innes's account, 138
Brooklands Museum agreed to house 'R for Robert', 128
Brough, Flight Lieutenant, bomber pilot, Heligoland Bight raid, 14.12.39, 39, 40
Brown, Pilot Officer Billy,
    second pilot, standing in for Sandy Innes, 21, 22
    crash in sea 89, 90
    Paul Harris's account, 130
Browning machine guns, 8, 40, 52, 74, 118, 131
Brummer, German ship hit, 3.12.39, 35-36
Brunsbüttel, 12, 20, 21, 23, 25, 26, 29, 50, 63, 124
Bryan-Smith, Squadron Leader M. DFC, crew, 'R for Robert', 116
Bulloch, Flying Officer H. L., pilot, 3.12.39, 32
    N2943, 58
    Battle of Heligoland Bight, 60
    landing at Mildenhall, 93
    2.1.40, 102, 107, 108, 109, 111, 113

C

Catalina, 127
Catt, Squadron Leader, Heligoland Bight raid, 14.12.39, 39
Challes, Flying Officer,
    Battle of Heligoland Bight 18.12.39, 60, 72, 84, 162, 163
Chamberlain, Neville, 14, 15, 17, 19
Chandler, Sergeant, trainee navigator, 128

Chapman, Lieutenant Commander, 109
Churchill, Winston (later Sir), First Lord, 19, 30, 52, 119, 124, 130
City of Edinburgh Squadron No. 603, 29
City of Glasgow Squadron No. 602, 29
Civilians not to be attacked, 17, 21, 28, 30, 64, 120, 130
Coalter, AC1, tail gunner, 63
Coastal Command, 26, 37, 116, 121
Coltishall, 60, 82, 92, 139
Cooper, Flying Officer, 39, 40
Copley, Corporal, 32
Copley, Leading Aircraftman J., 36
Cunningham, Wing Commander J.C., 27
Cuxhaven, 23, 25, 63, 68, 70

D
Dabinett, Squadron Leader, 50
The Dambusters, 9, 47, 117
Dawson, Pilot Officer M.B., crew, 'R for Robert', 116
Daylight raids, 6, 13, 29, 41, 43, 45, 53, 90, 98, 99, 101, 102, 103, 107, 110, 118, 122, 129, 141
Demer, Leutnant, 39
Dickore, Hauptmann, 32
Diehl, Leutnant Hermann, 68, 69, 70
Dietrich, Dr., 153
Dingle, Pilot Officer (later Flying Officer) A.C. crew, 'R for Robert', 116

pilot, 'R for Robert', 115
Dombrowski, Oberfeldwebel O.K.,
radio operator/rear gunner Me 110, 86
claims, 87
personal recollections, 129, 149-152
Acknowledgements, 169
Doran, Flight Lieutenant K.C., Wilhelmshaven 4.9.39, 8, 20, 23, 26, 27, 28
Dornier 17 bomber, 16
Dornier 18 flying boat, 26
Douglas-Cooper, Flying Officer J.S., 168
crew, 'R for Robert', 116
pilot, 'R for Robert', 115
Douhet, General Guilo, *The Command of the Air*, 118, 119
Downey, Flight Sergeant, 39, 40
Doxsey, Aircraftman First Class, front gun turret, 'R for Robert',
training, 52
front gun turret, 58
Battle of Heligoland Bight 18.12.39, 75, 134, 137, 140, 141
injured, 81, 82
missing, 104
Sandy Innes's diary 2.1.40, 108
Bunny Austin's account of 2.1.40, 112
Duguid, Flight Lieutenant A.G., pilot, N2984,
4.9.39 raid, 22, 25

INDEX

3.12.39 raid, 31, 32
Battle of Heligoland Bight 18.12.39, 58, 59, 60, 62, 75
'Dustbin' retractable under-turret, 42, 62, 73, 74, 79, 111, 131, 133, 134, 144, 146, 147, 148
Dyer, Flying Officer, Heligoland Bight raid, 14.12.39, 39

E

(East India) Squadron No. 149, Mildenhall, 20, 21, 22, 25, 30, 31, 32, 33, 36, 37, 44, 46, 47, 48, 49, 50, 51, 52, 54, 55, 57, 58, 60, 61, 81, 83, 84, 93, 110, 113, 114, 115, 116, 122, 125, 129, 130, 131, 132, 135, 144, 160, 169
Erillas, 92

F

Fairbanks, Douglas Jnr, 125
Falck, Staffelkapitan (later Oberst) Wolfgang,
    background 68
    Battle of Heligoland Bight 18.12.39, 70, 71, 72, 84
    lands at Wangerooge, 86, 88
    press conference, 94
    Dombrowski's account, 152
    Memories of Peace, 153-154
    meeting Paul Harris in 1984, 154-155
    The Marienkäfer Squadron, 156-159
    claims, 162-163

Acknowledgements, 168-169
Feltwell, 21, 44, 49, 57, 59, 60, 70, 77, 93, 115, 138, 144, 161
Fensome, Sergeant, Rear Gunner, 128
Five Years in the R.F.C., Jimmy McCudden, 154
Fleischmann, Oberfeldwebel, 84
Flying Barn Door, 10
Flying Fortress bombers, 9, 10, 114, 118
Ford, Sergeant, trainee navigator, 128
Frankland, historian, 118, 119, 169
Frazer-Nash, Archie, 51, 52, 131, 134, 141
Freya, early-warning radar, 37, 68, 69
Fuhrmann, Oberleutnant, 75, 84, 86, 163

G

'G for George', Lancaster bomber, Mohne Dam, 9
Geddes, A/C, tail gunner, N2889
    body recovered from wreckage, Battle of Heligoland Bight, 18.12.39, 80, 161
    buried with full military honours, 103
Geodetic design, 13, 14, 40, 74, 93, 111, 117, 137
German fighter defences 1939, 43, 67

German fleet, Wilhelmshaven, 17, 18, 20, 23
Gibson, Wing Commander Guy, VC, Dam Buster raid, 9
Glencross, Squadron Leader, 65
Gneisenau, 18, 20, 23, 25, 64, 70
Goebbels, 19, 94
Gollob, Oberleutnant Gordon,
   Battle of Heligoland Bight, 18.12.39, 76, 84, 88
   Ace, 101
   claims, 152, 161, 162
Goodwin, Group Captain, SASO at 3 Group HQ, 44
Göring, Hermann, 15, 16, 19, 27, 28, 29, 39, 83, 94, 112, 123
Grant, Cary, 125
Grant, Flight Lieutenant (later Wing Commander) Peter,
   4.9.39 raid, 23, 25
   Battle of Heligoland Bight, 18.12.39, 55, 60, 74, 76, 81, 97, 124
   lands at Honington, 93
   lectures on daylight attacks 103
   Paul Harris's account, 132, 133, 135
   Petts's account, 149
   claims, 161
   Acknowledgements, 168
Grey, C.G., 11
   Memories of Peace, 153-155
Grey, Mr, editor of *The Aeroplane*, 158
Griffiths, Flying Officer, pilot, 'R for Robert', 115, 116

Griffiths, Wing Commander J.F., 37-38
Gruppe I/ZG76, German fighter group, 39, 67, 68, 76, 84, 88, 101, 107, 113, 152, 167
Gun turret, power operated, 10, 16, 49, 53, 118
Guthrie, Squadron Leader,
   Battle of Heligoland Bight, 18.12.39, 60, 63, 73, 84
   breaks formation, 65, 97, 100
   under attack, 72
   casualties, 149
   claims, 162, 163

H

Halifax bombers, 9, 10, 102, 114, 116
Hampden bombers, 16, 27, 97, 102
Handley Page Harrow, 48, 57, 70, 129
Harris, Air Marshal Arthur T., 107
Harris, Mr, National Heritage Memorial Fund
Harris, Kit, 93
Harris, Squadron Leader (later Group Captain) Paul Ivor DFC,
   pilot 'R for Robert' 8, 21, 116, 127, 128
   Preface, 6-7
   Brunsbüttel raids, 1939, 8, 20, 21, 22, 23, 49
   Heligoland Bight raid, 3.12.39, 31, 32
   transferred to 149

INDEX

Squadron, Mildenhall, 1939, 25
background and experience 1939, 49
described by Bunny Austin, 22, 35
The Lion Has Wings, 48
takes charge of 'R for Robert', 53
tight formation philosophy, 51, 54, 98, 99, 100, 124, 162
formation flying and high level bombing, 54
summoned to Group Headquarters 17.12.39, 54, 55
flashback to childhood, 56
at Battle of Heligoland Bight, 18.12.39, 60, 65, 115
  account, 74-76, 89
  on formation flying, 65
claims, 83, 87, 88, 89
account of meeting with Ludlow-Hewitt, 100-101
pneumonia, 103, 110
subsequent career, 103
DFC, 103
sends 3 aircraft on daylight sweep, Heligoland Bight, 2.1.40, 107
personal recollection of Battle of Heligoland Bight, 129-136
meets Oberst Falck, 154-155
Acknowledgements, 169-170
Harrison, Sergeant, Wellington pilot, 25
Hayes, Pilot Officer, crew, 'R for Robert', 116
Healey, Flight Sergeant, Heligoland Bight raid, 14.12.39, 39, 40
Heathcote, Ginger, second pilot,
  Battle of Heligoland Bight, 18.12.39, 73
  Petts's account, 145-148
Heays, Sergeant
  Brunsbüttel, 4.9.39, 25
  Heligoland Bight raid, 3.12.39, 32
Heilmayr, Unteroffizier,
  Battle of Heligoland Bight, 18.12.39, 71, 84, 152
Heinkel 111 bomber, 16
Held, Feldwebel Alfred,
  Luftwaffe pilot, 23
  Decorated, 25
Heligoland Bight,
  target, 17
  The First Battle of Heligoland Bight, August 1914, 18
  4.9.39, 20
  map, 24
  reconnaissance missions, 26
  2.12.39, 52
  3.12.39, 30, 31, 32, 37, 53, 115, 131
  14.12.39, 37, 39, 42, 149
  Battle of, 18.12.39, 35, 44, 45, 60, 61, 119, 56-106, 132-133, 136, 141, 144, 158
  see also Battle of Heligoland Bight, 18.12.39

daylight sweep, 2.1.40, 107
'R for Robert' 117, 122, 128
outcome, 123, 125
900 bomber raid, 123-124
German fleet, 143
Harris and Falck discuss, 155
Historical significance, 168
Henderson, Sergeant Harry, ground crew, 602 Squadron, 29
Henz, Oberleutnant, 39, 84
Herget, Leutnant, 107, 113
Hetherington, Flight Lieutenant, 39, 40, 43
His Majesty's Submarine *Salmon*, hits German cruisers, 37, 38
Hitler, Adolf, 10, 11, 13, 14, 15, 19, 47, 112, 119, 124
HMS *Arethusa*, 18, 45
HMS *Ark Royal*, 27
HMS *Courageous*, 26
HMS *Edinburgh*, 29
HMS *Emden*, 18, 26, 123
HMS *Hood*, 27, 28
HMS *Mohawk*, 29
HMS *Nelson*, 27
HMS *Renown*, 27
HMS *Rodney*, 27
HMS *Royal Oak*, 27-28
HMS *Southampton*, 28, 29
Hogan, Flight Lieutenant H.A.V., 52
Holley, Sergeant Tom, 79, 103
Hough, Sergeant, navigator, 59, 62
Hue-Williams, Squadron Leader,

Battle of Heligoland Bight, 18.12.39, 60, 65, 84
losing formation, 76, 77, 100
Air Vice-Marshal Baldwin's report, 97
claims, 161, 162

I
Innes, Pilot Officer (later Flying Officer) Herome Alexander (Sandy) DFC, 21, 35, 36
diary entry 15.12.39, 53
account of 14.12.39 raid, 42-43
diary entry 17.12.39, 54
second pilot, 'R for Robert' 53
joins RAF 1939, 57
posted to No. 149 squadron, 57
Battle of Heligoland Bight, 18.12.39, 142, 143
aims bombs, 65
lands Coltishall, 92
account, 92-93
claims, 96
decorations, 103, 134
daylight sweep, Heligoland Bight, 2.1.40, 107-110, 113
death, 104, 134
Christmas Day diary entry, 105
last diary entry, 105
pilot 'R for Robert', 115
crew 'R for Robert', 116
in Paul Harris's recollection, 136-141
Acknowledgements, 169
International Aviation

INDEX

Exhibition, XXVth, Brussels, 48

J
Jever, 32, 39, 67, 68, 69, 70, 71, 72, 78, 86, 88, 101, 151, 157
Jones, Harry
    Battle of Heligoland Bight, 18.12.39, 78-79
    prisoner of war, 80, 103
    Acknowledgements, 168
Junkers 87 bomber, 16

K
Kellett, Wing Commander (later Air Commodore) Richard, DFC, AFC,
    Heligoland Bight raids, 6, 31, 36, 37, 40, 52, 54, 56, 59, 60, 63, 66, 123, 131, 132, 133, 134-141, 162, 163
    attacks Wilhelmshaven, 67, 70
    joins 149 Squadron, 52
    prewar flying career, 52
    World Long Distance Record, 52
    summoned to Group Headquarters 16.12.39, 54
    formation flying, 54, 62, 96, 121, 133
    Scharnhorst and Gneisenau, 64
    claims, 69, 83, 87, 88, 102
    report, 82, 101
    landing at Mildenhall, 93
    survives Battle of Heligoland Bight, 97
    Paul Harris's high opinion, 99-100
    outcome, 102
    prisoner of war, 102
    death, 102
    DFC, 109
    picked up by radar, 122
Kelly, Flight Sergeant,
    4.9.39, 25
    Heligoland Bight, raid 3.12.39, 32
    18.12.39, 60, 75
    pilot, N2894, 58
    Wellington pilot, 59
Kemp, Bob,
    Battle of Heligoland Bight, 18.12.39, 73
    Petts's account, 147, 148
Kidd, Corporal,
    Battle of Heligoland Bight, 18.12.39, 76, 160
Kiel Canal, 21, 22, 23, 95

L
'Lady Bug' Squadron, 68, 73, 155
    account by Wolfgang Falck, 156-159
Lamb, Squadron Leader L.S.,
    Brunsbüttel 1939, 8, 20, 27, 28
    attacked by German fighters, 23
    dropped bombs on Merchantman, 25
Lancaster bombers, 9, 10, 114, 117, 124
Leipzig, 18, 37, 121
Lemon, Flying Officer 'Cheese', 184

landed Feltwell, 93
  approaching
  Wilhelmshaven, 66, 76
  Battle of Heligoland Bight
  18.12.39, 60, 63
  Wellington limps home, 77,
  87, 132
  prisoner of war, 103
  Berlin Airlift, 103
  Acknowledgements, 168
Lent, Oberleutnant Helmut
  claim, 152, 161
  interviewed, 78-81, 84
  press conference, 94
  war service, 101
Lewis, Flying Officer,
  Battle of Heligoland Bight
  18.12.39, 60, 77, 161
  shot down, 80, 84
Lewis, Pilot Officer,
  Heligoland Bight raid,
  14.12.39, 40
  crash, 39
Liberator bombers, 114
Liddell, Alvar, radio announcer, 46
Lindley, Squadron Leader W.J.H., 27
Lines, Pilot Officer,
  Battle of Heligoland Bight,
  18.12.39, 60, 72, 84
  Sandy Innes's account, 138,
  claims, 162, 163
The Lion Has Wings, 47, 95, 124, 125
Little, Sergeant, trainee
  navigator, 128
Littlejohn, Pilot Officer, crew,
  'R for Robert', 116
Loch Ness, 114, 115, 126, 127, 128, 168
Loch Ness Wellington
  Association Ltd., 128
'Lord Haw-Haw', 94
Lossiemouth, 'R for Robert'
  stationed, 115, 126
Lucton, Pilot Officer, Trainee
  Navigator, 128
Ludlow-Hewitt, Air Chief
  Marshal Sir Edgar,
  Commander-in-Chief
  Bomber Command, 15
  force strength, 16
  Wilhelmshaven attack, 44
  flies to Norfolk to hear
  reports, 96
  formation tactics 97, 98
  arrives at Mildenhall, 100
  de-brief, 101
  discusses tactics with
  Baldwin, 120, 121, 122
Luftwaffe,
  early days, 6, 11, 15, 16, 153
  blitzkrieg, 19
  4.9.39, 23, 25
  26.9.39, 26, 27
  strength in 1939, 28, 29
  3.12.39, 32
  14.12.39, 39, 43
  propaganda, 48
  bombing accuracy, 51
  Lipetsk, secret base, 68
  responsibilities, 69
  Battle of Heligoland Bight,
  18.12.39, 69, 70, 71, 78, 81, 87, 92, 101
  discrepancy of losses, 83, 86, 88, 94
  after the battle, 88, 94

Battle of Britain, 105
  2.1.40, 113
  daylight raids, 118
  British triumph, 119

M

McCudden, Jimmy VC, DSO, MC, 154, 155
McKee, Squadron Leader, 37, 39, 40
McLaglen, Victor, 125
McPherson, Flying Officer, 19-20, 26
Macrae, Flying Officer Bill,
  Brunsbüttel raid, 20, 21, 25
  18.12.39, 60
  report, 72
  emergency landing, 73-74
  return journey, 87
  Innes, 93
  death, 103
Marienkäfer, see 'Lady Bug' Squadron
Marwood-Elton, Squadron Leader (later Group Captain) David,
  pilot, 'R for Robert', 126, 127
  ditches in Loch Ness, 114, 115, 126
  Acknowledgements, 168
May, Tom
  Battle of Heligoland Bight, 18.12.39, 65, 80
  prisoner of war, 103
Merton, Air Chief Marshal Sir W.H. KCB, CBE, OBE, CB, 116
Merton, Wing Commander, 115

Messerschmitt 109, 16, 25, 27, 32, 34, 36, 38, 39, 40, 42, 62, 66, 68, 70, 71, 75, 76, 77, 84, 86, 88, 99, 137, 141, 142, 144, 145, 147, 151, 156, 158, 160, 163
Messerschmitt 110, 32, 39, 40, 42, 67, 68, 70, 72, 73, 76, 78, 79, 86, 87, 88, 99, 101, 107, 108, 110, 111, 113, 134, 136, 137, 142, 146, 147, 148, 149, 150, 151, 156, 158, 161, 162, 163
Metz, Leutnant, 23
Miers, Flying Officer (later Wing Commander) G.P. DFC,
  pilot, 'R for Robert' 115
  crew, 'R for Robert' 116
Mildenhall, 62, 70, 93, 95, 100, 104, 105, 125, 141
  No. 99 Squadron, 14
  No. 149 (East India) Squadron, 20, 21, 23, 25, 30, 37, 44, 46, 49, 50, 51, 56, 57, 58, 59, 60, 115, 129, 144
  Target for Tonight, 46-47
Miller-Trimbusch, Leutnant, 67
Morrice, Sergeant, 107, 108, 111, 113
Mosquito aircraft, 9, 10, 47, 112, 114, 117
Muirhead, Pilot Officer G.H., 116
Mullineaux, Aircraftman First Class (later Flight Lieutenant) Jimmy J.
  tail gunner, 'R for Robert', 23, 52, 58, 82
  background, 58

186   THE BATTLE OF HELIGOLAND BIGHT 1939

Battle of Heligoland Bight 18.12.39, 82
  at debriefing, 100-101, 140
  career after, 103, 104
  personal account of raid, 141-143
  DFM, 103
  in Paul Harris's recollection, 133, 134
  Bunny Austin's account, 111, 112
Munich Agreement, 14
Murdoch, Sergeant, 59
Mustangs, 112, 119

N
National Heritage Memorial Fund, 128
Niemeyer, Unteroffizier, 84, 94
Nordholz, Luftwaffe group, 23, 25, 32, 68, 88
Nurnberg, 37

P
Perioli, Flying Officer (later Wing Commander) W.N., OBE, DFC, 115, 116
Petts, Sergeant (later Flight Lieutenant) F.C., DFC and Bar
  Battle of Heligoland Bight, 18.12.39, 60, 63, 162
  account of attack, 72-73
  landing at Sutton Bridge, 74, 93
  personal recollection of raid, 87, 143
  career after, 103
Pickard, Group Captain, P.C., DSO, DFC, 47
Pinkerton, Flight Lieutenant George, DFC,
  visits Captain Pohle, 29
Pocket battleship, Heligoland Bight, 20, 30, 53, 64, 119, 133
Pohle, Captain, 28, 29
Pointer, Oberleutnant, 94
Prien, Leutnant Gunter, 27
Pughe-Lloyd, Group Captain Hugh, 96
Purdy, Sergeant,
  Wellington pilot, 4.9.39 raid, 25
  Battle of Heligoland Bight, 60, 149
  landed at Honiton, 93
  no trace found, 103

R
'R for Robert', N2980,
  Preface, 6
  Introduction, 8
  new Wellington named, 30
  Paul Harris takes charge, 53-54
  cleared for take off, 58
  Battle of Heligoland Bight, 59, 62-64, 74, 81
  crew (medals awarded), 103, 116
  end, 112, 117
  14 mission, 115
  radar, 122
  recovery, 127-128, 168
Radar defences, German,
  early acquisition, 12
  Wangerooge, 68-69
  first used, 22

INDEX

Radio Direction Finding loop, 66
Ramshaw, Sergeant (later Wing Commander),
  Battle of Heligoland Bight, 18.12.39, 60, 74, 81, 92-93, 149
  death, 103
Reinecke, Captain, 68, 76
Restemeier, Captain, 39
Richards, Denis, *The Fight at Odds, 1939-1941*, 123
Riddlesworth, Flying Officer A.F.,
  4.9.39 raid, 25
  3.12.39 raid, 32
  Battle of Heligoland Bight, 18.12.39, 58-60, 75, 84, 93
  death, 102
  Me 109, 163
Roosevelt, Franklin D., 17, 18
Rosyth, 28
Rotherham, Lieutenant Commander, 63, 132
Ruhr Plan, 13, 17, 48, 98, 122
Ruse, Sergeant Herbie,
  Battle of Heligoland Bight, 18.12.39, 60, 65, 77-80, 84
  crash lands Wellington, 88-89
  captured, 88
  explanation for no bombs on board, 99, 120
  prisoner of war, 103
  N2936, 160-161

S

Sawallisch, Feldwebel, 39
Scharnhorst, 18, 20, 23, 25, 64, 70
Schillig Roads, 20, 31, 38, 44, 63, 64, 65, 71, 72, 77, 80, 144
Schuhart, Leutnant, 26
Schulze, Hauptegefreiter, 39
Schumacher, Oberstleutnant Carl,
  Luftwaffe pilot, 23, 25
  Wilhelmshaven, 67
  Battle of Heligoland Bight 18.12.39, 80, 81, 84, 86, 88-89, 152-153
  interviewed after, 94
  claims, 101
  2.1.40 raid, 107
  Sandy Innes diary, 110-111
  Wolfgang Falck recollection, 158
  N2889, 161
Scott, Flying Officer A.A, 116
Seliger, Captain, 68, 88
Shirer, William L., 94
Sinclair, S., 92
Slatter, Pilot Officer, 126
Smith, Flying Officer, 32, 39
Snagge, John, radio announcer, 46
Specht, Pilot Leutnant Gunter, 32
Speirs, Flying Officer J.H.C., 56, 60, 75, 84, 88, 162
Spitfires, 12, 15, 29, 78, 112
Squadrons:
  No. 9, badge and motto, 55
  Battle of Heligoland Bight, 25, 39, 59, 60, 61, 65, 71, 73, 74, 81, 87, 92, 96, 122, 131, 132, 135, 140, 144, 149, 162, 163

No. 37, badge and motto, 55
Battle of Heligoland Bight, 44, 54, 59, 61, 65, 66, 76, 77, 78, 81, 87, 93, 97, 115, 116, 122, 132, 133, 144, 145, 146, 160, 161
No. 107, 20, 23
No. 110, 20
No. 139, 20
No. 214, 48, 49, 57, 58, 65, 70, 129
No. 149 *see* (East India) Squadron
Squadron commanders, 1939, 54
Steinhoff, Staffelkapitan 'Macki',
  C.O. German nightfighter squadron 68, 70, 71
  Battle of Heligoland Bight 18.12.39, 84, 152
  decorations, 101
Stewart, Flight Lieutenant (later Wing Commander) J.B.,
  pilot 'R for Robert', 115, 116
  Wellington pilot, 20
  4.9.39, 25
  Heligoland Bight raid, 3.12.39, 31, 32, 34, 50, 53, 131
Steigler, Leutnant Roman, 76, 77, 84
  crash, 86, 87, 160
Storp, Leutnant, 27
Strachan, Squadron Leader A.J., 105
  crew 'R for Robert', 116
Summers, Mutt, 30

Swift, Pilot Officer J.R. 53, 108, 109, 111, 116

T
Tangmere, 78
Taylor, A.J.P., 11
Taylor, Corporal, 103
Taylor, Fred, 79
Templeman, Pilot Officer Paul, 66
Thompson, Flying Officer,
  Battle of Heligoland Bight 18.12.39, 60, 65, 77, 78
  shot down, 79, 84, 160, 161
Thompson, Captain E.G., 52
Tilley, Sergeant, 80, 103
Trenchard, Sir Hugh (later Lord), 10, 15, 47
Troitsch, Feldwebel Hans, 23, 25, 86
Tucker, Professor, 127
Turner, Flying Officer F.W.S.,
  Heligoland Bight raid 3.12.39, 32
  search for German fleet, 50
  Battle of Heligoland Bight 18.12.39, 56, 60
  attacked, 63
  landed at Mildenhall, 60, 93
  reported missing, 116
Turner, Pilot Officer, crew, 'R for Robert, 116

U
Uellenbeck, Leutnant,
  Battle of Heligoland Bight 18.12.39, 84
  attacked and wounded, 87

INDEX 189

attacks Wellington, 87
claims, 88
in Dombrowski's recollections, 86, 150-152

V
Vetter, Captain, 27
Vickers Wellesley monoplanes, 52
von Bülow-Bothkamp, Major Harry,
    1939 Messerschmitt pilot, 38, 68, 69, 78
    Battle of Heligoland Bight 18.12.39, 86
Von Richthofen, 110, 154, 155
    Richthofen Geschwader, 153

W
Wakcham, Mrs, 111
Wallis, Sir Barnes, 6, 9, 13, 14, 117
Walz, Feldwebel, 70, 73
Wangerooge, 22, 38, 68, 69, 72, 80, 84, 86, 87, 158
Watson, Aircraftman First Class 'Jock'
    wireless operator 'R for Robert', 57, 141
    fixes Briden's position, 90, 92
    believed shot down, 104, 112
Watt, Pilot Officer,
    crew, 'R for Robert', 116
    pilot, 'R for Robert', 115
Watt, Sergeant,
    Pilot, 'R for Robert' 115

Way, Flight Sergeant,
    Heligoland Bight raid 3.12.39, 32
Webster, historian, 118, 119
Wellington MF 628, 8
Wellington bomber,
    Barnes Wallis, 6
    in action, 6, 12, 16, 20, 21, 22, 23, 25, 30, 31, 32, 37, 38, 43, 44, 45, 50, 56, 58, 59, 63, 65, 67, 69, 76, 77, 87, 112, 113, 126, 131, 132, 141, 155
    under attack, 6, 72, 73, 78-81, 86, 93, 99, 102, 107, 150, 158
    at outbreak of war, 8, 48
    Mk 1A, 8, 30, 31, 141, 148
    number built, 8, 117
    history, 10, 14, 16, 46, 116, 117
    defence weapon, 10, 43
    claims and losses, 39, 40, 41, 43, 71, 72, 83, 87, 89, 101, 102-104, 109, 123, 149, 150, 151, 160-163
    formation flying, 42, 76, 89, 98, 150
    ventral gun turret, 42, 131
    high altitude bombing, 51
    blind spot, 71
    armour plating and self sealing tanks, 71, 92, 96, 107, 113
    propaganda, 95
    last built, 117
    Loch Ness Wellington Association Ltd., 126-128
    illustration, 164-165
Western Air Plan 7B, 17

Whitley bomber, 10, 16, 45, 122
Wilhelmshaven, 6, 8, 12, 17, 18, 19, 20, 23, 26, 29, 30, 37, 44, 45, 48, 62, 63, 64, 65, 67, 69, 70, 72, 76, 77, 88, 95, 96, 102, 105, 115, 121, 124, 131, 133, 136, 141, 145, 158, 163
Williams, Flight Sergeant, 39
Wimberley, Flying Officer,
   Battle of Heligoland Bight 18.12.39, 60
   crash, 77, 80, 81
   claim, 84, 161
   explanation of no bombs found on board, 88, 89, 99, 120
   prisoner of war, 103
Wolff, Generalleutnant, 88, 89
Wright, Flight Lieutenant Bill, 168